The Reader-friendly Library Service

First published by:

The Society of Chief Librarians
Tony Durcan, President
Newcastle Libraries and Information Service
PO Box 88
Newcastle upon Tyne
NE99 1DX

A CIP catalogue record for this book is available from the British Library.

ISBN: 978-0-9559028-0-2

Book designed and typeset by Paul Miller, shootshoot.me.uk

The Reader-friendly Library Service

Rachel Van Riel, Olive Fowler & Anne Downes

FOREWORD

Reading remains the key means by which we all seek to make sense of a complex world and try to understand the emotions that drive human behaviour. This skill is often taken for granted by a wide range of professionals including, on occasions, librarians.

Branching Out sought to reinvigorate the importance of reader development and mainstream the work throughout the public library service. Initially 33 authorities were selected to participate in a three-year initiative managed by the Society of Chief Librarians, delivered by Opening the Book and supported by the National Lottery through the Arts Council of England. From 2001 to 2006 the programme of face-to-face and online training was rolled out to all 149 English library authorities, again managed by SCL in partnership with Opening the Book. It says a great deal about the Arts Council that financial support for this ambitious programme was seen as a priority for its then Literature Department.

Branching Out enabled the Arts Council to put reader development through libraries at the heart of its literature policy, based on the belief that in public libraries we have a nationwide network of literature centres, democratically accessible venues where readers and reading can flourish. It was clear that if the potential for reader development was to be realised fully, the skills of the librarian needed to develop. Branching Out provided the means to make this happen; it challenged librarians across the country to make reader development central to the library offer.

Branching Out took a hugely imaginative approach to training in its efforts to transform library culture, broadening the skills base and engendering confidence in frontline staff without whose commitment so little might have happened. It is this transformational approach that makes the initiative so unique. Branching Out provided leadership, strategic thinking and creativity in ways that will benefit libraries, readers and reading for a long time to come.

This book aims to maintain the impetus, by promoting best practice in library services throughout the country and also encouraging debate. Varying views on many of the topics covered will no doubt come to the fore. That is to be welcomed for debate on reader development is central to a vibrant, challenging, ambitious and relevant library service.

Patrick Conway, Chair Branching Out Board 2001-2006
Director Culture and Leisure, Durham County Council, 1991-2007
Gary McKeone, Literature Director, Arts Council England 1996 - 2006

CONTENTS

INTRODUCTION

The reader-centred approach has changed the way public libraries in the UK engage with their users. Library staff recognised the potential of reader development as a professional tool at a time when a rekindling of interest in reading, especially reading fiction, began to spread in the wider UK culture. The practice released new energy in public libraries as staff rediscovered what they came into the job for and readers responded with delight to new opportunities provided. The reader-centred approach has generated international interest from libraries, literature promoters and educational organisations in countries across Europe from Norway to Hungary to Portugal, as well as in Australasia, Africa and North America.

Reader development practice has grown at an extraordinary rate since its inception in 1990 and there is very little documentation of the philosophy and approach. Most of what is available is project-specific and takes the form of reports to funding bodies or short accounts online. This book sets out to explore the thinking behind reader-centred practice and to present a sustained argument for its benefits.

The Reader-friendly Library Service is written for middle and senior managers of public library services but will be of interest to arts and education professionals as well as those responsible for cultural policymaking. Reader development is still a relatively young field where mistakes are inevitable and lots of potential remains. This book sets out to bring clarity to discussions of reader development to help library managers as they make day-to-day and strategic decisions.

Branching Out was a private-public sector partnership between Opening the Book Ltd and the Society of Chief Librarians, funded by Arts Council England and contributions from Opening the Book. We are grateful that support from Branching Out has enabled free copies of the book to go to every public library service in England.

We should make it clear that the opinions expressed here are solely those of Opening the Book and do not represent the views of any other body. Please get in touch with us if you would like to continue the discussion, whether in agreement or disagreement - we believe important ideas are always strengthened by debate.

Rachel Van Riel, Olive Fowler and Anne Downes
Opening the Book
2008

Chapter One

STARTING WITH THE READER

The major difference that reader development has introduced to library practice and services is the shift away from the product to the user. Reader development offers a new approach to promoting the library service's core product by drawing on a basic principle which has underpinned the advertising and marketing industries for decades - 'sell the sizzle, not the sausage!'

Advertisers promote products and services by helping consumers imagine themselves using them. You will be healthier/more successful/a better parent if you use product X. Advertising plays on the aspirations of the consumer - we all want to be that good-looking person with an attractive home, perfect partner and successful career. Imagining how much better your life will be after you've purchased the miracle product clinches the sale.

In the same way, telling a reader they will be thrilled, amused, riveted or challenged by a book will win them over more convincingly than, 'This is the third book written by the prizewinning, young British author....' The reader-centred approach offers the potential reader a vision of what they will experience as they read a book, how it will make them feel, what it will make them think about and why they should commit several hours of their lives to reading it.

Starting from how people use reading

Motivating people to pick up a book means thinking about how reading fits into their lives. For example, recognising that people are busy, bored or swamped with the minutiae of day-to-day living led to a unique approach to an online reading promotion for Welsh libraries. *Give me a Break* did not set out a list of recommended titles to browse, instead it offered reading as a break from all the stresses of life. Whether you are overloaded at work, fed up with domestic chores or dreaming that there must be more to life than this, the site offers a solution. Readers can discover fiction and non-fiction titles, in Welsh and English, which are categorised according to what kind of break they offer.

*Give me a Break** shows how thinking about the way people use reading in their lives, rather than what the book is, can provide a good starting point. Scottish libraries created *Bite-sized*, a promotion which offered a selection of short novels, non-fiction and poetry for busy people who don't have much time to read. The collections were placed on the counter

* Created as part of the Society of Chief Librarians' Estyn Allan (Branching Out) programme. The site is archived at: **www.openingthebook.com/archive/givemeabreak**

Give me a Break

About this site
English | Welsh

do you fancy...
a short break
a long break

surprise break

give me
a break from....
boredom
everything
my life
stress
the email
the ironing
the kids

Give me a break from everything

31 Songs
by Nick Hornby

A blast from the past that will have you searching the depths of your musical memory bank. Share Hornby's secret delight at the tacky tunes and guitar solos that have mysteriously attached themselves to your memories.

Tri Chynnig I Blodwen Jones
by Bethan Gwanas

It was good to open Blodwen Jones' diary once again – for the third time. This is an easy to read story and one that is full of humour when she describes life's tribulations, work and relationships – problems many of us are familiar with! This is not just a story for learners but an exciting book that will give pleasure to many others.

Hokkaido Highway Blues
by Will Ferguson

It is much, much easier (and probably more fun) to read this book rather than to try hitchhiking across Japan. This trip was the result of a drunken bet. It's such a thrill to be with the first people to hitchhike the whole length of Japan. It's what reading is for!

Click here to borrow one of these titles from your local library
Don't fancy these? Try again for a different selection

Give me a Break

About this site
English | Welsh

do you fancy...
a short break
a long break

surprise break

give me
a break from....
boredom
everything
my life
stress
the email
the ironing
the kids

Boss getting you **down?**

Kids driving you **nuts?**

Bored out of your **skull?**

It doesn't have to be like this!

Whatever it is that's getting you down, we've got the antidote. Choose what it is you want a break from and find yourself an escape route. Or click on Surprise Break and leave it all to us.

Supported by an 'Arts for All' Lottery grant from the Arts Council of Wales

designed by Opening the Book for Estyn Allan

in small, concentrated displays and functioned in the same way as supermarkets present high turnover items by the checkouts to tempt queuing customers to take something extra.

The *Take your seat* feature of **www.reader2reader.net**, part of the *Read* strand of The People's Network Service, presents routes to books linked to the situations where they might be read - 3 am reads for sleepless nights, relaxing and fresh reads in the garden, familiar reads on a comfy armchair. This site offers readers an alternative to the traditional author and title searches, where you need to know a name in order to use the search facility.

Audience development for literature

Before the rise of reader development in the 1990s, fiction was a low priority in library strategic management, left to tick over as it always had done without any investment in professional training or representation in senior management teams.   Information, ICT and community services were seen as much more important, despite the fact that fiction generated 70% of adult loans. In 2008, after more than a decade of innovation, library managers can see the benefits of a reader-centred approach in increased take-up of services, greater qualitative involvement of customers and a new cultural role for public libraries which has brought respect from government, education and the book trade.

Before reader development, arts funders supported literature as an art form through grants to writers, to independent presses, and, in the 1980s, to new distributors in a cultural industries model. Reader development showed it was worth investing at the consumer end too. Moving readers beyond brand loyalty to individual authors, helping people develop the confidence to try something new, builds an expanding audience, willing to take risks, make commitments and be entertained, challenged or perplexed. This has benefits for the whole literature industry and arts funders in the UK were quick to perceive this.

Starting from the reader offers a new approach to audience development. The traditional model of audience development in the arts identifies ways to attract more visitors, sell more tickets and to increase the audience at professional events and venues. This gives the consumer a relatively passive role.   The community arts movement sought to overturn this thinking in the 1960s and 1970s, claiming that everyone is an artist, and rather than watch other people perform the art of the past, it was better to make your own. This led to some exciting projects but ultimately faced two flaws - not everyone wants to do it themselves, some people prefer to watch professionals, and, of course, not everyone has the talent either.

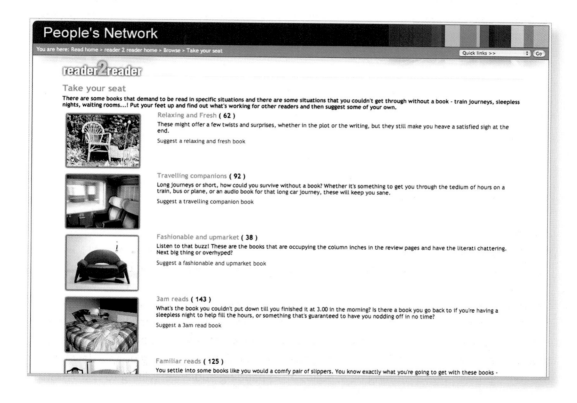

Reader development offers a new concept of the audience as actively participating but making a different contribution from the writer, not imitating or usurping their role. It cuts through the tired distinctions of highbrow and lowbrow, elitist and popular. It offers a way to achieve quality and access together by shifting attention to the quality of the reading experience rather than the quality of the book or the writer.

Reader development has grown to encompass many different activities so it may be helpful to begin with the first definition when the term was invented by Opening the Book.

Reader development means active intervention to:

- increase people's confidence and enjoyment of reading
- open up reading choices
- offer opportunities for people to share their reading experience
- raise the status of reading as a creative activity*

Principles first formulated in *Report to the Arts Council Literature Department on Creative Reading Training in Libraries*, Van Riel, Rachel 1992.

The concept was created in work with adult library borrowers and had no connection with literacy or learning to read. It combined a professional aspiration to develop audiences for literature with a recognition that many people wished to use reading for personal growth. (*Opening the Book - finding a good read** by Rachel Van Riel and Olive Fowler was written for individual readers who wanted to get more out of their reading.) Libraries had always been key places for self-help and self-development but the professional culture contained no activating role in relation to adult readers. Once that was animated, the energy released was huge.

Reader development begins from valuing and respecting individual reading preferences; each reader is expert and judge of their own reading experience. Sometimes, though, we feel trapped inside our own choices - aware we could be missing something we'd love to read or simply wanting help to know what else is out there. Opening the Book's mission statement for reader development, taken up by many library services, expresses this clearly:

The best book in the world is quite simply the one you like best. That is something you can discover for yourself but we are here to help you find it.

Embedding this approach in library services gives libraries an important new role at the centre of the cultural landscape. Promoting reading as a creative activity confirms the status of readers as the largest arts audience in the UK and promotes the role of libraries as having regular contact with hundreds of thousands of them. Libraries provide the ideal location for promotions and activities aimed at readers. This, in turn, creates a new, energetic role for library staff. Staff can directly engage with their core customers to understand what drives them, not only to fulfil declared customer needs but to anticipate and tempt. The resulting benefits to readers are clearly demonstrable; they enjoy the chance to participate, are relieved to have help negotiating the collection and appreciate the un-pressured nature of library promotions, with no commercial or other agendas attached to the books on offer.

When built into a larger programme involving librarians from across different authorities, working together to develop new skills and new practice, the reader-centred approach has the potential to transform the library service from passive-responsive to a more confident active role. In the UK, this is what happened with the Branching Out project in England, from 1998 to 2001, and then mirrored in Estyn Allan (Branching Out in Wales) and the Reader Development Network in Scotland.

Van Riel & Fowler *Opening the Book - finding a good read*, 1996. *

The Branching Out project consciously set out to invest in 33 librarians from different parts of England as agents of change and ambassadors for the reader-centred approach. This resulted in a programme of projects and promotions which was rolled out not only to the participating authorities but to all other library services in England. All projects, details of training sessions and other resources were available through the Branching Out website[*] set up to disseminate outcomes to all English libraries. These national training programmes became the seedbed for many new styles of library promotion which are today almost standard practice, all starting from the reader and the experience of reading.

WAKE-UP CALLS

Misunderstandings, however well-intentioned, undermine reader-centred practice. If you recognise the views below, use the arguments in this chapter to challenge them.

" *Reader development will influence people to read better books.* "

" *Reader development is patronising – people should be left to choose for themselves.* "

" *Reader development is dumbing down – as if there's no difference between quality and trash.* "

Understanding reader psychology

Most readers - possibly all readers - have an in-built resistance to one (or more) authors or genres. 'I don't read books written by women,' is the kind of sweeping statement familiar to many library staff. 'I don't like poetry/SF/romance...' are also commonly expressed. As readers we protect ourselves from the kind of read we think will not interest us, won't offer the kind of experience we enjoy, will be dull, too highbrow or too lowbrow. This resistance provides a huge challenge for library staff, not only in helping individual readers to find 'a good read' when all the books written by a favourite author have been read, but also in achieving increased issues from existing book stock. 'What's in it for me?' can be turned into the most powerful motivator in the world. Giving a reader an image of what's in it for them for any particular book begins to unlock any resistance they might have to trying something different.

Traditional promotion presents a collection of books by author, genre or subject-related theme. This draws attention to specific titles (in a bookshop they will be new titles, although not always in a library). This works best for readers who already know the author, genre or subject. A reader-centred approach can reach much wider, beyond those who are already hooked. A reader who has read everything by their favourite author, or who has worked her way through a small branch library's entire collection of her favourite genre, needs to be convinced that there are other books in the library to tempt her. Tapping into why the reader chooses a particular kind of read (for challenge, for indulgence, for enlightenment) gives scope to introduce the reader to other books which offer the same experience. A reader coming to a dead-end in the library may walk out empty-handed. Fifty such readers in a small branch can have a significant impact on issues.

When the Branching Out programme planned the first national reader-centred promotion in the UK it was important to demonstrate these principles. The skills audit undertaken in preparation for the Branching Out programme showed that librarians lacked confidence and knowledge in dealing with a wide range of fiction. One of the stated aims of Branching Out, particularly attractive to the Arts Council who funded the project, was to skill librarians to be able to promote less well-known authors, non-mainstream genres and books from independent presses. It was widely recognised that these areas were under-represented in library collections and it was an explicit aim of the Branching Out programme to encourage library services to buy more of these titles and promote them effectively. Creating readership for these books meant that the service offered a richer experience to individual readers but was also playing a more important role in the wider culture.

For Branching Out's first major promotion the area of stock chosen to be promoted was one which could be said to be weak across the wider culture of books and the media in the English-speaking world and not just libraries. Translations from another language make up between 13% and 40% of fiction publishing in countries across Europe. In Britain and America translations account for just 2% of fiction output. How to tackle an area where big-name publishers, with all the marketing tools at their disposal, clearly feared to tread? This is where the reader-centred approach proved its worth.

A traditional approach to promoting world fiction and fiction in translation would select authors and arrange them country by country, with a bit of text about their importance, their history and context, under a title like *Great Authors from around the World*. The problem with this is that it doesn't speak to a new audience who might enjoy these writers. If you're not sure you're up to the demands of 'Great Authors', it sounds pretty intimidating. If you recognise some names as ones that have been on your 'ought to read list' for years, it's likely to make you feel guilty. Guilt and inadequacy are not good motivators to tempt readers to pick up a book.

The Branching Out promotion of world literature was called *Open Ticket*. The colours and images used in the print publicity connected to world travel and conveyed the excitement, beauty and challenge of visiting other countries. *Open Ticket* presented readers with an opportunity to explore places through the pages of a book that they would love to visit in real life.

A ticket empowers the reader and the word 'open' conveys the freedom of choice to go where you like. In the early days of reader development, many library staff were worried that the new approach required them to 'tell' people what to read. A reader-centred approach is always about tempting not prescribing and it was important the first national promotion embodied that philosophy. *Open Ticket* seduced and empowered the reader to make choices; it didn't tell them what to think. Readers were welcome to hate books in the promotion as much as love them - and some did. The job of the reader development librarian is to remove the barriers which stop readers from experimenting, not to change or 'improve' readers' tastes.

The *Open Ticket* promotion was run by the 33 Branching Out authorities and by a further 51 library services across England. The concept, promotional materials, book selection, supporting website and training sessions changed what thousands of library staff thought promotion could be. *Open Ticket* took an area of stock perceived as 'difficult' and of limited interest and, using reader-centred principles, moved it from the dusty corner at the back of the library to a high-profile position. The success of the *Open Ticket* promotion in terms of book issues, staff and customer reaction, and introducing readers to new reading experiences, created a template for many imaginative reader-centred promotions which followed.

Opening up choices

Traditional book displays and promotions in libraries are put together using a book-centred approach. What genre is it? Who wrote it? What's the theme? Is it a prizewinner? All displays have value in that they throw a spotlight onto a smaller selection and therefore give the browser a focus in the sea of spine-on shelved books. But book-centred promotions have major limitations, especially in libraries. The first is that they aim to the centre of established audiences. This is common retail practice, of course, but libraries who have embraced the philosophy of reader development are looking to open up reading choices, to tempt people past those reading cul-de-sacs we all fall into.

The second problem with the book-based promotion is that libraries simply do not have enough copies of the single titles most in demand. Driving customer focus towards these few titles is self-defeating. A reader who spots something he is keen to read may well discover that the book has already been borrowed and there is a waiting list. The lasting impression might well be, 'They never have anything I want in that library,' and the reader votes with his feet. There are thousands of books worth reading in every library; the reader-centred approach to promotion finds ways of bringing more of these to the fore.

On Valentine's Day, for example, the traditional approach puts together a display of romantic novels. This will tend to appeal to an existing audience for romance and will exclude most male readers. It misses the opportunity to fulfil the reader development aim of introducing a wider range of books to a wider range of readers. Take a focus like Valentine's Day and approach it from a reader-centred perspective and a much wider range of options opens out. 'Books we're passionate about' enables staff and readers to draw attention to personal favourites and will result in a much more eclectic mix. 'Go on a blind date with a book' challenges readers to take a risk outside their normal preferences. 'Choose a book women should read to understand men better' mixes humour and seriousness across the gender divide. Each of these promotions can contain titles from any area of stock - fiction, audiobooks, poetry, non-fiction. The mix of books under one banner introduces the browser to authors, titles and genres they might have previously bypassed completely, offering a much richer variety than a straightforward romance promotion. Regular romance readers might find something to try but so will lots of people who loathe the idea of romance.

Reader-centred promotions use colloquial language to signal they are different from the formality of library subject guiding. *Get Lost, Get a Grip* and *Get a Life* are three punchy straplines from Opening the Book Promotions which grab the attention by using casual insults unexpectedly. All three themes also represent and celebrate the nature of the reading experience - selling the sizzle of completely losing yourself in a story, having an edge of the seat experience or stepping totally into somebody else's shoes. This opens up many more options for the range of titles to be included than the more traditional Fantasy, Thriller and Biography promotions would have offered.

Raising the status of reading

Reading is a private and individual activity. Hundreds of thousands of people may be reading the same book, far more than share a theatre, music or sports experience at the same time. But reading takes place in living rooms and bedrooms; there are no grand halls or arenas where readers congregate for specific events. Even in large libraries, the flow of customers is spread through the day, they are not all there at the same time. Because reading is largely invisible, its importance is easy to overlook and undervalue.

A good way to take the temperature of attitudes to reading in any culture is to look at how books and readers are depicted in advertising. No paperbacks were shown in UK adverts for living room interiors in the 1980s, despite the dramatic growth of Waterstone's bookstores. The assumption among advertisers that books were passé and uncool is made explicit in a typical bank advert to students in the 1990s. The headline runs: 'We were going to offer Book Tokens. Luckily we woke up.' (A Book Token is a gift voucher which enables someone to give a book as a present, the receiver gets to choose whatever title they like to the value of the gift.) The copy continues: 'Open a Student Bank Account and we'll give you lots of goodies. Unfortunately a Book Token won't be one of them. Sorry but this year we've decided to give you things that you may actually want.' These turn out to be a music storecard and a travel card. The insult to readers, to books and to students would be unthinkable today. Now many advertisers of sofas, interior design, kitchen or bathroom furniture will have a pile of books included in the picture. If the product is expensive, the books will be art and style books; if it's more homely, there will be a mix of bestselling paperbacks. Books have become a way of signalling aspiration and attraction, they are now part of the 'sizzle'.

You may think negative attitudes have completely disappeared but they still recur. It is not uncommon to find readers represented as unadventurous, in retreat from life, compensating for their lack of action, power, friends and sex by reading about it instead. The newspaper adverts for online travel firm, Opodo, used the same old put-down of reading in 2006 with the strapline, 'Don't just read about it, travel'. Old-fashioned ideas of reading as lazy and indulgent have not gone away. Marketing expert, Jeremy Bullmore, writes for *Management Today* and *The Guardian*, where he runs a column giving advice on problems people experience at work. In August 2007, he featured a letter describing how 'Along with the July 1 smoking ban, our bosses have decided to ban the reading of books, magazines and newspapers during our organised tea breaks. Is this fair?' Worse still for those working in public libraries, the writer was employed by a local council in the customer services department.

Old-fashioned images of reading also persist. Look at the backdrop for the typical school portrait photo. This is a commercial offer, made by every UK school to raise income; your child is photographed and a copy sent home to tempt parents to buy more copies for all the relatives. The background setting for most of these photos is a row of bookshelves. Presumably the intention is to convey something serious and scholarly. The books are hardback, old-fashioned, undifferentiated and totally boring - what a negative message to send home with every child.

The effect of thinking more about how books fit in people's lives is shown in the changes to advertising campaigns for Book Tokens during the 1990s. In the campaign for 1991, the image presented three individuals sitting on piles of hardback books, each reading a book. Three ages are represented in the image; one is a girl of about seven; one is a young woman, about 20, wearing an academic cap and gown so, quite clearly, a graduate; the third is an astronaut, in full space suit, therefore implying an individual in their 30s-40s and a high achiever. The caption reads 'Who knows where a Book Token might lead?' The not-so-subtle message of the campaign is that reading equates to education and achievement. The campaign may have been successful in terms of persuading anxious parents and grandparents to buy books so children do well in their studies, but it would never convince a reluctant teenager that reading is an enjoyable pastime.

A couple of years later, the Book Token campaign took a much more reader-friendly approach and used more powerful 'sizzle' messages for a contemporary audience than those of education and achievement. The adverts present scenes of individuals who are so engrossed in their books that they can't bear to put them down for anything. This campaign implies that reading is pleasurable, gripping, a private and personal thing that can be done anywhere, any time. It adds a liberating element of down-to-earth humour about everyday life; it is human and extremely witty. It also associates reading with taboo and transgression - toilets, sex, disobeying your parents - rather than respectability and success.

When Opening the Book Promotions came to design its first library promotion aimed at children, in 2003, it added a sense of mischief and fun to the reading experience with the strapline 'The book made me do it'. This carries the same vein of humour and transgression, steering clear of the message that books are good for you - a guaranteed turn-off for most kids.

Getting the message right

Because there have been so few positive, attractive images associated with reading, libraries have been forced to use what they could get. There is no good picture of a contemporary paperback on clipart. In an age where most fiction is sharply designed and the range of good-looking non-fiction books has never been greater, from coffee table interiors to photo-reality information books, the chief representation of books in clipart is three undistinguished hardbacks piled on top of each other at different angles, with an old-fashioned forked silk ribbon bookmark trailing out of one of them. This image has been reproduced on countless promotional leaflets, websites, conference programmes and reading campaigns without thought as to what it conveys. This image will undermine any presentation of reading as an exciting and contemporary activity; text without any illustration is far preferable.

Some of the most traditional images associated with reading are not, when you come to think about it, that attractive. Every reader knows that the act of reading is an exciting and challenging activity. Reading is a creative partnership with an author, providing a way to embrace different lives, cultures and new experiences as well as supporting us in confronting the things we fear. But when we come to represent this imaginative inner experience graphically, one of the most frequently used images is the bookworm. The bookworm has appeared on television programmes, children's projects, letterheads, websites, and is a common logo for many book-related projects. It has been given a new lease of life in recent years through clipart. Pause to consider what the bookworm image is suggesting about readers.

Bookworms send a negative image of reading

One of the key principles of reader development is to present reading as a creative activity and to challenge old stereotypes of readers as dull, reclusive, socially inept individuals whose only friends are books. Bookworms are regularly used as a logo or as a name for a group, website or promotion and this is subtly undermining to readers. Bookworms are nasty little grubs that burrow into books. Calling somebody a bookworm in our society isn't usually meant in a respectful way. It automatically conjures up an image of dusty old books and dusty old codgers reading them. This image is quite at odds with the pleasure and complexity of the reading experience.

Libraries themselves are guilty of reader put-downs. The library service has diversified into offering imaginative experiences not just in print but also in audio and DVD formats. Similarly, routes to information are now provided online as well as offline. Summarising this diverse range to convey to a potential audience the richness of the library offer is not easy. A common way to solve the problem has been the use of the phrase 'More than just books'. For a service with readers at heart it is worth examining this slogan more objectively. The use of the word 'just' devalues the core product of the service and dismisses the customers requiring that product as unimportant.

A slogan like 'More than just books' does not work well to attract the non-readers it is aimed at. It is a classic example of trying to sell something by what it's not. Customers who are not interested in books have no idea what it is you're offering. Promotions of ICT, DVDs and other services are excellent in themselves but negative marketing is not a successful method of attracting customers to your product. As well as failing to convey an attractive message to potential customers who might enjoy computers or DVDs, it has the effect of putting down and alienating your core customers who enjoy books.

The phrase 'more than just books' can work if followed by positives. For example, 'More than just books - a rich collection of the best that's been thought and written since printing was invented.' This may not be a punchy marketing slogan but it celebrates exactly what it is that's exciting and unique about public libraries. Marks and Spencer's very successful campaign unpacked the headline 'This is not just food, it is M&S food' by making the product more enticing with juicy details not by ditching food to advertise something else. Some library services incorporate the phrase 'Much more than books' as part of the library brand without any follow-up phrase. The comparison is left hanging and has a damaging implication that the books are somehow inadequate. This is in danger of coming across as a slap in the face for every keen book borrower who values books and the reading experience. The phrase left hanging also conveys a lack of faith in the libraries' book offer. Is there a worrying assumption that the non-user couldn't possibly be interested in the books, therefore we have to lure them in with the tempting delights of internet access, DVDs and CDs?

WAKE-UP CALLS

Misunderstandings, however well-intentioned, undermine reader-centred practice. If you recognise the views below, use the arguments in this chapter to challenge them.

" The head of service says we really need to get over to people that the library is about more than just books. "

" The bookworm logo gave our mobile a new image - it's a fun way of branding the service. "

" Everybody is doing reader development now - publishers and bookshops are all putting the reader at the centre. "

Making readers visible

It is admittedly very difficult to source strong images to use for a reading promotion. The reading experience is internal, private and unique - how can you possibly capture that in a photograph? The strongest images associated with reading have been those which celebrate the portability of books and the capacity of reading to create personal space in any environment - on trains, at bus stops, on park benches.

Many libraries in the UK have made displays by taking photos of individual borrowers posed with the title they have chosen to borrow. This is a great way to show the range of people using the library - different ages, fashions, lifestyles. It also showcases the range of books available. At its best, it may undermine stereotypes and get people thinking about who reads what as there is always at least one face and book which are an unexpected match. Celebrating readers in this way conveys an important message about how the library values its customers in a context where photos of the author would be the more familiar approach.

Durham Libraries produced an entire calendar starring their own borrowers with their chosen books. The calendar is a powerful way of demonstrating to customers, staff and elected politicians the role of the library in the community and the cross-section of people they serve.

Insomnia
Stephen King

Chosen by **Marc Carne**
of Peterlee

"Sleep is the overlooked hero and the poorman's physician.'

Joe Wyzer to Ralph Roberts regarding his insomnia

Nov

Mon	Tue	Wed	Thur	Fri	Sat	Sun
				1	2	3
4	5	6	7	8	9	10
11	12	13	14	15	16	17
18	19	20	21	22	23	24
25	26	27	28	29	30	

Clan of the Cave Bear
Jean M Auel

Chosen by **Pamela MacDonald** of Chilton

'The bear waded into the squad of spear-wielding men who closed in on him. A swing of the raging animal's powerful fore leg cleared a swath, knocking down three men and catching a fourth with a ripping gash that tore the muscles of his leg to the bone.... Ayla clutched Durc in horrified awe, petrified that the bear would reach them. But when the man fell, his life's blood spilling on the ground, she didn't think, she just acted. Shoving her baby at Uba, she dashed into mêlée...Leaning hard on the pressure point in his groin with one hand, she held the end of the thong of her wrap in her teeth, and cut off a piece with her other hand.'

September

Mon	Tue	Wed	Thur	Fri	Sat	Sun
30						1
2	3	4	5	6	7	8
9	10	11	12	13	14	15
16	17	18	19	20	21	22
23	24	25	26	27	28	29

DURHAM COUNTY COUNCIL

In order to raise the profile of reading with a male audience, Danish libraries launched a promotion called *Det Laeser Disse Maend!* (What do men read!). The promotional materials included posters, bookmarks and an A5 booklet, featuring a range of Danish men from various walks of life and their chosen books. The route to motivate men to try the library was not a list of authors or a set of book reviews. Instead the promotion stimulates curiosity as to what others are reading and allows men to identify with people like themselves who are using the library.

Marco van Engeland 22 år Murer

Efter skolen kom jeg i lære som murer. Jeg blev udlært i 2004 og har fortsat mit arbejde i samme firma. I min fritid er jeg sammen med vennerne og elsker at høre musik. Jeg har bl.a. været på Roskildefestival flere gange. Jeg er meget stor Brøndbyfan, spiller dog ikke selv fodbold, men basketball på hyggeplan. Når det gælder bøger er jeg "fantasyfan". Det er helt klart den type bøger, der har sat mig i gang med at læse romaner.

Dragonlance-bøgerne
Jeg har læst rigtig mange Dragonlance-bøger, som består af flere serier, f.eks. Dragonlance-forhistorier, -heltesagn, -legender, -krøniker En del er skrevet af forfatterne Margaret Weis og Tracy Hickman, men også andre forfattere er kommet med.
Det specielle ved bøgerne er, at de er baseret på de såkaldte Dungeons & Dragons rollespil, hvor forskellige figurer går igen i bøgerne. Det kan være elver, drager, kendarer, bjergdværge, troldmænd, riddere o.s.v.
En fantastisk eventyrverden, hvor der altid foregår en kamp mellem det gode og det onde.

Stephen King: Det mørke tårn, bind 1-3.
De tre første bind i serien *Det mørke tårn: Revolvermanden, Udvælgelsen og Ødemarken* førte mig ind i et spændende univers, man bestemt ikke er vant til. Det er et fantasyunivers med spring mellem flere verdener og mellem fortid, nutid og fremtid.
Den gennemgående hovedperson i bogen er Revolvermanden Roland, som i sin søgen efter Det mørke tårn bevæger sig gennem bizarre og kaotiske landskaber, hvor ham møder ukendte, mystiske væsener og farer. Rigtig spændende og anderledes.

Frans G. Bengtsson: Røde orm
Min morfar anbefalede mig at læse bogen. Den foregår godt nok i en virkelig verden, men i en helt anden tid, nemlig vikingetiden. En spændende tid, som jeg rigtig kunne leve mig ind i.
Den handler om bondesønnen Orm fra Skåne, der ved et uheld kommer med på vikingetogt til Irland først som fange, senere som kriger. Herefter bliver det til rigtig mange eventyrlige togter videre ud i verden. Jeg synes så godt om bogen, at jeg har anbefalet den videre til min fætter.

11   12

This approach opens up many opportunities for promotional campaigns and enables library services to show an appreciation of their borrowers. It makes a refreshing change from the campaigns in which celebrities are used to promote books and reading, where it is the celebrity that provides the focus, rather than the book. The celebrity approach has produced some toe-curling embarrassments where, for example, a major pop star has been photographed with a book aimed at an eight year-old, and another in which a smiling celebrity was holding their book upside down. It could appear that no-one involved in the photoshoot knew or cared anything about books or reading.

Local libraries have successfully used pictures of their own borrowers in many promotions. Matching the reader to the book, like many reader-centred ideas, can be adapted to suit different situations and run at different scales. It has been run in single libraries and across whole counties; become a six-week project in a school, a feature in a council newsletter, and an intranet competition.

Reader-centred promotion from Glasgow Libraries

WAKE-UP CALLS

Misunderstandings, however well-intentioned, undermine reader-centred practice. If you recognise the views below, use the arguments in this chapter to challenge them.

" My regular borrowers love the genre displays - they go mad if we don't have them. "

" Who Else Writes Like? is a really useful reader development tool. "

" The management team expects every library in the city to display the Top Ten lists from The Bookseller in a prominent position. "

Opportunities to share reading experiences

Taking a reader-centred viewpoint on traditional projects and activities presents lots of potential for fresh and accessible events and promotions. For example, the most common library event for adult readers is the author visit. The pattern for this has been unchanged for years; the author is introduced and reads from his/her latest publication, then questions are invited. The level of reader involvement on offer is clear from the two questions asked at every author peformance. 'How do you get an agent?' comes from the aspiring writers who make up more than half the audience, interested only in finding out how to get their own work published. Then the reader, confined to the role of admiring from a distance, enquires in a small voice, 'Where do you get your inspiration?' Colin Bateman satirises this situation in his book *Chapter and Verse* in which the author-protagonist, Ivan Connor, records his stock reply to this question as: 'A small shop in Covent Garden.'

Author events are worth scheduling in if there is a member of staff available to put in the time needed and the author is well-known enough to pull an audience. Some library services have built audiences to support annual programmes or festivals. This requires sustained marketing effort, beyond the reach of many small branches. Writer and broadcaster, Ian McMillan, tells the story of turning up to a library for an appearance where he was confronted by a homemade poster on the front door announcing 'Funny writer here tonight'. The librarian confidently assured him that the full force of the local marketing machine had been called into action: 'I've put a poster on the back door as well as the front.'

Author events are not the heart of reader development. They are easier for library staff to understand because there is a perceived focus for the event and a faith in the pull of the celebrity, even though libraries find that many London-based publishers will not bring authors to other parts of Britain. In promotional terms, the author event is usually an extremely labour-intensive and nerve-wracking endeavour for the organiser, which showcases the work and backlist of only one writer and may result in an embarrassingly low turn-out. If staff invested the same amount of time and energy in changing stock displays, this would impact on a far wider group of library users, not to mention loan figures.

No-one should feel that they are failing their readers if they are not able to offer a regular programme of author events. It may be more important from the libraries' perspective to maintain a series of small reader-centred events than to host author tours. This should not be taken to mean that reader development is anti-writer - on the contrary it's about creating the ideal audience that any writer dreams about: readers who are able to open up to the experience the writer offers, readers who are confident enough to take a risk on a new experience. Reader development starts with readers and aims to enrich their experience in ways which are not on offer anywhere else.

The experience of a rural festival is instructive here. Swaledale Festival in Richmond, North Yorkshire, encouraged a mix of art forms and usually included an author visit. The library service was considered the natural host and it always fell to library staff to organise the event. The writer's fee was paid by the regional arts council and the library contributed all the other expenses and time needed. The writers usually put in a good performance but they were not well-known and, despite the best efforts of library staff, it was hard to tempt more than a few loyal borrowers to turn out, especially if the weather was bad. After a reader development training session, library staff took a different proposal to the festival committee. Instead of offering an author event in the evening, they wished to respond to the way people already used the library at times when it suited them. They proposed that readers would be able to book one-to-one slots with another enthusiast to discuss their reading all through the designated festival day. Individuals could suggest the areas they wished to explore and would be matched with a suitable discussion partner drawn from volunteers among library staff and users. In the three years of author events, the audience involved had never been higher than 12. In the year of one-to-one conversations about reading, the number of participants jumped to 45. It is clear that a reader's experience with a book gives them more in common with another reader than with the author. It was creating this initial point of contact between readers that resulted in the setting up of North Yorkshire Libraries' first ever reading group, which is still going strong and still run by the reader volunteers.

Shifting the focus from the writer to the reader and the experience of reading opens up the potential to promote a wide range of books and writers at the same event. The reader event is cheaper to organise and makes the reader the star, offering an opportunity for the exploration of their own creative contribution as a reader. Reader-centred events are not always one-to-one or group discussions; it is possible to raise the bar and create a good night out using only the talents of your own borrowers.

In 1997, the first library Wine and Book Tasting was organised in Pontefract Library with the support of Opening the Book and Fiona Edwards, Pontefract Library's new reader-in-residence. The aim of the event was to promote literature in translation to a wider reading audience in a small ex-mining town in West Yorkshire. Finding a way to promote these books to a non-traditional audience was not easy. The wine and book tasting presented the books as desirable by drawing on the retail practice of adjacency - placing a new, unknown product alongside a more familiar one to reassure the customer. Most consumers in the UK now have a confidence about wine that would have been undreamt of 30 years ago.

The wine and books model focused on nine wine producing areas of the world such as Eastern Europe, Germany and South America. The local Tesco branch agreed to support the event, provided wine recommendations from each country and sent their wine buyer, and a generous supply of the wine. Six of the countries were introduced through their wine, everyone sipped and swirled as they followed the wine buyer's tasting notes. Then as they relaxed with glasses in hand, a reading group member read an extract from a book from the same country as the wine. The booklist accompanying the event, entitled *Real Corkers*, featured blurbs written by reading group members, in a way which reflected the wine theme. It included the recommended wine to go with the book and was distributed throughout the district's libraries to give the promotion a wider impact. The original event was a sell-out and has been successfully replicated in libraries from the Czech Republic to New Zealand.

Perfect Partners

Welcome to a wine and book tasting produced by Pontefract Library Readers Group. What could be better than unwinding with a good book and a glass of wine? Why not match the length and finish of a good Rioja with the sophistication of a Spanish detective story, or enjoy the delights of a best-selling Italian novel with a lightly aromatic, smooth Italian white?

We have catered for a variety of palates. Everyone knows their particular favourite, something tried and tested, that won't let you down. Could you be tempted to try something different: visit another area of the shelves; pause and examine another label? You may discover the one you've always been looking for. If the experiment doesn't work for you, and one sip was more than enough, don't worry: there is no pressure to finish the bottle. Return the novel and choose again.

However, some novels, like wines, are an acquired taste. You can always put the one that didn't hit the spot back in the cellar for another occasion, or mention it to a friend with a different palate.

In compiling this selection, we have gone into previously unknown territory, tasted new and sometimes strange flavours, and had lots of surprises.

So, we propose a toast - good health and happy reading!

NORTH AMERICA
Idoru by William Gibson

This is a vintage that you've never tasted before. Imagine a world where rock stars fall in love with computer creations and passport control checks the DNA in your split ends. Underneath the matt-black surface, this is a conspiracy thriller with a freelance information surfer and a 14-year-old pop fan taking on the big corporations. But, it's also an exploration of what it means to be human in a technological age; how can any of us retain privacy when every move we make generates information for the databank? This is a read with mouth-filling flavour and lean acidity. If you're not ready for the Gibson taste yet, put it in the cellar and test its freshness in ten year's time.

Tesco recommends:
Ernest and Julio Gallo Colombard at £3.99

SOUTH AMERICA
Like Water for Chocolate
by Laura Esquivel

Produced in the tradition of old Mexican families, this is a novel rich in local colour, with a spicy, full-bodied bouquet, and an explosive after-taste. Tita, the youngest daughter, is condemned to spend her life looking after her tyrannical mother, instead of marrying her sweetheart, Pedro. Banished to the kitchen, Tita prepares huge feasts to celebrate many family occasions: her sister, Rosaura's marriage to Pedro, to name just one. Her magical touch, with amazing ingredients, often ignites more than the appetites of her guests. Once uncorked, this story requires rapid consumption. An easy read and a good choice to share with friends.

Tesco recommends:
Tesco Mexican Cabernet Sauvignon at £3.19

FRANCE
Empire of the Ants by Bernard Werber

If you have a taste for thrills and horror and can take a swift kick in the perceptions, then enter the world of the ants. Pursue adventure, do battle, uncover intrigue, and fall in love in an alien world that isn't thousands of light years away - all below ground level. The human angle here is slightly corked, but the whole goes down easily without being lightweight.

Tesco recommends:
Tesco French Merlot Reserve at £3.69

AUSTRALIA
Oyster by Janette Turner Hospital

Set in the Australian outback town of Outer Maroo, this is a novel with a very strange nose. The time shift from this week to last week to two years ago means it is not easy at first to work out what's happening - but stick with it - it's worth the effort. A strange 'religious' cult; an isolated, frightened and frightening community; horrific happenings to those who don't stay silent - all ferment to make a powerful, scary, and unusual novel with an astonishing bouquet.

Tesco recommends:
Tesco Australian Shiraz/Cabernet Sauvignon at £4.29

SOUTH AFRICA
You Can't Get Lost in Cape Town
by Zöe Wicomb

This novel lets you choose from a mixed case of South African vintage. Poignant short stories intertwine to relate the bittersweet memories of a Cape coloured girl. We follow Frieda, as she grows to maturity through the years of apartheid, including her transfer to a white school, and her journey to have an abortion. The natural flavours of the stories are both melancholic and exotic, creating a collection which is intensely palatable.

Tesco recommends:
Tesco Cape Colombard (Chardonnay) at £3.49

ITALY
Follow Your Heart by Susanna Tamaro

A thoughtful and thought-provoking product, developed over four generations in a family vineyard in Italy. A grandmother breaks a long barrier of silence and speaks from her heart in a letter to her absent granddaughter. She blends news of her day-to-day routine and shares memories of things past, some she regrets, others she rejoices in. This is a story of remarkable vintage; any suggestion of sourness has been banished and replaced by the flavour of mature and mellow fruit, evoking the scent of flowers and the compassionate warmth of human love. Serve at room temperature and then relax and reflect.

Tesco recommends:
Tesco Colli Lanuvini at £2.99

WAKE-UP CALLS

Misunderstandings, however well-intentioned, undermine reader-centred practice. If you recognise the views below, use the arguments in this chapter to challenge them.

" Yes, we have a reader development programme. We already have 16 reading groups. "

" Our head of service believes the City Read is an excellent way of engaging readers. "

" The Readers' Days are a great success because the readers love meeting authors. "

The explosion of reading groups in the UK, particularly library-based groups, has provided a ready-made audience for the new generation of reader activities. These groups are in continuous contact with reader development staff and are easy to target. Many reading group members contribute to the planning and organisation of events, as well as providing the much needed core audience on the day.

A new approach to creating large-scale reader-centred events has been the Readers' Day. Many library services have successfully staged these one day programmes of workshop-style activities and presentations. These days always involve authors but the creative reading focus gives a context in which the authors become engaged in discussions as readers as well as writers. Many authors relish the opportunity to face an audience of well-informed, articulate readers who may ultimately challenge their own view of how their work is interpreted or received.

'Readers' Days are quite uniquely wonderful. I can think of nothing more gratifying for a writer than having a room full of several hundred people who have taken the trouble to read, know and understand your work. I was touched by their curiosity and dedication and went away feeling inspired both as a reader and a writer.'

Julie Myerson - author

These events blur the demarcation between the roles of creative artist and audience as the buzz created by enthusiastic readers sharing their experiences becomes the highlight of the day rather than individual contributions by authors.

The Readers' Day includes sessions which put contributions made by readers on a par with contributions from published writers. There should be no suggestion that the writer is the expert just because they are published and famous. To make the day a success, participating writers need to completely understand the nature of the event. James Nash, an experienced organiser and master of ceremonies for Readers' Days says:

'I always make sure that I talk with the authors before the start of the day. That way I can ensure that they understand what the day is really about and I stress that, although they are writers, they are also here to contribute as readers. Most writers love this as they often don't get the chance to talk about their reading habits and preferences in public - and readers love it too. If a writer stands up and delivers what they always say at literature events, it just doesn't work within the Readers' Day structure or its philosophy.'

There is a useful guide to planning and running a Readers' Day written by Jane Mathieson, the Regional Reader Development Co-ordinator for the North West, on **www.time-to-read.co.uk/toolkits/**.

National promotions

There have been many successful promotions which have taken a book-centred approach. These have played a big role in raising the profile of reading in UK national culture and reader development professionals are grateful for that. There is a downside for libraries, however, because the projects drive the reader towards a small number of titles chosen by publishers, critics, judges - the reader follows somebody else's selection rather than what they choose for themselves.

The BBC's *Big Read* in 2004, for example, placed reading for pleasure prominently on the public agenda. This promotion presented a particular challenge for libraries, however, because the list contained so many classics, including children's classics. The result of this was that many libraries gave their best promotional space to tired, battered copies of old books which hadn't seen the light of day for years.

An interesting import from the US, first taken up in the UK by Bristol and now adopted by many other library services, is the City Read concept. The City Read aims to get the public discussing the same book in workshops, reading groups and online forums. The idea has been successfully used to connect across boundaries, for example, the Western Education and Library Board of Northern Ireland linked across the border with Donegal County Libraries to read *Divided City* by Theresa Breslin, a book which deals with sectarianism in Glasgow.

In 2007, a reading campaign to mark the 200th anniversary of the abolition of the slave trade brought together residents of Bristol, Liverpool, Glasgow and Hull, former centres of the slave trade. The chosen titles were *Small Island* by Andrea Levy, *Refugee Boy* by Benjamin Zephaniah and Mary Hoffman's *Amazing Grace* for younger readers. Fifty thousand free books were handed out via schools, libraries, shops, local companies and community groups. The Edinburgh UNESCO City of Literature project in 2007 included a City Read of Robert Louis Stevenson's *Kidnapped*. Print copies of the book were distributed via libraries in three editions including a graphic novel, a simplified retold version and the classic paperback. An online audio version and e-book were also available.

As well as raising the profile of reading as a creative activity, a key principle of reader development, these events highlight reading as a participative activity. The stereotyped image of the reader as a sad and lonely individual, escaping into the pages of a book is seriously challenged by an entire city's readers buzzing about one book.

This distribution of free or cheap copies of the books goes some way towards countering the constant problem faced by libraries involved in book-centred campaigns which focus on a limited number of titles - once all the books have issued from the Orange Prize display, what can they be replaced with? Astute library staff, and those experienced in reader development, will look to previous years' shortlists, other titles by the authors of the shortlisted books, widen it out to other prizewinners or ask their own customers to nominate their own shortlists/winners. If they don't take these routes, the display will very quickly start to look picked over and unappealing.

It is easy to see why libraries get drawn into participating in these events, offering as they do the attraction of a ready-made promotional opportunity, a sense of connection to a national/international activity and the chance to tap into wider publicity and hype.

However, it is worth thinking about how far a promotion opens up reading choices, before deciding whether to invest energy in it. Many book-centred, and author-centred, promotions do not fulfil this basic principle. The book choices in the City Read examples above are crucially important, the Breslin in Northern Ireland being a particularly brave and successful one in opening up discussion. A 2007 publisher initiative to enlist librarians' help to promote Stephen King seemed to overlook the fact that King has been on the most borrowed author list for decades and scarcely needs extra help. Other fallbacks deployed in the traditional promoter's armoury of loosely-book-related-but-not-reader-centred activities include the literary quiz, an excellent tool for finding out if the small percentage of readers who will bother to do it have read the tiny number of titles you are able to include.

Lists of Top Books always generate media interest and a reader-friendly librarian can find ways to piggyback reader activity on this. In 1997, Waterstone's list of the *Top 100 Books* created a lot of controversy and column inches and also achieved a great deal in terms of getting readers talking to each other. The only drawback of list conversations is that they tend to follow the line of, 'How many have you read then?' None of these lists offer readers a route for analysing or sharing their own experience of reading; this is what the library can add.

A primary tenet of the reader-centred approach to promotion is that value judgements are made about the quality of the reading experience enjoyed by the individual rather than about the book. It doesn't matter whether it's Anthony Trollope or Joanna Trollope, as long as the reader is satisfied. To have a promotion which forces people into quality debates, measuring one book against another, contradicts the fundamental truth about reading: no two readers will have exactly the same experience reading the same book. A book does not arrive as a pre-determined experience in which you are guaranteed to laugh/cry/despair/ rejoice, or your money back. Our own life experience, prejudices, preferences and mood at the point when we read the book determine our response to it. It is this which makes talking about books so interesting. Book discussions would be very short and terribly bland if opinions never differed and members often cite the fact that reading groups provide a safe context for argument as a key motivation for attending.

Trust the reader

After years of approaching promotion and events in a traditional way, it can be hard to believe that a new direction is going to work and is worth the investment of time and resources. However, thousands of librarians across the UK can testify to the impact and success of reader-centred work. The enjoyment of the readers, the way staff attitudes change and the new energy that's released all have considerable, lasting impact, not least on staff morale. Success in one small project gives staff the confidence to arrange more.

This nervousness will not come solely from library frontline staff. The reader development librarian will regularly find her/himself having to explain the approach to colleagues, senior managers, funding organisations and publisher partners. Whichbook.net was launched in 2000; a site to choose what to read which starts from the qualities a reader might be looking for rather than an author or title. The largest group of critics were librarians who felt it was a poor substitute for a proper catalogue search. Whichbook in no way replaces the catalogue and is no threat to it; it offers a quite different way to choose. Interestingly, when the Norwegian version, ønskebok.no, launched in 2007, its editors had to deal with exactly the same objection from a similar range of colleagues.

In 1999, Opening the Book and Waterstone's worked with lots of reading groups to create and test a Reading Group Toolbox to support libraries in their development of reading groups. When the Toolbox was finished, Waterstone's and their PR company, whose experience with this type of event rightly told them that this was hardly a story which would attract much in the way of media attention, wanted to create impact by involving authors in a more traditional format. Opening the Book worked hard to persuade them that a party for the contributing reading groups was the way to go. An evening event was therefore planned to take place on the top floor of the new Waterstone's in Piccadilly. Waterstone's were nervous about the event involving readers only and invited a number of authors to attend. Opening the Book wanted reading to be the focus and not writing. The evening proceeded, therefore, on a compromise which absorbed the guest writers into the event, rather than making them the stars. Each reading group was allocated to a table and one author was placed at each. The groups were then given a Toolbox each and left to get on with it.

Waterstone's and the PR company were clearly anxious about a reader-directed event and believed it would be hard to get off the ground. However, as the reading group members began to assemble after their London shopping sprees, and the wine and chat began, the evening turned into such a riotous success, nobody wanted to go home. The authors enjoyed getting direct feedback from readers, even if it wasn't about their own books, and relished the experience of being involved in discussions as readers themselves. The conversation never flagged and at least one of the reading groups decided to read a book by their guest author at their next session. Readers have such a lot in common with each other that whenever they are given space to explore that commonality there will rarely be a dull moment.

Putting the reader at the centre

Any new practice needs to invent its own vocabulary. Creative reading, making an explicit parallel with creative writing, was the first description used by Rachel Van Riel and Chris Meade, while working at Sheffield Libraries in the 1980s, to claim the creative role of the reader in literature. Schools and educational projects have found this term useful.

Opening the Book invented the term reader development in 1993 to claim a wider role for public libraries in audience development for literature. 'Reader' was used instead of 'reading' to signify the activity was about the person rather than the skill. The term evolved to become a description for the body of work undertaken by library and literature staff to promote reading actively and to engage readers in new ways. It can be found in policy statements, reports, job titles and job descriptions throughout UK libraries as well as in government reports. It has become a useful shorthand as a description of professional practice though it is not a phrase to use to market initiatives aimed at readers. Some library services have always preferred to use reading development as a description of their reading promotion activities and have moved the work closer to literacy than to literature. Opening the Book also uses the term reader-centred as a simpler and more direct phrase than reader development.

Whatever you call the activity, the most important thing is to do it. Putting the reader at the centre has brought a new energy to UK library services and it is important as it becomes more successful and embedded that the originating dynamic is not lost.

WAKE-UP CALLS

Misunderstandings, however well-intentioned, undermine reader-centred practice. If you recognise the views below, use the arguments in this chapter to challenge them.

" *Our newsletter, called 'Reader Development' goes to all the reading groups in the county.* "

" *We photocopy lots of book covers - they make great displays.* "

" *You can get lots of stuff from authors' websites for your readers' noticeboard.* "

As reading promotion gains a higher profile nationally, small-scale reader-centred activities may seem unimportant and unglamorous. In pursuing a promotional programme it can make good sense to build in space for the high profile, media attention-grabbers that occur annually. You will be able to benefit from the recognition drawn from coverage in the press, TV and radio. However, to give the best service to your customers and get a return on the inevitable investment of your own and your colleagues' time, you need to add value for your readers. It is the reader-centred activity you devise around these pre-packaged, book- and author-centred events which will improve the quality of the experience and offer long-term returns in audience development objectives.

The temptation to deliver a series of short-term, low-value book-centred promotions when under pressure from senior management, or your own lack of time and resources, will be great. It is counter-productive, however, to punctuate a solid reader development programme with these one-off activities which occupy valuable time and offer few tangible outcomes. It makes much more sense to focus energy on a small number of good quality, reader-centred activities which will help towards achieving objectives. Maintain

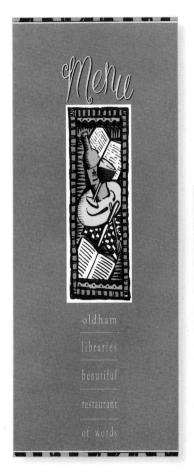

Starting from the reading experience jazzes up the traditional booklist

Main Course

Seriously hungry for words? Why not try one of these main course reads guaranteed by library workers and borrowers to satisfy the biggest appetite.

Some Kind of Black
by Diran Adebayo

An exhilarating multi-flavoured odyssey through the soul kitchens of millennial London. A coming of age story about Dele, a young student, and his sister Dapo, as they glide and stumble by turns through violence, love and politics. A sophisticated, elegantly presented meal which communicates a rare incandescent energy in witty, moving and refreshing language.

Crusader by Nigel Tranter

A Highland Fling. To be savoured in a Scottish castle (real or imagined) after a Burns Night banquet. For adventurous and romantic eaters, or for those who love to travel through time. A meal to share with friends over a glass of single malt whiskey. Savour the history.

The Last Continent by Terry Pratchett

Neighbouring nosh - an Australian barbeque. A meal to share with your friends. A light alfresco eating experience best accompanied by fizzy champagne or a couple of your favourite "tinnys". A rib tickling, hilarious taste of New (Old) World cuisine.

The Godfather by Mario Puzo

A rare steak read. Grilled with olive oil, garlic and bullets of black pepper, having all the ingredients to raise your temperature and inflame temperament, this is not a book for the faint hearted, but if you like your books thick and bloody this is for you, best devoured alone!

Postmortem by Patricia Cornwell

With it's bloody murders and sizzling plot this sirloin steak of a story is a perfect main meal read. Protagonist Kay Scarpetta gives her suspects a grilling they won't forget. A feast for the unrepentant meat eater.

The Stallion by Harold Robbins

Essentially meaty with all the sizzling ingredients of lust, greed, sex and intrigue. Garnished with a sauce of explosive passion to titillate the tastebuds and leave you hungry for a second helping.

About A Boy by Nick Hornby

A delightful main course that will prove enjoyable whether wolfed down or slowly savoured. An insightful and witty tale about the relationship between a man and a boy, both of whom are having trouble growing up.

Monkey by Wu Ch'eng-en

An ancient dish of Chinese legend, translated into modern English by Arthur Waley. A highly satisfying and accessible main course read, Monkey tells the story of Tripitaka's journey to India, but being an allegory is really concerned with what it means to be a human being. Unlike many such works, however, Monkey is also hilarious, and the characters of Pigsy, Sandy, Tripitaka, and of course Monkey himself are unforgettable.

The Holder of the World
by Bharati Mukherjee

Blend together old and new worlds, east and west, present times, past times, a modern day asset hunter, Beigh Masters, who is definitely not Indiana Jones, and the quest for a fabulous ruby, and you have the basic recipe for a wonderful story which really does illuminate 17th century puritan New England, London, and the court of Indian princes. A really satisfying main course read.

Beirut Blues by Hanan al-Shaykh

A genuine Lebanese experience. Asmahon transcends her situation in war torn Beirut by composing letters to her friends, to famous jazz singers and even to the very war that is raging around her. Sensuous and luxurious, Asmahon's responses to family, cityscape, love, and of course food, provide a far more human taste of Beirut than the fast food productions of News programmes.

quality, reader-centred activities which will help towards achieving objectives. Maintain your confidence, and your focus on the reader and the experience of reading, and your time will be well-spent. Investing in reader-centred activities provides your service with a solid and sustainable core of informed and enthused users.

Libraries are still the leaders in prioritising and delivering reader-centred activities amongst all the players in the field. Some publishers and booksellers are investing in supporting reading groups, they use positive images of readers enjoying their books and they display reader comments on the shelves to promote specific titles. But it is still the public library which has the best, consistent access to the reading audience and is carving a unique role in offering reader-centred activity to support and enrich the reading experience.

Libraries can replicate the promotional work already being done by publishers and booksellers; this can lead to some excellent promotions but when there is already such a substantial commitment to it, libraries can only ever play a supporting role. In the wider literary, education and media world, libraries are small beer. They carry little power in the relationship with bigger players and are engaging from a position of gratitude.

When libraries undertake reader-centred work, not only are they giving their readers more but they are also claiming a unique role for the public library which, if nothing else, is a justification of their public funding separately from the commercial sector. With the excellent reader-centred programmes being implemented by many library services in the UK, libraries are doing something different and exceptional. The reader-centred approach is a natural fit for public libraries.

Chapter 2

FINDING OUT WHAT READERS WANT

The information available to libraries to help plan customer services is sometimes limited or one dimensional. Libraries are well-placed to gather basic quantitative data such as issue statistics and footfall. How useful is this level of information, however, if we're trying to plan how many staff members we need on the counter after 5.30pm? Or whether a particular branch library would be a suitable venue for a promotion aimed at 18-25 readers? What if that library doesn't have anyone from this age group coming through the doors?

It is easy to slip into the habit of basing decisions like these on perceptions instead of evidence. During a temporary promotion aimed at men in one branch library, staff were quite certain that the book display was being visited and borrowed from by a majority of female users. When a formal observation of the use of the display was carried out, it was found that the books were strongly attracting male users and their borrowing outweighed that of female users.

In a popular exercise run by Opening the Book trainers in many library services, library staff members were asked to list which sections of the public were missing when it comes to book borrowing. Top of the list were usually teenagers and next were men.

A follow-on exercise then set participants the task of drawing who they saw as the typical library borrower - the person seen most often borrowing fiction from libraries. Picture this person now, in your mind. Is it a she? Is she over 65? Is she sporting a perm, spectacles, and a shopping trolley? The style of the clothing varied according to the wealth of the area served by the library branch, but the gender and age profile, as well as the list of books this person was borrowing, was frequently the same in this exercise in libraries all over the UK.

The second most popular stereotype drawn was a more confident, demanding library user who knew her way round the requests system and made heavy use of it. If it had been in *The Mail on Sunday* reviews page, she'd be there Monday morning demanding it and bemoaning the fact that it was available in bookshops but the library didn't have it yet. This is the borrower whose presence was keenly felt not only in the library building but in the letters page of the local newspaper, by heads of service and elected politicians. If this borrower didn't like something, everyone heard about it. The challenge here is to remember that there are many more library users whose opinions go unexpressed and are not taken into consideration. The individuals who do express an opinion, therefore, have a disproportionate impact on the service.

While this may seem to support thinking in stereotypes, these exercises were a useful way to get staff to start thinking about who their borrowers are. The exercise asked them to focus on this individual and think about what else was going on in their daily life. Did they come to the library by bus or car, or did they walk? What else were they doing while they were out and about? Going to the Post Office, meeting friends, supermarket shopping? Where were they most likely to go on holiday - Majorca, Margate or Miami? It's a short step then to start looking more closely at what their existing reading habits are and what kind of triggers might tempt them to try something different.

Library staff are sometimes resistant to analysing their customer base in this way because they feel it too easily reduces people to stereotypes and the whole point of the library service is that it caters for everybody. Although that is an understandable value position it can be a cover for an unwillingness to think harder. If any retail business took the same attitude to finding out about their customers, they would go bankrupt.

Targeting audiences within the marketplace is essential to the success of any business. The difficulty for public services is that they can't target in this way, simply picking off specific groups, because they have a statutory duty to supply an equal service to all those who live or work in their district. There is no commercial provider with this range. Even the most dominant player in the UK does not have the whole market. Tesco took £1 of every £8 spent in shops in England in 2005 but not everybody shops at Tesco, even for groceries. Some people don't have a branch handy and some people choose a different brand or style, whether this is a more upmarket brand like Waitrose, a value supermarket such as Aldi, a farmers' market or a village shop.

Refusing to analyse your audience can, if you're not careful, lead to complacency where you continue to supply to your existing users, whoever they are, and assume everything is all right. Understanding commercial marketing will always strengthen your service. You don't have to use the knowledge in the way a commercial firm would. For example, a library can identify its best promotional space and use that to promote unknown writers, not mainstream bestsellers.

WAKE-UP CALLS

Misunderstandings, however well-intentioned, undermine reader-centred practice. If you recognise the views below, use the arguments in this chapter to challenge them.

" Staff believe that the library service is here for everyone and that nobody should be put into pigeonholes. "

" We know who our borrowers are, we don't need anybody else to tell us. "

" People who come into libraries know what they want - it's our job just to give it to them. "

Information gathering

Neighbourhood statistics taken from census and other data are freely available online in the UK through **www.statistics.gov.uk**. These give information on local populations by age, ethnicity, economic activity, educational attainment and a host of other factors. Central council departments may well hold further analysis; check what is already available before rushing off to do your own. Many authorities also have in-house expertise in the council who will assist in questionnaire design, sample size advice and statistical analysis though libraries may have to pay for this.

Some library services may have access to more sophisticated marketing tools such as MOSAIC lifestyle analysis. MOSAIC's system was developed by Richard Webber, a visiting professor at University College London's geography department. He says socio-economic classification based on job title, such as A1 or C2, has been weakened by a proliferation of work grades, along with an increase in dual-income couples and pensioners. MOSAIC is a classification system which divides Great Britain into postcode-based neighbourhood types such as Stylish Singles, Low Rise Council, or Independent Elders. The geo-demographic types are based on census data, electoral rolls, commercial credit information and other marketing data. MOSAIC includes categories concerned with job types (such as 'Corporate Chieftains'), others focus on housing ('Coronation Street'), age, family structure, ethnicity ('South Asian industry') and whether the area is urban or rural. This approach can help libraries target more successfully.

The introduction of free internet access has changed the user profile in many libraries in the last ten years. Libraries see a lot more young people and more students. Many also see larger numbers whose first language isn't English. This may be to do with local employment, manufacturing or agricultural workers recruited from Eastern Europe, for example, and also refugees and asylum seekers from many different parts of the world. The basic book borrowing profile has not shifted nearly as much as the overall footfall.

You may be able to access research commissioned by private firms. W. F. Howes, suppliers of large print and audio books, worked with Loughborough University and many library services to gather and analyse responses from large print book borrowers in UK libraries. Over 19,000 valid questionnaires were returned, making this the largest data bank ever gathered from large print readers. The results showed that large print borrowers shared many of the characteristics of the wider reading population - crime was the most popular genre and browsing was the preferred method of choosing what to read by a very large majority. Less expected was the discovery that half of respondents also read standard print books and nearly one third were aged between 51 and 70. The traditional picture of the very elderly romance or western reader as the only consumer of large print was proved to be way out of date.

The quality of the information gathering process you establish will affect the quality of the information you collect. There are many options available, some more time- and labour-intensive than others. The key question to ask at the outset is, 'What do we really want to know?' The follow-up question then has to be, 'Are we prepared to act on whatever we find out in terms of shifting our emphasis, targeting resources or revising the products and services we provide?' If the answer to this last question is negative, why waste time and resources on research in the first place? It is insulting to your users to perpetuate the con trick in which the fact of having undertaken public consultation is seen as having addressed a problem satisfactorily.

Customer consultation

The plain truth is that we already know what most people think about the public library service. The MORI report, *Perceptions of Libraries*, (MORI/Audit Commission, February 2002), carried out for the Audit Commission report *Building Better Library Services*, is one of the largest summaries of national and local data on attitudes to libraries from both users and non-users. There were four areas of concern identified by both users and non-users. Everyone wanted better books, better opening hours, better environments and better marketing.

Many authorities have also commissioned MORI to carry out research or they have undertaken user/non-user surveys themselves. Kent County Council, for example, commissioned MORI to investigate the views of Kent residents and the key findings were the same. The areas of improvement needed to persuade more people to use libraries were again better books, better opening hours, modernising the library environment and better marketing of what libraries offer. Playing a social and community role was also mentioned but not as frequently.

Some authorities have used inventive ways to find out the views of harder to reach groups. The independent consultancy, Book Communications, worked with one authority, for example, to facilitate sessions with primary school children, teenagers, Surestart users, users of voluntary services and asylum seekers. The methodology included workshops with movement games and also phone and face-to-face interviews. The strongest single finding from all of them was that everyone thought that books were the most important thing from the library service.

In all of these surveys, it is clear that the image of the library is as much a barrier as the reality. Reader development techniques are vital in addressing this. The most common reason given for not using libraries after 'I don't have the time,' is, 'They don't have the books I want.' Given what we know about how few people are looking for specific titles, this must be a perception more than a reality. Most libraries carry such a range that whatever a reader wants they will have something to meet that preference. It's just that nobody standing at the door can see this.

So the first question with consultation is 'What do you want to know that's different from what all the other surveys have found out?' You may need to have local information for political reasons. Or you may have specific aspects where knowing more would be really helpful. But do think hard about whether you can use the information already available from other sources and don't spend your valuable energy and resources on finding out what you already know.

In planning your consultation, which part of your audience is most likely to supply the information you need? A scattergun approach which involves all users will result in a flood of information which may not be relevant because of the variation in age profiles, patterns of use, purpose of visits. It is useful to consider targeting smaller communities of users if their relationship to your products and services is more likely to give you an accurate picture of customer awareness or satisfaction. For example, a 24 year-old man visiting the library occasionally to check his emails will have quite a different view from a young mum with a baby in a buggy bringing her older child to choose some picture books.

WAKE-UP CALLS

Misunderstandings, however well-intentioned, undermine reader-centred practice. If you recognise the views below, use the arguments in this chapter to challenge them.

❝ *We run a friendly library service - staff always know who's coming and going.* ❞

❝ *Staff don't expect to get a lot of men in the branches because men don't read that much.* ❞

❝ *The book sale is the most popular thing in this library.* ❞

Questionnaires

Probably the most widely-used form of user consultation is the questionnaire. These are excellent for gathering basic quantitative data. They have their shortcomings, however, in that it is difficult to phrase questions exactly right to get the information you need. Authorities using questionnaires to gather audience response have found that the information they provide can be too general to be helpful. In a survey in East Dunbartonshire, for example, common responses to the question 'What do you like to read?' included 'fiction' and 'a wide range of interests'.

The other problem is that, unless you target very specifically, use of questionnaires is self-elected. People with an axe to grind love to fill in questionnaires! It's a great outlet for them to get creative with their grievances against the service, the books, the staff and all the rest of life's disappointments. At the other end of the spectrum, the regular borrowers who form the bedrock of library audiences and who are responsible for a high percentage of the issues, when presented with a questionnaire, will feel that their beloved branch is under threat and may well ask staff, 'What would you like me to put, dear?'

To make questionnaires really work for you, you need to focus on what you want to know and compose the questions very carefully. Questionnaires can be quantitative, qualitative or a mix of both. If you want to find out what a lot of people think about a fairly straightforward question, phrase the question so it can be answered with a tick box Yes or No. 'Do you always finish a book if you start it?' and 'Do you read just one book at a time?' are questions which work like this. Avoid questions which will frustrate respondents. 'Do you use books to help you sleep?' does not give space to anyone wanting to record that they read in bed but not in order to fall asleep.

If you want a deeper, qualitative response, make sure questions are phrased so they cannot be answered Yes or No. 'Do you like reading?' can only be answered two ways and would give no further insights into the respondent's thoughts. Follow up questions would be required to winkle out any really useful data. 'What do you like about reading?' offers an opportunity for someone to give a response about the quality of their reading experience, how they use it in their life and the sort of books they read. Be aware, however, that this response cannot be easily collated into a statistical analysis; it's an individual response which contributes to qualitative understanding.

It's easy to confuse a PR exercise with finding out information you really want. Journalists and public relations professionals are always looking for statistics that can make a story. This can raise the profile of a particular service and may be well worth doing for that reason as long as you are aware that the need to find one statistic which is newsworthy will drive the work and may outweigh the other more subtle factors you are interested in. Also you may not be able to control the way the news story is used. For example, a question 'Are you attracted to people who read a lot?' may turn into a statistic that '75% of women say they are attracted to men who read a lot.' Before you know it, this may turn into a piece about stereotypical sex-starved spinster librarians fantasising about men who don't exist.

Sample size

The sample sizes used in market research are often quite small. Sufficiently accurate data can be obtained as long as the sample is a representative balance. Recording television viewing figures is a good example here, one hotly debated as advertising revenues follow on audience share. The Broadcasters' Audience Research Board (BARB), responsible for viewing figures in the UK, uses a panel of 5100 homes, that's less than 0.001% of the 60 million UK population. This is higher than in the US where a panel of 5,000 is used to represent a population of 250 million. Of course, professional marketing organisations like BARB spend a lot of time and expertise ensuring their sample is a representative balance. If the sample is representative then the results from 5,000 households will not be different from the results from 10,000.

In using a questionnaire, you can ensure that you get a good demographic representation in your responses by tasking staff to give the questionnaires to targeted groups, rather than passing them out to everyone. For example, you might decide that a fair sample of your customers would have to include 25 women aged approx 25-40, 25 men from the same age range, 25 women approx 70+, and so on.

A good example of how a questionnaire can be used is provided by the Emrald project where nine East Midlands library services participated in a user consultation supported by Briony Train of the Centre for the Public Library in the Information Society, Department of Information Studies, University of Sheffield. The original focus of the research was on the impact of *Black Bytes*, a promotion of Black British writing with a 16-30 appeal, which was implemented across the region in 2003. In order to avoid giving leading questions and obtaining biased responses, it was decided that the evaluation should have a more general focus, investigating people's reading choices, and factors that may affect these choices. Rather than couching the consultation in terms of 'Did the *Black Bytes* promotion interest you?' a more general questionnaire was designed on 'What do you like to read?'

The questionnaire was distributed to 16 libraries which had hosted the promotion plus five which had not as a control group. A fixed number of questionnaires were distributed to each venue and they were given a venue code so that information could be collated on the type of library the respondent was using; urban or rural, high or low Black and Asian communities, etc. Forms were handed out as books were issued and staff were asked to specifically target a good cross-section of users and not to give the forms to the same profile of person each time. The questionnaires were distributed twice at all venues, once before the *Black Bytes* promotion and once after. 1047 valid questionnaires were completed, a sufficiently large sample size to enable the collection of statistically significant data.

WAKE-UP CALLS

Misunderstandings, however well-intentioned, undermine reader-centred practice. If you recognise the views below, use the arguments in this chapter to challenge them.

“ We don't need questionnaires - our borrowers tell us when they're not happy. ”

“ Our management team ran a questionnaire two years ago and it showed 96% were happy with what we do. ”

“ We ran a questionnaire two years ago but I never found out what happened with it. ”

Interpreting results

The results provide a good picture of the reading habits of library borrowers in the first years of the 21st century. For staff involved in reader development, it was very encouraging to find that how the stock is displayed in the library was the most important factor influencing choice. It was also more important to the majority of respondents to have a well-sited and well-stocked display which changes frequently than to have lots of displays at once.

There was a remarkable consistency in results across age, gender, class and the rural/urban/ suburban differentiation. There were some detailed differences, for example men were more influenced by reviews and women by friends' recommendations but men and women share the same top three preferences, this is just a shift of what is in second and third position. (Both put display in the library first.) Borrowers in working class areas were less likely to read literary fiction than those in middle class or mixed areas but they were more likely to read Black British and Asian fiction. The full report is available on **http://cplis.sheffield.ac.uk**.

In the key area of attitudes to Black British fiction the results were extremely interesting. 3.5% of the sample usually read Black British fiction and 32.2% would not consider reading it, leaving 64.3% who did not usually read it but did not rule it out. Library professionals who believe that library stock should follow popular demand would argue from this that if only 3.5% want Black British fiction, only tiny amounts should be bought. Library professionals who believe the library's role is to open up reading choices would argue that if 64.3% don't read Black British fiction but would consider reading it, there is a great need for active promotion to draw it to their attention. A further figure from the survey results would support this; Black British fiction was 4.3% less unpopular with respondents to the second questionnaire, a significant increase which could suggest the *Black Bytes* promotion had affected their response.

What do you like to read?

1. During your visit to the library TODAY, what type(s) of book for yourself were you looking for (please tick all that apply)?
Please exclude any music CDs, DVDs or videos.

Science Fiction/fantasy	☑	Crime fiction	☑
Gay/lesbian fiction	☐	'Chick lit'e.g. Lisa Jewell, Jane Green, Marian Keyes	☐
Black British fiction	☐	Asian fiction (in English)	☐
Family sagas	☐	Audio books (books on tape/CD)	☐
Non-fiction	☐	Literary fiction	☐
Romance fiction	☐	War/spy/adventure	☐
'Lad lit' e.g. Nick Hornby, Irvine Welsh, Mike Gayle	☐	Other **(please give details)**..	

2. Where did you look for these books (please tick all that apply)?

Displays of new books	☐	Other displays or promotions	☐
The returns trolley	☐	On the shelf	☐
The library catalogue	☐	Other (please give details).................................	

3. What type of books would you USUALLY borrow from the library (please tick all that apply)?

Science fiction/fantasy	☐	Crime fiction	☐
Gay/lesbian fiction	☐	'Chick lit'e.g. Lisa Jewell, Jane Green, Marian Keyes	☐
Black British fiction	☐	Asian fiction (in English)	☐
Family sagas	☐	Audio books (books on tape/CD)	☐
Non-fiction	☐	Literary fiction	☐
Romance fiction	☐	War/spy/adventure	☐
'Lad lit' e.g. Nick Hornby, Irvine Welsh, Mike Gayle	☐	Other (please give details).............................	

PLEASE TURN OVER.

4. In the following list, are there any types of book that you would NOT consider reading (please tick all that apply)?

Science fiction/fantasy	☐	Crime fiction	☐
Gay/lesbian fiction	☐	'Chick lit'e.g. Lisa Jewel, Jane Green, Marian Keyes	☐
Black British fiction	☐	Asian fiction (in English)	☐
Family sagas	☐	Audio books (books on tape/CD)	☐
Non-fiction	☐	Literary fiction	☐
Romance Fiction	☐	War/spy/adventure	☐
'Lad lit' e.g. Nick Hornby, Irvine Welsh, Mike Gayle	☐	Other (please explain)...............................	

5. What factors usually influence you in your choice of library books (please tick all that apply)?

Display in the library	☐	Library staff recommendation	☐
I saw it/them on the returns trolley	☐	Friends' recommendation	☐
Internet	☐	Current events	☐
Newspaper/magazine/TV review	☐	'Prizewinners' e.g. Orange prize, Booker prize	☐
I saw it in a bookshop	☐	Other (please explain)....................	

We would be grateful if you would complete this section.

Your gender   Male ☐   Female ☐

Your age   16-19 ☐   20-29 ☐   30-39 ☐   40-49 ☐   50-59 ☐   60-69 ☐   70+ ☐

This section is optional.
We are interested in knowing more about people's reading habits and choice of books from the library.
Are you prepared to give 10 minutes of your time so that we can phone you to ask a few more questions? Yes ☐   No ☐
If you answered yes, **what time do you prefer?** ☐ Morning (9-12) ☐ Afternoon (12-4.30) ☐ Early evening (4.30-6) ☐ Any

My name is Mr/Mrs/Miss/Ms......................................   **My telephone number is** (............) ....

East Midlands Libraries working together to promote   **N.B. All responses will be treated in the strictest confidence.**
books and reading supported by East Midlands Arts.   **Thank you very much for your help.**

The group who would not consider reading Black British fiction are also interesting to look at further. There was a strong correlation between reluctance to read Black British fiction and reluctance to read Asian fiction. There was a further definite correlation between respondents who would not read gay/lesbian fiction and those who would not read Black British fiction. Gay and lesbian fiction was the least popular reading choice with 63.4% of respondents not prepared to read books in this category. Black British fiction, Asian fiction and gay and lesbian fiction cover a huge range of kinds of reading experience; they have no literary qualities or other characteristics exclusively in common with each other. What's at work here is not just a reading preference. Clearly large numbers of library borrowers do not want to read these books not because of what they are but because of what they represent.

The extent of this reluctance was only uncovered because the questionnaire was open and non-judgmental. It was very careful to be neutral - it is not the job of the library service to tell people what to read. The answers clearly evidence the success of this approach as there is a high level of honesty in the responses - no-one is made to feel ashamed or to give what they think is the 'right' answer.

The evidence from the 'What do you like to read?' survey can be used to justify low levels of provision of Black British, Asian and gay and lesbian fiction. Or it can be used to highlight the importance of high profile purchase and promotion in these areas in order to overcome the barriers that exist around them.

It can also open up a wider debate about the importance of reader development in the cultural role of libraries. Reading prejudices and defences of all sorts abound - genre ones like science fiction or poetry which many readers will not look at; gender biases such as chick lit/lad lit or adventure/romance; and ones rooted in a sense of difference of culture, religion or sexuality. Reader development was invented in recognition of this reading behaviour - we all stick to known preferences and we're reluctant to take risks. Yet at the same time we are thirsting for that good read we've always wanted and we sometimes get bored with our regular favourites. The first reader development book published, *Opening the Book - finding a good read* by Rachel Van Riel and Olive Fowler*, aimed to help individuals overcome their prejudices and open up a wider choice. Reader development has always taken the approach that no-one should apologise for what they read or feel embarrassed or judged by others. The 'What do you like to read?' survey shows how

Van Riel & Fowler *Opening the Book - finding a good read*, 1996. *

important it is when introducing new titles to respect people's choice not to read them, and to tempt rather than preach.

Focus groups

Less common within libraries' customer consultation practice is the focus group. Pulling together a group of users into one room at the same time and asking them what you want to know can be a more time- and resource-efficient way of gathering in-depth feedback. Focus groups are structured discussions led by someone with reasonable interviewing skills. They usually involve between seven and ten people and should be comfortable and enjoyable to all the participants, so putting people at their ease is crucial. You will want to consider the location, the time of day and offer appropriate refreshments. A focus group gives participants a forum where they can bounce off and build on each other's opinions, providing an opportunity for deeper, qualitative exploration of a topic than would be provided by a one-dimensional questionnaire.

As with questionnaires, it is important to target the invitations precisely to get good demographic representation. Once again, if attendance is wide open, you are giving an ideal forum to your local, litigious zealot who enjoys nothing better than the opportunity to challenge the council on all aspects of its services.

You can draw together groups representing a mix of ages and backgrounds or you have the option of targeting specific groups appropriate to the topic/service you are researching. You can also use existing groups, such as reading groups and Friends of the Library groups, for focus research, as long as you bear in mind that these groups are likely to have a strong bias in favour of the service. Using these groups as sounding boards has the additional benefit of giving them an opportunity to feel involved in decision-making and they can become very strong advocates for the library service.

When targeting non-user groups, obviously it will be necessary to set up outreach contact with groups in the community, for example civic, voluntary or faith-based groups. If you are particularly exploring non-use of the library by specific groups in your community, attendance at focus groups may have to be incentivised in some way. Refreshments are a must, of course, but you may also wish to consider paying participants for 45 minutes of their time.

Arts-based consultation

Enabling equal access to consultation to all user groups offers particular challenges. Cultural, social and educational differences all affect how individuals perceive and are able to respond to traditional consultation methods. Even for confident, articulate customers who are comfortable with traditional approaches, there is a possibility that the very format of the consultation hampers any creative thinking.

In 2005, Bolton Libraries experimented successfully with using arts-based techniques to consult the local community about a project to demolish an existing library and to replace it with a new library building. This library was in a disadvantaged area with a large Asian population. Traditional consultation methods were considered to be potentially alienating and Bolton decided to test new and innovative ways of consulting with culturally diverse communities.

Bolton Libraries received funding from the Laser Foundation to appoint Book Communications to plan and implement the consultation programme using local artists to lead various sessions. These sessions enabled participants to think creatively about the library service, empowered those who are put off by formal approaches and didn't depend on high verbal skills.

Involving artists in these sessions is helpful but not essential. Following the consultation, a toolkit was produced to enable other authorities to employ these techniques and using this, members of library staff could deliver the exercises themselves. The toolkit and full details of the process are available on Bolton's website at **www.bolton.gov.uk**.

User observation

While customer consultation has its place in a service which prides itself on the quality of its public service and its responsiveness to customer demands, the most objective way of discovering what your customers are actually doing is by watching them.

This approach, widely used in retail environments, is far more inclusive and comprehensive. Asking your customers, directly, what they think about the service or a particular feature in a library may result in a bland response - nobody particularly wants to be aggressive or offensive in this situation so they may say whatever they think you want to hear! For instance, asking a customer if they like a particular book display in a library will probably result in a range of positive responses. However, if you monitor the display closely and watch how many of your users actually look at it, how many approach it for a closer look, how many pick up things from the display and then how many actually borrow from it, your picture of how that display functions as a promotional tool is much more complete and accurate. What observation can't tell you, of course, is whether the customer is satisfied with the display itself or with the book chosen from it - only follow-up interviewing would do that.

Opening the Book introduced this technique to English libraries from the work of Paco Underhill, the analyst who revolutionised global understanding of shopping behaviour.[*]

WAKE-UP CALLS

Misunderstandings, however well-intentioned, undermine reader-centred practice. If you recognise the views below, use the arguments in this chapter to challenge them.

" Customers ask us for help all the time. "

" Most people wouldn't use self-issue, they'd much rather talk to a human being. "

" Our borrowers really appreciate the little genre labels we put on the spines. That's how most of them find what they're after. "

[*] **www. envirosell.com** and Underhill, Paco, *Why We Buy - the Science of Shopping*, Orion 1999.

Involving staff in undertaking observations was initially simply a training exercise developed through the Branching Out project. It was a good way for professional staff not working on the shop floor to get a feel for what was going on in their library spaces. Staff from 33 very different authorities across England came together to share their findings and the results were explosive. Across counties, cities and London boroughs, the findings were the same. Whether staff had tried observation in small or large libraries, and whatever the time of day, the results remained broadly the same.

The key findings were:

- the average length of visit was between 5 and 9 minutes
- 90% of people entering the adult lending area visited the returns trolley first, where there was one
- fewer than 1 in 10 people approached staff members for help
- fewer than 1 in 20 used the library catalogue

In 1999 these results were surprising to everyone. Most people guessed the average visit to be 20-25 minutes at least. Staff assumed far more of their customers spoke to them than actually did. This is natural when you think about it - if you are focussed on serving the people who ask, you will not be aware of those who don't.

Thinking further about the results drove the need for change home. The average length of visit includes all those who stay two or three hours to study and all those who book computers in slots of 30 and 60 minutes. This means that many people must be staying less than five minutes for the average to fall between five and nine. What do libraries offer to people who drop in for only a few minutes?

Observing spaces and people

Since that first trial, Opening the Book has run similar training sessions across another 40+ English library services. Every authority in Wales and Scotland has also joined in through their reader development networks, Estyn Allan (Branching Out in Wales) and the Reader Development Network in Scotland. What set out as a training exercise ended up producing substantial evidence of library use and changing practice in many libraries.

◇	A	B	C	D	E	F	G	H	I	J	K
1	Data Sheet No....										
2											
3	Library..				Date..............		Observer..............................				
4											
5											
6											
7			Age				Gender		Borrowed		
8	Time In	under 25	25 - 40	40-60	over 60	male	female	yes	no	Time Out	
9											
10											
11											
12											
13											
14											
15											
16											
17											
18											
19											
20											
21											
22											
23											
24											
25											
26											
27											

Data collection sheet | Comparison of day totals | Analysis in half-hours

Sample data collection sheet for observing time of day, length of visit, age, gender and whether the person borrowed.

Sample data analysis sheet for a small library comparing time of day totals. Use this to analyse which age group and gender use the library at what times.

◇	A	E	F	G	H	I	J	K	L	M	N	O	P
1	Library												
2													
3													
4	Date	Duration of Visit			Gender		Age				Borrowed		
5		< 10	10-30	30 >	Male	Female	< 25	25-40	40-60	60 >	yes	no	
6	10.00	1	2	1	1	3	0	0	0	4	2	2	
7	10.30	1	2	0	0	3	1	0	1	1	1	2	
8	11.00	2	4	1	6	1	0	1	4	2	5	2	
9	11.30	0	4	0	1	3	1	1	1	1	2	2	
10	12.00												
11	12.30												
12													
13													
14													
15													
16													
17													
18													
19													
20													
21													
22													
23													
24													

Analysis in half-hours

Date	Time of day			Duration of Visit			Gender		Age				Borrowed
	am	pm	eve	< 10	10-30	30 >	Male	Female	< 25	25-40	40-60	60 >	
23-Nov	289	156	78	387	82	54	195	328	93	127	157	146	235
24-Nov	212	170	94	318	96	62	217	259	118	106	123	129	224
26-Nov													
27-Nov													
29-Nov													

Library ....

Data collection sheet \ Comparison of day totals \ Analysis in half-hours

Sample data analysis sheet for larger library over a week showing most visits are under ten minutes. The morning is the busiest time and more women than men use the library.

Another approach to user observation is to monitor one particular space in the library. For example, you could use the approach to determine how well a Quick Choice area is being used. Plan in advance what you want to find out and design your data collection sheet accordingly. Do you want to know how many people out of the total visiting your library use the Quick Choice area? This will mean one person counting numbers entering the library for the chosen time period and another person counting numbers entering the Quick Choice area. Or you can track the age and gender of users if you want to find out if your Quick Choice area is appealing more to one user group than another. This can be used to plan changes to library layout and identify best location of displays. Or observe at different times of day to find out when it is busiest in order to plan topping up routines.

Another approach which delivers a different perspective on how your library is being used is to track individual borrowers as they travel round the space. A user is discreetly followed from the point where they enter the library. Their arrival time is noted and the observer then makes careful notes about where the visitor goes, what they look at, what they pick up, whether they borrow anything and, finally, their time of departure.

	Observation Sheet No: .... Date: .... Location:							
No	Time arrive	Person	Type	Moved	Looked	Touched	Borrowed	Time left
1								
2								
3								
4								
5								

© Opening the Book Ltd 2003

Sample data collection sheet for observing users in one space.

Case study 1 - Using observation to help plan the look and feel and the stock of a small library

Surrey Libraries undertook a review of its 24 community libraries in order to develop a new model that reflected the needs of the people the libraries serve. Two libraries would be refurbished as demonstrations of what the new model could be like. The first step was to find out who actually uses these libraries. The expectations of everyone involved - staff in the branches, library management and Opening the Book as external consultants - was that the dominant group would be elderly. Opening the Book was planning to design an excellent library for fit, active over-70s but suggested a more accurate picture of the age ranges of the users could be gained from a detailed observation exercise. Surrey felt this was important to inform the work on the next phase of change in library design and stock selection.

Opening the Book helped Surrey libraries to structure a programme of user observations in each of the community libraries. These took place on two different days, at different times and in different weeks. The aim was to discover the age and gender of the borrowers who used the libraries at those times. This survey was a very simple model, carried out by staff on the counter alongside their other duties.

The observation was first carried out in five libraries and then extended to all 24 of the smallest libraries in the county. The results were similar across all 24.

	A	B		D	E	F	G	H	I	J	K	L	M	N
1								Age						
2				0 - 5	5 - 10	10 - 15	15 - 20	20 - 30	30 - 40	40 - 50	50 - 60	60 - 70	70 +	Total
3														
4	Bramley Day 1			2	7	4	4	5	8	23	17	16	23	109
5														
6	Bramley Day 2			10	7	0		6	26	11	10	8	16	94
7														
8	Chertsey Day 1			9	11	14	9	26	29	21	27	18	24	188
9														
10	Chertsey Day 2			10	10	9	7	37	22	16	18	19	3	151
11														
12	Cobham Day 1			22	16	12	17	72	41	40	40	27	33	320
13														
14	Cobham Day 2			11	14	12	3	43	46	36	22	22	27	236
15														
16	Frimley Day 1			27	7	7	7	14	29	23	24	33	26	197
17														
18	Frimley Day 2			6	10	7	6	14	20	9	21	21	23	137
19														
20	Merstham Day 1			13	16	2	3	13	5	4	5	8	21	90
21														
22	Merstham Day 2			3	5	0	3	2	3	2	1	3	10	32
23														
24	Total			2007 20/12	103	67	59	232	229	185	185	175	206	
25														

Sheet1 | Sheet2 | Sheet3

Results of age observation in five libraries.

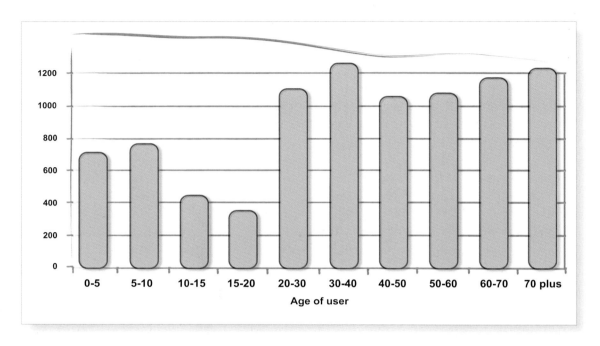

Results of age observation in 24 libraries.

The observation showed very clearly that the largest user group across all 24 libraries during the period of the survey were the 30 to 40 age group. There were an appreciable number of over 70s, as anticipated, but there were a lot more adults under 70 than over 70. Surrey Libraries used the results of the survey to inform stock selection for these libraries. They recognised that they were buying the majority of stock aimed at older age groups and were in danger of neglecting titles for the 20s to 50s. The balance of stock in the two refurbished libraries has been shifted to the younger user group. The brief for the design of the interior layout - the overall colour scheme, the look and feel of the spaces - was similarly shifted. Had Surrey Libraries gone ahead on their initial assumption that over 70s were the majority users, they would have planned a library model for the wrong generation.

Case study 2 - Using observation to compare visits and issues

Warrington Libraries undertook a week-long observation exercise in two libraries resulting in over 200 observations of individual users. They then looked in more detail at the short-stay visitors to see how many of them had borrowed something from the library on that visit. Of the people who were in the library for nine minutes or less, 43% had borrowed. 57% - well over half - had not.

Of course, people come in to the library for lots of different reasons and may be perfectly well satisfied with their visit without borrowing. But is this true of short-stay visitors? It takes longer than nine minutes to use a computer and you often have to wait till a daily newspaper is available. You can look up something in a book fairly quickly but a more complicated enquiry could well take more than five to nine minutes. Staff were left to wonder what these people had come into the library for? Was it that they had come in looking for inspiration and temptation - that elusive good read - but had been unable to find it?

Listening to your customers

Knowing how many and how often is very useful but won't tell you everything you need to know. Statistics can evidence trends in patterns of reader behaviour but they won't explain the reasons behind the change. To check whether short-stay customers had failed to find a tempting book or had come into the library for a different purpose, you would need to ask a representative sample on the spot.

Sometimes library staff can assume they have things right for certain borrower needs but further checking can often reveal that there is room for improvement. In one particular library, for example, staff followed the common practice in the UK of putting the large print fiction near the entrance so that it was convenient for the elderly people who used it. Conversations with borrowers revealed that this wasn't a comfortable experience for older people because it was draughty near the door and there was nowhere to sit down.

The library staff moved the large print section to a space much further into the library which had been dark and little used. They added some chairs and a small table and installed a large flood spotlight with a warm-coloured bulb. They then weeded the large print books thoroughly and added some audiobooks to a much slimmer collection of books. The area was immediately voted a great success by the elderly ladies who were the main customers for the stock and became a meeting place for them. Library staff were particularly surprised by comments from a number of the large print borrowers saying they were so grateful for 'All the new books'. No new stock had been bought but because the presentation of stock had improved, readers were able to find books that they hadn't seen before.

Meanwhile, the vacated space in the prime display spot in the library was reorganised to showcase new fiction, popular paperbacks and a range of DVDs. Issues of contemporary fiction and DVDs went up as younger adults in a hurry could choose much faster without having to navigate round the large print users who had previously dominated the space.

Qualitative data takes longer to collect and cannot be gathered by observation alone. All library services offer basic feedback mechanisms such as comments and suggestions boxes. Reader development practice has taken this further by encouraging borrowers to share comments on what they've read through readers' noticeboards or message slips inside books. This kind of data can be very useful in revealing how the customer is using the product and what they are getting out of it.

The largest qualitative data sampling in the UK from 2006-2009 is being created by thousands of staff taking an online training course used by most library services in England. Chapter Six discusses the Frontline course in more detail.

The first task given to all library staff on the course is to talk to five different borrowers in the library about how they choose what to read next. Staff record what the five people say and also their own reactions to undertaking the exercise. The purpose of the exercise is individual learning for the staff taking the course but data about thousands of library readers is being gathered as a by-product.

Common themes emerged strongly from the first 2000 borrower interviews. The first lesson is about the relation of staff and customers in UK public libraries. Most staff are unused to approaching customers and find this a very big change of role which is quite

WAKE-UP CALLS

Misunderstandings, however well-intentioned, undermine reader-centred practice. If you recognise the views below, use the arguments in this chapter to challenge them.

" I don't have time to talk to the borrowers. "

" My manager thinks I'm gossiping if I stop to talk to the readers. "

" Our head of service has sent a memo to all our staff instructing them to talk more to the customers. "

demanding to carry out. Library staff feel more comfortable interacting over the counter and responding to direct enquiries. They are also nervous of starting a conversation about books; if they want to be sociable, they feel safer talking about the time of year, the difficulties of parking, the weather.

So the first surprise for many staff was just how many people were willing to talk about their reading and how enjoyable the experience was on both sides:

> 'I was really surprised that everyone I approached was happy to talk to me. I thought they would ignore me, or think I was intruding.'

> 'I did expect to have at least some resistance or negative comments but everyone was really keen to talk about what they do and don't like reading.'

The conversation was not enquiry-based and did not revolve around recommending specific titles. Staff found that starting from a general question around reading was much easier than starting from making recommendations and opened up more interesting discussions too. The conversation quickly became two-way, instead of the staff member taking the expert role:

> *'I asked the people that I spoke to if they could recommend a book to me. I got lots of good suggestions. I'd never thought of doing that before.'*

What has been discovered about what readers want through all these thousands of conversations? The most common finding is that people are in a hurry and that this impacts not only on the way they use the library but what they choose. The majority of people interviewed use face-on display, promotions or returns and this is a shock to library staff who mostly think that borrowers browse the shelves. There is also a real sense of surprise about who chooses what; it was harder to guess what any individual might be reading than staff expected.

> *'I was amazed to find that so many people liked science fiction - people you just wouldn't expect!'*

Another common discovery is that people are very prejudiced about what they will not read but not so definite about what interests them. This is where library staff can begin to define a new role for the service:

> *'By far the best conversations were about what people would never, ever read. But it was funny that when we talked about those books, that readers often were quite curious about them. I would like to think up a way of showing readers that the books that they think that they hate might turn out to interest them if they gave them a chance.'*

> *'I think the best question I used was 'Do you ever take a risk with a book - try something you wouldn't normally touch with a bargepole?' The responses ranged from 'I've never thought about doing that' to 'I'd like to try other things but I wouldn't know where to start'. It feels like a really different way of working with readers, and really positive. It's something I'll do again.'*

> *'Most people began by telling me they know the authors they like. But when*

*I asked them how they found these authors the conversation developed quite
differently as they talked about how difficult they find it to discover new
favourites. Clearly there is plenty of need for our work.'*

Preconceptions about what is happening in a library, what regular customers are thinking
and the barriers which prevent people finding what they want, are being directly
challenged by simple questions about their reading experiences. The reader-centred
question, 'How do you choose what to read next?' leads into greater awareness of bigger
issues such as display, stock arrangement and signage, and opens up many challenges to
the traditional way of organising public libraries. This is justification in itself for investing
in a reader-centred approach. Reader development professionals are only just beginning to
unlock the full potential offered by this radical shift of focus.

Chapter 3

REACDER-FRIENDLY ENVIRONMENTS

In the age of the make-over no surface has been left unmolested. Interior design became the new rock and roll and celebrity designers stippled, stapled and MDF'd everything they touched. Fed a constant diet of magazines and TV programmes about the desirability and achievability of change, the British public's aspirations towards environments shifted upwards. Add to this an increasing sophistication in commercial marketing and advertising, and huge improvements in retail layouts, and suddenly you have an audience that expects more.

It is hardly surprising, therefore, that the reality of the typical British library interior fails to inspire or impress, particularly with a young audience. Years of under-investment have taken their toll and many library buildings are shabby and uninviting. The number of products and services offered by the library add to the pressure on space. The amount of visual information the eye has to deal with when entering an average lending library can be confusing, even overwhelming; a plethora of public information posters and leaflets; confusing directional signs in different colours and styles; boards with opening hours information; greeting cards and spectacles for sale; and behind all this shelves of spine-on books stretching as far as the eye can see. There's no way a reader can take it all in. One visitor, interviewed on exiting the local library about what she'd borrowed, sighed: 'Oh, I just gave up. I grabbed a book on knitting - I don't even knit!'

Strengths and weaknesses of library culture

Public libraries are unpressured environments. You can do what you want, stay as long as you like and nobody will bother you. You don't have to spend money, you are in the warm out of the rain, there is no dress code and nobody will challenge what you are doing. There is also plenty to occupy yourself with if you're killing time. There are very few public places in 21st century Britain with these characteristics. Parks and squares are subject to weather, churches are locked, shopping centres are patrolled by security staff, briefed to move on anyone they think undesirable.

The public library is free, warm and safe. Friendly informality is a great strength of the UK public library tradition and is why libraries have been safe havens for all kinds of people who are uncertain of their welcome elsewhere. Libraries should be proud of their record here. They have always tolerated eccentricity. They have provided space for people who sometimes don't have other options, whether students who can't afford heating bills or asylum seekers newly arrived in a strange country.

Library staff tend to see themselves as people first - the person comes before the job. This is true for the specialist librarian with a love of a particular subject and for the part-time library assistant who gives more than the hours she is paid because she takes pride in 'her' library. There are clearly strengths in this tradition but there are also problems. Branch libraries can come to reflect the personal tastes and idiosyncrasies of the staff who work in them. Staff bring in plants, ornaments or soft toys and see this as humanising the space and making it more welcoming. Counters get cluttered not only with objects relating to work tasks but with things relating to personal habits. This blurs the boundary between the personal and the professional, making public space into personal territory. It assumes that others share the same tastes as you. Where budgets are also tight, it sometimes leads to an acceptance of shabbiness, untidiness and unfinished tasks as the normal library environment.

WAKE-UP CALLS

Misunderstandings, however well-intentioned, undermine reader-centred practice. If you recognise the views below, use the arguments in this chapter to challenge them.

" The 'You don't have to be mad to work here' notice behind the counter really makes everybody laugh. "

" Our window space is well used by community groups. The operatic society had its 50th anniversary display there for months, they were so pleased. "

" We bring plants in to make it feel more homely. "

Some customers, particularly those who have been using the library for many years, find this a comfortable experience; they see it as relaxed and informal. They feel at ease with the staff and are likely to stop for a chat. But others will find this environment unattractive and down-at-heel; they see it as messy and confused with nothing to offer. They don't feel comfortable or welcome moving into space which expresses personal taste very different from their own. They will keep their transactions to a minimum.

Library environments can feel like the personal fiefdom of the individual manager; the environment is personality-related as much as service-related. This is true of all organisations to some degree, of course, but it is more visible in libraries than in most. It is common in UK libraries for staff to choose the carpet and the colour of the paint on the walls in a way which is unheard-of in the brand-conscious retail sector. This may seem charmingly democratic but it results in poorly designed environments for customers.

There is sometimes resistance to corporate initiatives to change this environment from staff who value the informality and individuality of library culture. It is true that heavy-handed corporate branding can be off-putting to customers, particularly if it obscures the product offer. But there needs also to be a recognition that informality and individuality can lead to amateurism where the customers who happen to share tastes with the staff are those who feel most comfortable. A professional service is one which gives all customers an equal service.

An example of where putting reader needs first conflicts with the individualism of traditional library culture is the vexed question of uniforms. The idea of a staff uniform causes revulsion and outrage to many library staff who see it as an infringement of personal liberty and a formalisation of a customer relationship they wish to keep more informal and human. But from the customer point of view some means of identifying staff is crucial.

In traditional libraries, customers know the staff are the ones behind the counter. But reader-centred libraries are moving staff out from the counter to be more available in the public areas. The old line that the staff are the ones with no coats on is not true in an age when most young people don't wear outdoor coats. Badges are too small to be seen from a distance and are completely invisible from behind. It isn't necessary to introduce a full uniform but a large enough visual signal is needed. Some services have introduced branded sweatshirts and T-shirts, others have opted for a staff colour (wear any style of top you like as long as it's in the colour). These are easily recognised ways of advertising staff identity. Other alternatives under discussion in the UK are the result of awkward compromise - bigger badges don't solve the problem unless they are so big as to be a source of comedy, a sash worn over clothes connects more to a parade than a customer-service situation.

Influencing customers

The retail sector invests a great deal of money in understanding what customers want and what makes them tick. Retailers transfer this acquired knowledge into action by developing sympathetic layouts which work with customers' natural browsing patterns to draw them through the store.

Store owners keenly monitor the demographic profile of their customers to find out who they're attracting. This information impacts on store layout, marketing, and what you're likely to find on the shelves there. Some retailers have used this profiling to ensure that the music played in-store matches the taste of the dominant customer group using the store at any given time of the day. It may not seem like much, but these subtle, mood enhancing tweaks add to making the customer feel comfortable, more likely to stay in the store longer and, ultimately, spend more. Libraries can learn from the same techniques to attract new customers and increase borrowing.

The use of smell in retail environments is also being keenly researched. For many years, store owners have been aware that particular smells piped into stores, such as fresh baking and coffee, will provoke a positive response from customers. In his RSA Lecture, 'Smell: Can we use it to manipulate behaviour?' Dr G Neil Martin, Senior Lecturer in Neuropsychology Cognition and Brain Sciences at the Middlesex University Research Centre, reported: 'An experimental study diffused either lavender, ginger, spearmint or orange odour into a mocked-up store as business studies students evaluated its environment and products. The students expressed greater intent to visit the store in the scented conditions and regarded the merchandise as more up-to-date, varied and of higher quality.'[*]

In a similar vein, an experiment conducted by psychologists at the University of Leicester researched the effect of music on shopping habits. Over a period of two weeks they played

Spangenberg, Crowley & Henderson, 'Improving the Store Environment: Do Olfactory Cues [*] Affect Evaluations and Behaviors?', *Journal of Marketing*, Vol 60 No2, 1996.

French and German music at a local branch of Asda. The results were clear. When French music was played, sales of French wine outnumbered sales of German wine by a third. Sales of German wine rose when German music was played. An experiment carried out in the US found that if classical music was played in off-licences, shoppers would gravitate towards more expensive wines and diners ordered more expensive food in restaurants if the piped music was classical*.

However Machiavellian you think these techniques are, there is an important lesson to be learned here. Libraries traditionally are quite passive towards their customers and establish layouts and systems which they expect the users to fit into, rather than building the systems to suit the users. In libraries we may not wish to manipulate our customers to the level that some retailers do but we can take the same approach of finding out as much as possible about the customers in order to treat them as individuals and directly target specific services and products to meet their needs and expectations.

Many library staff can tell stories of how demand was manipulated unintentionally. These usually revolve around situations where physical work is done in the library - redecoration or the floor is up to mend a pipe - so shelving has to be moved. Library staff recount these tales with astonishment: 'When a bit of the ceiling fell down in the corner and we had to rope that section off, we thought that the regular borrowers would be really fed up. Nobody complained, though, and they all just borrowed from other areas of the library.' Armed with this evidence of customer behaviour, it should then be a small step to making changes in the library layout which can reproduce the effect.

For example, in one East Midlands library, the most popular area was two bays of mixed popular genres. More books issued from this area than any other. When the library got a new carpet, the shelving was all put back in a slightly different order and the popular area was replaced by the last part of the alphabetical sequence. The staff reported with glee that for three weeks after they reopened, nobody noticed. Everybody who had previously used the popular genre section bowled up to their usual spot and just grabbed whatever caught their eye. Authors beginning with W, Y and Z had never been so popular!

A school librarian hearing this story put it to good effect in her own library. She carried out some observation research and realised that children were only penetrating halfway into the space. The A-L stock issued well but the M-Zs were dead. Students were looking at the first run of books inside the door and either borrowed from that or gave up and went out.

---

* 'Human Traffic', *The Guardian*, 09.03.2000.

It was a small enough library for her to initiate an overhaul of the layout which swapped the sequence around. This resulted in a substantial shift in what her users borrowed. The issues did not go up but readers were discovering authors and titles they had previously overlooked. Large libraries cannot undertake re-organising the whole stock arrangement very often but it's worth thinking how the principle can be used on a smaller scale to change what is in the most-used areas.

There is a considerable challenge to public libraries in the fact that the environments change so rarely. A borrower commented recently: 'The children's library hasn't changed a bit. It looks just the same as when I took my children in 10 years ago. In fact it looks just the same as when I was a child!' When something looks the same as it always has, it becomes very hard for the visitor to spot anything they might want in the undifferentiated mass.

Another customer, overheard chatting to a friend in the queue, was commenting on the library never having any new books. Her evidence for this was that every time she came in she could see Jean Auel's *The Clan of the Cave Bear*, with its distinctive thick red spine, sitting in the exact same place on the top shelf, where it had been for years. The small intervention of turning the book face-on, or turning the book next to it face-on, would have been all that was necessary to shift that customer's perception.

Importance of first impressions

On entering any new space, 80% of the impression we carry thereafter is based on what we see immediately. In the case of libraries, the view is often dominated by security barriers and the main counter, after which there is no real focus, just rows of similar-looking shelves, crammed into the space. Research shows that people are more inclined to linger in spaces which feel light and airy. Many shops manage much smaller spaces than libraries; it's not about having the space, it's about creating the illusion that you have the space.

Creating a welcome for visitors involves more than putting up a sign saying 'welcome'. Eye-contact and smiles from staff, clear signage and guiding, uncluttered surfaces and tempting points of focus created by well-stocked displays all help customers to feel relaxed, confident and comfortable. There is an added benefit to this initial acknowledgement of customers. US retail group Wal-Mart, now owners of Asda, have found that using in-store 'greeters' led to a 35% reduction in theft. It seems that once an individual is aware that their presence has been noted, they're far less likely to get up to anything.

These small changes are all within the control of staff in libraries of all sizes with very little budget. How often do you go out of the building and re-enter by the same door the customers use? Do you pause at the entrance and assess the condition of the space and try to view it as a new visitor might?

Many libraries are housed in buildings which are not designed for purpose. It is even more important to address the issue of first impressions in this situation. One library in the south of England was located upstairs in an ex-town hall building. The first impression as you came up a dingy flight of stone stairs was an unstaffed desk, submerged under leaflets and posters. The entrance to the library was through a pair of closed double doors to the right of the desk. The windows of both doors were covered with notices, the most prominent of which declared when the library would be closed for an upcoming Bank Holiday, so there was no view into the space before you entered. One of the doors held a permanent sign saying 'No Entry'. An entirely different welcome could have been created had even one of the doors been fixed open or if the notices had been cleared from the glass. Even better if the desk of leaflets was removed and replaced with a sign angled to be visible as you came up the stairs saying 'The library is open - please come in.'

The very least that public libraries can do, given the lack of resources, is to ensure that the overall impression of the space is not negative. How tidy is it? How many notices are displayed which aim to control visitor behaviour? Are staff members identifiable if they're not behind the counter and do they take a moment to raise their heads, make eye-contact and offer a smile to all visitors? And how does your library smell?

Any first impression starts from the street. If you are lucky enough to have windows facing out to the street, use them to convey important messages about the library and its services. Many libraries cover their windows with information notices and posters, which has the double effect of screening the space from outside view and blocking light to the interior. Check on what passers-by see when looking into the space. If it is the backs of books, leaflets piled on window ledges, the rear of the display boards for the local photography club's latest exhibition, you are not exploiting the windows to their best effect.

View into Builth Wells Library before and after refurbishment

To see people in the library, interacting with the books, computers or staff, presents it as a welcoming, busy environment and motivates passers-by to consider how they themselves might use the library.

It is worth thinking about which aspects of your service you most want to emphasise in your first impression. For example, it would seem very sensible to site stock aimed at readers with visual impairment or elderly customers near to the library entrance so that they don't have to negotiate the length of the building. However, what signals does this send about the nature of your service and your priorities? Making this area of stock so prominent could strengthen the commonly expressed perception that libraries only cater for the very old or the very young. In general, it is true to say that there will be a direct relationship between the stock that is missing, or invisible, and the audience that is missing. If you need to attract more 16-25s into the library, for instance, they will need to see pretty quickly the kind of books and services that interest them set in a context in which they feel comfortable and welcomed.

WAKE-UP CALLS

Misunderstandings, however well-intentioned, undermine reader-centred practice. If you recognise the views below, use the arguments in this chapter to challenge them.

" *Our management team never gives us the budget for smartening up the library and they wonder why it looks so shabby.* "

" *As an upgrade to our library environments, we will be placing plasma screens in every service point over the next six months.* "

" *The last time the manager came through the front door of Central was when she came for interview.* "

For years public libraries have acted as a repository for the posters and leaflets of all other local authority services and for every community group and activity. They also display tourist information, often for attractions located a considerable distance from the library. It is easy to feel a level of responsibility to promote activities by community groups but the truth is that the impact of print publicity on these events is very low and the lack of one poster in the library will not deprive the group of their audience. Word of mouth support from library staff will have much more effect.

The real impact of the rash of notices is on the level of visual static experienced by the customer. Notices are defended on the basis of their public information role but the fact is, if closely observed, these posters and notices are rarely read. One librarian taking up a new role in a medium-sized library was challenged by a long-standing member of staff to find the poster that had been on the wall for 12 years, since he had taken up post. She scoured the walls and decided it was impossible to distinguish the old poster since they all looked like they had been there forever. Staff in another library nervously removed 90% of its posters and leaflets in order to declutter the space and were amazed that nobody complained.

As libraries introduce electronically displayed information, the same issues arise with the new technology. A plasma screen with too much information, presented as a mass without consideration of its purpose and audience, will fail to engage just as a crowded noticeboard does. It is the quality of content that will determine the effectiveness of electronic communication.

Forward-thinking services are now formulating more rigorous policies on leaflets and posters, accepting only local groups and events, and organising them into accessible but contained systems, such as ring binders with a page per organisation or online directories.

Consideration should also be given to what the library service gets in return for all this free marketing of other people's services or activities. Could the local art club display a small collection of art books at their next exhibition? Can the local theatre give you a free small ad in their programme? How does the Housing Department or Social Services promote library services in their various offices and waiting rooms?

The first view of public libraries is often dominated by security barriers and counters. The impression created is of a controlled and supervised environment. Security barriers have become less obtrusive with better technology but many libraries still use strictly signed one-way systems where ugly barriers are made more visible by extra traffic-style signs with large directional arrows and No Entry notices. Major retail outlets have just as much to lose from petty pilfering as public libraries, yet they manage to integrate security gates relatively unobtrusively and keep their spaces welcoming.

Having overcome the first set of barriers, the customer in many libraries will then be confronted by a choice of counters. In smaller libraries, there may be a single point of enquiry, discharge and issue but in others the number can be as many as three or four within the same space. One city centre library in England boasts four, fairly new counters in the entrance area; one large, almost circular, sited immediately in front of the entry doors, and two smaller versions to the left and right, the gaps between them being bridged by security gates. The desk on the left is for returning books and the one on the right is for issues. The large central counter is rarely staffed, and no-one, not even senior management, is quite sure what its intended, distinct purpose ever was. It is not an enquiry desk, as this function is filled at another separate counter opposite. The result is that the library loses a considerable area of prime floorspace which is dedicated entirely to bureaucracy rather than promoting library products and services to the customers.

The problem with the traditional split between enquiry desk and issue desk is that most customers can't tell the difference and often get shunted from one to the other. All libraries who have undertaken any studies of the key enquiries at the enquiries desk have discovered that the majority of them are not high level. In a recent study in a higher education library 70% of queries could be answered by any member of staff. Libraries need a better way of utilising expertise than sitting highly experienced staff behind an enquiry counter.

The counter is the symbol of meeting customer need but it does so in a way which is on staff terms not customer terms. The counter expresses a power relationship - the person behind the desk is comfortable and secure and from this position they offer help to the person in front of the desk who identifies themselves as in need. It is revealing that on many architects' plans for library spaces, the counter is marked as 'control desk'.

Libraries need to understand that many people do not like to ask for help because they recognise this implicit power relationship. Everyone likes to think of themselves as intelligent adults who can find their own way. This applies as much to other areas of life as to libraries. In March 2006, motoring organisation, the RAC, published research which demonstrated people's reluctance to ask for help when lost while driving. Within this there was a marked gender difference. When they get lost, male drivers will wait, on average, 20 minutes before stopping to ask for directions. With women, the average was only ten. In a library, there may be an additional factor that the staff are mostly female and men are reluctant to ask women for help.

In many libraries, counters were designed with optimum usage in mind, to accommodate the maximum number of staff who might be working behind it at any one time. The reality of counter usage in day-to-day business is probably quite different and a counter designed for three staff, when only one person is likely to be on duty for most of the time, is more than unnecessary, it is a liability.

WAKE-UP CALLS

Misunderstandings, however well-intentioned, undermine reader-centred practice. If you recognise the views below, use the arguments in this chapter to challenge them.

" Customers come to the counter when they need help. They don't want us pouncing on them. "

" My borrowers don't like it when we change things. "

" They've spent a fortune on self-issue and nobody ever uses it. The customers don't want it. "

Self-service and changing staff roles

The necessity for large counters will reduce as more libraries introduce self-service issue and return systems. Self-service is often seen as relating only to cost and efficiency but it is also a key aspect of reader development and customer care. Self-service enables readers to keep their choices private, rather than have to offer up their chosen titles for the scrutiny of library staff. The lack of privacy in most library transactions must influence what some borrowers take. Staff know this from the books which are presented to them face-down with titles hidden and the way people hold books so titles are not obvious to others in the queue.

Good staff are careful not to look as if they are noticing the specific titles an individual has chosen but there are still areas of awkwardness. Readers can be self-conscious about choosing something they think will be judged as 'trashy' or 'pretentious'. Choosing gay books or erotic books can give rise to perceptions about your sex life, while choosing a book on divorce in a small village where everyone knows your partner is bound to start rumours. One member of staff gave the example of a young woman approaching the counter nervously and hiding the book from view as much as possible. The book was about anorexia and the customer was clearly suffering from the disease herself. How much easier that would have been in a self-service system.

The other great advantage of self-service is that it frees staff time for more reader-centred work. If staff are not restricted to activities behind the counter, they can be out amongst the shelves, refreshing displays and approaching customers to offer help, rather than waiting to be asked.

The move to self-service has a major impact on staff roles and there is a great deal of concern, not least from the staff members who may be affected, as to how new roles will develop. Senior management, having seen commercial examples of the success of floorwalking, are keen to introduce the concept into libraries but need to recognise what a huge shift in culture it is.

Library staff are, understandably, very nervous about floorwalking. Nobody wants to walk up and down looking like they've got nothing to do. Nor do they want to be forced to accost customers, seeing this as intrusive and at odds with libraries' image as an unpressured environment.

One of the first libraries to look at introducing floorwalking was Blackburn Central Library, following its refurbishment in 2003. During individual staff sessions prior to the library reopening, it was discovered that the term 'floorstalking' was being used instead of the common retail term 'floorwalking'. Staff had heard about user observation where individual customers are tracked to learn how the space shapes their behaviour (see Chapter Two, page 67). They had also picked up a distorted view of the reader development objective of opening up reader choices. Together, these gave rise to a nightmare picture of staff being required to walk up and down, pouncing on customers and persuading them to read something different. No wonder there was a marked lack of enthusiasm for the new role!

The best starting point for explaining their new role out on the floor is the common experience of all library staff when shelving books. Library assistants all know that customers ask questions while they are shelving more than when they are at the enquiry counter. The new role of floorwalking is nothing more than a formalisation and extension of this. The shift is not about being aggressive or intrusive, it is about staff becoming more available and approachable.

It may be difficult for some staff members to imagine what a significant impact this might have on library users as it's not always easy to understand that someone else might find the prospect of approaching you or one of your colleagues behind the counter daunting. The counter feels a very comfortable place from the staff point of view. Staff are relaxed, in control and ready for anything. They know they will give a friendly and helpful response whatever they are asked; they know this personally and they know it from customer satisfaction surveys.

It's useful to consider an equivalent situation where, despite having an urgent or important question to ask, the circumstances are so intimidating that you can't quite bring yourself to speak up. For example, many people will recognise the experience of the consultant ward round in a hospital from a patient's point of view. As a patient you may have a key question you need to ask about your treatment and you know this is your chance to ask it. But when the consultant, and accompanying retinue of junior doctors, nurses and medical students sweeps in, you're aware of their importance and lack of time. Everything is on their terms, not yours and somehow you don't articulate the question you've been meaning to ask. It isn't that the consultant would be unwilling to answer, it's just that the circumstances in which you have to ask the question are disempowering.

If it feels safer and more natural for the customer to approach a member of staff while they are out on the floor, and staff feel less exposed if they are actually performing a clear task while they are floorwalking, then there is an obvious solution. Apart from shelving and tidying, staff can be involved in the very basic promotional technique of using on-shelf stock display, dressing the shelves to make them look good. Breaking up the rows of spines by turning one or two books face-forward looks attractive and increases their chance of being borrowed. Responsibility can be given to staff while floorwalking to monitor and maintain book promotions. This means keeping existing displays topped up with appropriate stock, resiting them to better positions or dismantling ones that have run their course. Other valuable tasks like editing out time-expired leaflets and posters and general decluttering can also be carried out.

Whatever the designated task is, the manner in which it is carried out will hugely influence whether customers will feel able to interrupt. One of the most common explanations given by library users for not wanting to approach staff is, 'They always look so busy.' Keeping your head down and focused on a task is bound to put anyone off approaching you. Relaxed and open body language, making eye contact and smiling at customers as they pass sends a signal that you can be interrupted. Keeping your head up and being aware of what's going on around you also gives you the chance to intervene with a friendly approach if you see somebody looking a bit lost: 'Are you after something in particular?' or 'Can you find what you're looking for?'

The *Bothell Herald* newspaper in Washington (USA) reported recently that two libraries, Mukilteo and Lynnwood, had introduced a private sector sales concept which was improving service. 'On busy afternoons, a librarian walks around and is available to anyone who needs help, as opposed to having staff stationed at reference desks.' Mukilteo Library had seen an increase of up to 25% in the number of reference questions asked and this was attributed, at least in part, to the roving librarian programme[*].

Norfolk Libraries were one of the first in the UK to move services away from counters. Floorwalking staff deal directly with enquiries wherever they arise. This has changed the relationship between staff and customers. The transaction is seen as problem-solving together rather than one person with all the information handing it over to another who has none. Norfolk Libraries see the role of the staff as enabling, not gate-keeping.

[*] 'Librarians on the move', *Bothell Herald*, 13.01.06

At East Sheen Library in the London Borough of Richmond, the refurbishment in 2004 involved rethinking staff roles. All staff were timetabled for three different work areas; the backroom, the counter and out on the library floor. The backroom was where all necessary library tasks were carried out. In many libraries it has become the custom to have a pile of work at the counter to do at quiet times. This may seem on the surface a sensible efficiency measure but in practice it led to increased clutter in the public space and staff who had their heads down working on tasks instead of looking up and making eye-contact.

At East Sheen the rule was very clear: while serving on the counter, staff were not to undertake any backroom tasks, they were to be available to customers at all times (the library did not have self-service). If the counter area fell quiet, staff were encouraged to use the counter terminals to explore the online resources the Borough subscribed to so they could better explain what was available to customers. When out on the floor, staff were asked to do the normal shelving tasks and to top up the displays. They were also asked to be aware of customers who might appreciate help; the example given was that if a member of staff saw a harassed parent with a two-year old on the verge of throwing a tantrum, they should offer to sit down and read a story.

WAKE-UP CALLS

Misunderstandings, however well-intentioned, undermine reader-centred practice. If you recognise the views below, use the arguments in this chapter to challenge them.

" We need the No Smoking signs - how are staff supposed to challenge someone who lights up without them? "

" We don't want mobile phones. It disturbs our customers. "

" We put the children's artwork up - it really gives the place a lift. "

Public display of library rules relate to how staff understand their role and how confident they are within it. Negative notices are part of a policed environment. They set up a relationship of censure and anticipate bad behaviour before it's occurred. Customers who take books home do anything they like with them. They can eat, drink, smoke, bathe at the same time as reading a library book. It seems illogical that they cannot be trusted in the library environment in the same way as they are trusted at home.

Notices are not an effective way of controlling behaviour. If you are the type of person who will do it, you'll do it anyway. The inefficacy is observable in situations where multiple notices have been put up all saying the same thing. Clearly the first notice had no effect so staff have put up a second notice which will also have no effect - except to irritate your law-abiding customer who had no intention of using their mobile phone and enjoying a cigarette while rollerskating through the library accompanied by their dog.

The reason the notice is there is often so that staff can point to it in the event of having to deal with unacceptable behaviour. The notice is an aspect of staff support more than customer control. This should be addressed through staff training where it's important staff learn to negotiate behaviour situations rather than to escalate them. Heavy-handed notices have an instant effect on some customers; people who had no intention of being awkward are antagonised by the suggestion of policing and react by wanting to break what they see as absurd rules.

We need to be very careful that rules are not discriminatory. The common rule of no mobile phones in many libraries discriminates against young people for whom switching off their phone is unthinkable. The issue here is volume, not technology. Two pensioners having a loud conversation, or staff behind the counter answering a telephone query, can easily make more noise than a 14 year-old mumbling into their mobile phone. Focusing on the technology alone discriminates against the group of people most likely to use it. Young people are also more likely to be texting than talking on their phones. In 2005, UK National Statistics showed that there was a strong link between age group and the reason for owning a mobile phone. 94% of adults aged 16 to 24 had sent text messages compared with 15% aged 65 and over, who tended to keep mobile phones only for emergencies.

Rather than banning mobiles altogether, it would be much more customer-friendly to accept responsible use of phones, encouraging visitors to have them on silent mode. Cutting off a teenager's major form of communication adds to their perception of the library as unwelcoming and it becomes a clear choice for them - phone or library? There are already websites which will text book recommendations direct to mobile phones. It would be ironic if the only place you couldn't receive these was in a public library.

Some libraries have recognised this and have changed policy. Adopting this stance, as well as relaxing rules on eating and drinking, resulted in the Norwich Millennium Library having more users aged 14-20 than most other institutions of equivalent size. Their teenage-friendly reputation led to as many as 150 young people lounging in the Express area on Saturdays. This has not been an entirely happy experience for other users; complaints have been received about bad language and parents with buggies have had difficulties navigating around the groups to get to the children's library. However, Norfolk Libraries are maintaining their commitment to providing a welcoming environment for all by redesigning the ground floor and taking space from counter and staff areas to create more social space, working towards the concept of the living room in the city. Norfolk Libraries also prefer to integrate teenage stock into the Express area of the library, rather than separating it into a 'teenage zone', as a way of drawing the young adult audience into the mainstream of the library.

Different customers - different needs

The complexity of the libraries' offer - information, leisure, study, social - provides considerable challenges when it comes to accommodating different user needs. Further complications arise when considering that it's possible that customers using the library for leisure might find some parts of the information or study offer appealing and useful. Organising materials by format or subject category controls and restricts the user's options for discovery and full exploitation of all the materials available.

Traditional layouts have evolved through custom and practice. For example, children's stock is always separated from adult stock, although children under seven will be accompanied by an adult or older child. The library forces any adult with children to decide whose needs are met on any one visit. In the children's space there is nothing for adults and in the adult space there is nothing for children. As the influence of reader development has spread, collections of quick pick, relaxing adult fiction have successfully been introduced into some children's areas to counter this.

Another problem is the way books are often separated from computers as if use of one precluded use of the other. Accommodating the People's Network Service computers was a major challenge to UK libraries in the last ten years. The spatial problems already existing in some library buildings forced some difficult decisions for library managers and removing books to make space for computers was an uncomfortable choice which caused unrest amongst some staff and borrowers, despite the benefits of free internet access. The People's Network is now a huge success across the library service, attracting new visitors and being used to capacity in almost every library. But most libraries force a choice on the customer very near the entrance - do I want computers or do I want books? New library layouts should consider how best to present books and computers as routes to the same thing.

A customer-centred library will differentiate spaces by focusing on patterns of use, bringing together the appropriate stock and resources and providing the space and furnishings to support the users' immediate need. The library therefore has to consider how to accommodate the needs of the short stay and long stay visitor; the impulse browser and the focused borrower; the person requiring independence and minimum contact and those expecting a social experience; those who need quiet space to reflect or study and those who like a bit of background buzz.

Most library spaces would be hard-pressed to offer defined areas for all of these different needs but many could accommodate some and make occasional nods towards others. Spaces can also be managed through time. The problem of noise leakage, for example, is hard to overcome in small community libraries housed in one room. You can accommodate noisy events like babies' Bounce and Rhyme as long as other customers know when it's going to happen. If it's once a week and lasts half an hour it is not unreasonable to expect other library users to avoid it, if they object.

When the new High Street Library opened in Bolton in 2007 it was hugely successful with the local Asian community. For customers looking for a quieter visit, staff were recommending they drop in around 4.00pm when many Muslims attend mosque and library usage dipped. If you are serious about attracting more young people into the library, could you define a time slot, perhaps 4.00pm to 5.00pm, when you could signal a different appeal and ownership of the space by playing music. Even better invite two or three of the target age group to select the radio station to be played. If you have the appropriate licence, you could extend this to playing CDs from your collection.

Informing borrowers who prefer the library quiet in advance about occasions when it may get unusually noisy acknowledges the needs of this part of the audience - they can choose whether to visit the library at that particular point.

Helping customers navigate

In their book, *The Support Economy**, business gurus Shoshana Zuboff and James Maxmin outlined their theories about consumers being overburdened by choice and that the key to business success was to implement ways to help the customer navigate products and services. The business that wants to survive will have to be aware of the changing lifestyles and the corresponding shifting demands of their customers.

The Dutch library designer, Aat Vos, undertook a project with ten year-old regular library users to explore how easy they found it to navigate the library. Children worked in pairs where one child was given a task and the other was given a video camera to film them doing the task. The first task was to find a book on dinosaurs. One boy went immediately to look under D in the A-Z sequence, not understanding that fiction was organised alphabetically but non-fiction wasn't. The children took much longer to find a book on dinosaurs than any children's library staff would expect. The same group was then taken to a large DIY store and given a rawlplug and asked to locate the same item in the store. This involved going through a similar process of understanding how the space was organised and classified. Would the rawlplug be with timber or nails or decorating items? All the children found the rawlplug, even though it was an unfamiliar item, much quicker than they found the book on dinosaurs. The conclusion has to be that the DIY store's approach to product organisation and classification made it easier to navigate than the library.

Does everyone understand the difference between fiction and non-fiction? During a user observation exercise in a large branch library, one male customer was observed browsing very carefully in the fiction A-Z, in the Ps. He scoured the shelves for some time then left

Zuboff & Maxmin, *The Support Economy*, Penguin, 2004. *

the section empty-handed. When the member of staff observing happened to see him later at the issue desk, he had borrowed a book on plumbing. Clearly, he had been looking for plumbing in the A-Z sequence. The basic library organisation of fiction into alphabetical sequence by author surname and non-fiction into subject categories had passed him by.

Public libraries have a tendency to undersign globally and oversign locally. A visitor can find a real lack of directional signs at the higher level - Fiction, Internet, Children - to guide them to what they want. But if they persevere till they get to the shelves they will find that individual books can have as many as three or four different labels on the spines - a catalogue number, the first three letters of the author's name in capitals plus a mysterious coloured dot or a small pictogram. These icons tend to have very old-fashioned designs and their use can come across as patronising to readers. To label all contemporary crime with a crude Sherlock Holmes deerstalker or a badly drawn gun is off-putting to readers looking for a sophisticated, cutting-edge new author to try. It suggests the stock is all old-fashioned and traditional even when it isn't. The labels are often there to help staff shelve books in the right place although they are justified as helping readers. The answer to this is to invest more time in stock awareness training and to trust to the abilities of staff to tell what's a crime book and what isn't. If you must have a category label, recognise that its purpose is to help staff, not readers, and put it somewhere discreet - inside the book, for example.

Children's sections are amongst the hardest to comprehend for those not accustomed to library traditions, as Aat Vos' project demonstrates. The children's section is often the most cluttered visually; publisher posters, children's artwork and home-produced displays leave no inch of wall space uncovered. This means there are no clear overall messages about the purpose of the space. In commissioning a new signage package for the children's section in Spellow Library, Liverpool Libraries went for attractive, dynamic signs which are age appropriate and which convey the magic and unlimited potential of reading.

The shelves in children's sections are often packed tight and hard to differentiate; as children's books are generally thinner than adult books, the spines blend into a solid block. Shelf-headers can be unhelpful - what does Young Readers or Easy Readers mean in this context? Every library service seems to have its own classifications - Short Readers, Easy Stories, Early Readers, First Readers - and they are all equally meaningless to the uninitiated. It is impossible to know whether Picture Books for Older Readers means over five years, over seven, over ten or over 14.

Graphics for children's libraries by Opening the Book as used in Liverpool Libraries

In 2004, Book Marketing Ltd, the UK's main book industry research group, undertook research looking at non and light book buyers and readers. Their *Expanding the Market* report[*] found that people were baffled by the sheer number of books and didn't know where to start. The research identified a clear need for more help on what to choose and found this to be especially true in relation to children's books. 41% of people who were reluctant to give books as gifts would be encouraged to do so by better guidance on suitable age and reading ability.

Children's Libraries
How the books are arranged:

NON - FICTION, OR *INFORMATION* **BOOKS**	**SPACE** *(PURPLE)*
ALL ABOUT ME *(WHITE)*	**SPORTS, HOBBIES & PASTIMES** *(DARK BLUE)*
THE ARTS *(CREAM)*	**THE SUPERNATURAL** *(PINK SPOT)*
COMMUNITY *(RED)*	**TRANSPORT** *(BLACK)*
COUNTRIES *(GREY)*	**FICTION, OR** *STORY* **BOOKS**
THE EARTH AND ITS RESOURCES *(LIGHT BLUE)*	**BOARD BOOKS** *(NO LABEL)*
FAIRY TALES, MYTHS & LEGENDS *(ORANGE SPOT)*	**UNDER FIVES** *(YELLOW SPOT)*
FAITHS & FESTIVALS *(DARK PINK)*	**PICTURE BOOKS** *(NO LABEL)*
HISTORY *(ORANGE)*	**PICTURE BOOKS FOR OLDER CHILDREN** *(SILVER SPOT)*
LANGUAGE AND LANGUAGES *(YELLOW)*	**BEGINNING READING** *(GREEN SPOT)*
PLANTS & ANIMALS *(GREEN)*	**STORIES** *(NO LABEL)*
POETRY AND PLAYS *(LIGHT PINK)*	**TEENAGE** *(BLUE SPOT)*
REFERENCE BOOKS *(NO LABEL)*	**LARGE PRINT** *(GOLD SPOT)*
SCIENCE & TECHNOLOGY *(BROWN)*	

Over-complex labelling in a typical children's library

Of course, children's librarians have the expertise to help here; they have long experience in suggesting books to meet different stages in a child's reading development. But to use this help, the librarian must be available (most are responsible for more than one branch and have off-site tasks as well) and the customer must be willing to ask. As these two factors

❋ Book Marketing Ltd. *Expanding the Market - Summary report on a research project funded by Arts Council England and a consortium of publishers and retailers, looking at non and light book buyers and readers*, 2004.

will not always be present, it is crucial that the library is better organised for people to manage by themselves.

Using the book covers as navigational aids makes choosing easier. Nursery rhyme books are easy to spot if a few strong covers are turned face-out; a large book with a tiger on the front helps to define the animals section. Publishers convey the target age group and type of reader through the cover design and young customers can pick up on this. Using cover designs in this way is preferable to introducing systems of colour-coded dots on the spines. It takes a child's attention straight to the book instead of having to decode an unnecessary layer of complexity first.

There is resistance to the use of age-ranging in library signage from the understandable perspective that each child is different and should be treated as such. But there is no doubt that customers - both adults and children - would find the library easier to understand if some broad age signing was used. Toys and clothes are age-ranged and can be just as sensitive to handle. Any parent of a child who is larger or smaller than the average learns how to judge the age-labels of different clothing stores. Children and parents may not like having to do this but it is better than having no guidance at all. Imagine trying to choose from a children's clothes section with no age or size labels - this is what the library feels like to many first-time visitors.

Breaking the sequence

The history of library classification and labelling shows the contradictory impulses of giving access and retaining control which lie at the heart of library culture. Committed librarians want to make the labelling system transparent in order to empower readers. Supermarkets have their classification systems too but most of us when buying from a supermarket never look at the barcode, we don't care about the way the supermarket manages its stock as long as the product that we want is there on the shelf when we want it. Libraries see their role as making all knowledge accessible to everybody so they want to share the secrets of their labelling system with the customer. Libraries offered self-service of this kind long before it was introduced in retail. At the point where all shops had counter service only and the man in the brown coat would fetch the goods for you, libraries were the only self-service institutions. But when the whole of the retail world moved to self-service the library version got left behind. Most customers don't want to understand the system, they just want to find their type of book easily. This is a great disappointment to traditional librarian-educators.

Of course, wanting customers to understand can be about self-justification rather than empowerment - 'look at all the work we do to bring the books to you.' At its worst, the educational impulse is debased into blaming the borrower for not understanding the system. The retail store that organised its products in a way that customers found difficult to understand, and then bemoaned the lack of effort and intelligence customers were willing to exert when they visited, would not last long.

Library stock has to be organised. Dewey, although far from perfect, is the system most used.   A reader-centred approach will seek to compensate for the drawbacks created by Dewey.   There is no need to rigidly follow the 0-900 sequence round a space. You can keep the benefits of Dewey subject organisation within larger global areas which match the size

WAKE-UP CALLS

Misunderstandings, however well-intentioned, undermine reader-centred practice. If you recognise the views below, use the arguments in this chapter to challenge them.

" *There are loads of signs showing which way they should go and they still get it wrong.* "

" *Our borrowers are really lazy, they never go to the back of the library.* "

" *How will staff ever find anything in the Quick Choice section?* "

of the subject holdings with the available space or move popular categories to short-stay zones. This helps to avoid the absurdities of Dewey organisation where the shelves in the same bay will appeal to completely different audiences. In one central library, for example, neighbouring shelf labels read 359: Naval warfare and 361: Counselling.

Many libraries are breaking and mixing Dewey to meet specific audience needs. Shelving sporting biographies with sport, for example, rather than biography and creating Travel sections which mix geography and history. When a sub-genre becomes popular, libraries can benefit if they are willing to move with the times. After the success of mind, body, spirit in bookshops, some libraries introduced the concept even though it includes parts of Philosophy (the 100s), parts of Religion (the 200s) and parts of Health (the 600s). When sited prominently, this section achieved the highest loan rate of any non-fiction, making the effort of cross-shelving easily worthwhile.

The shortcomings of Dewey classification were particularly highlighted with the explosion in mass market narrative non-fiction titles that was precipitated by the success of Dava Sobel's *Longitude*. Where exactly should Mark Kurlansky's *Cod: a Biography of the Fish that Changed the World* be shelved? Is it in natural history, history, economics, the environment, biography or, even, cookery? If you put it in history, then science readers will never discover it; if you put it in biology, then economics readers won't find it. Of course, the focused user who already knows of its existence can track the book down wherever it is shelved by using the catalogue. But what about all those curious readers who never use the catalogue and who cannot ask for the book as they don't know its title or author?

Whatever organising system the library uses, there will always be a need to have cross-cutting displays and ways of bringing stock which is buried at the back to the front. For example, the first national reader-friendly non-fiction promotion to be available in public libraries, *The Mind's Eye*, brought a range of narrative non-fiction publishing to the attention of an audience who might never have considered venturing into the individual subject categories. Of all the promotions to come out of the first wave of reader development, this non-fiction promotion in 2001 was reported as having the greatest impact on issues across England and Scotland. Clearly the non-fiction impulse reader had been even more poorly served than the fiction browser. Offering a tempting collection in a prominent position - even if it was just one cardboard dumpbin - had a dramatic effect.

New Ash Green Library, Kent

When refurbishing New Ash Green Library to appeal better to 20-40s and young families, Kent Libraries worked with Opening the Book to rebrand the library experience to connect into people's lives and aspirations. Instead of the traditional Dewey classifications, the library is organised into five areas to define different kinds of appeal. Each area has a retail-style display wall with the branding clearly visible above each bay. *Making time* contains the fiction while *Making choices* offers film, audio and large print formats. *Making changes* includes non-fiction relating to personal aspirations, from house and garden makeovers to mind, body, spirit and business skills. *Going places* covers travel, history and biography and the children's area is called *Family-friendly*, indicating it has something in it for everybody. Kent Libraries tested customer response to the library and found that 89% of users said it was easy to find the books they were looking for and 96% liked the way the adult non-fiction books were organised. Kent Libraries have since experimented successfully with using broad subject areas for adult non-fiction in larger libraries.

The Quick Choice section has now become a staple in libraries of all sizes. A Quick Choice section brings together paperbacks from all areas of library stock, mixing fiction and some narrative non-fiction, and presents these close to the entrance and, preferably, face-on to the browser. This section offers an immediately accessible, tempting choice. From a reader development point of view, it also offers the opportunity for readers to try something different as they see authors and genres they may never have discovered before.

Quick Choice sections were first pioneered in English libraries through the Branching Out reader development programme. The first sections of this type were branded *unclassified* to make it clear to staff and borrowers that this was a random collection of books without order and to hint at the subversive and adventurous nature of this approach within a library context. All the books were paperback and with an appeal to under-40s. The issue rate from the *unclassified* section was so successful that the concept has moved from the subversive to the mainstream in many libraries since. Because the turnover of books in the

Sutton Central Library

Quick Choice section increases dramatically compared with books presented spine-out on traditional shelving (75% as compared to 35% in tests by some Branching Out librarians) it follows that library work processes have to adjust to ensure top-up stock is regularly fed in. It also follows that the library needs to have sufficient stock in good condition to keep the Quick Choice section supplied.

When Sutton Central Library was refurbished, a large area on the ground floor was devoted to a quick choice paperback section, given an identity as Page One. The area holds between 800 and 1000 paperbacks at any one time and displays are changed every week. Page One represents approximately 0.5% of the total stock in the library. This small area has consistently achieved between 30% and 40% of the library's fiction loans every month since January 2005. It is the pumping heart of the whole collection. This compares to figures quoted by a fiction manager in a flagship Waterstone's store that the tables located nearest to the entrance accounted for 45% of the sales of the entire three-storey bookshop.

Next generation added value services

In recent years high street banks have moved many of their services to being handled by telephone and online banking. In 2006, however, their research showed that although customers were happy to carry out basic transactions on the phone and online, more complex discussions on savings, investments, loans and insurance, all highly lucrative products in the financial industries, were preferred face-to-face with a sympathetic advisor. From a policy of closing as many branches as possible, they are returning to positioning themselves very visibly in the high street.

The new-style banks, however, are very far from their security conscious, queue-managed predecessors in terms of atmosphere and design. Banks are aware that they have to foster a more relaxed selling environment for their new push on products and are learning lessons from the retail sector. In the new-style banks you are likely to be greeted by the sound of soft music and the aroma of freshly brewed coffee. There are self-service machines near the entrance for fast transactions such as payments and withdrawals. Further in, there are seats to relax in to browse the product offers. Staff do not sit in rows behind glazed partitions; instead one person tactfully approaches you. Once engaged in conversation, it is suggested you sit with them at a small curved table which gives a little privacy but is still open to the room. The computer monitor is angled so that you can read everything on the screen. This transparent, friendly approach is completely different from the old-style fortress environment where customers sometimes had to remind themselves the money in question was actually their own. The parallels with changes beginning to happen in libraries are striking.

The other big change for banks is the recognition that people's lifestyles demand a new look at opening hours. One of the major banks is opening its Edinburgh Waverley station branch at 7.30 in the morning because that's when a high volume of potential customers are passing through the station. Similarly, the refurbished UpFront section of Bolton Central Library now opens its doors at 8.15 am to catch people who are on their way into work.

New libraries in the UK are now mostly planned as co-locations with other services as local councils seek to maximise efficiencies. This may be with other council services such as one stop shops, tourist information or sports facilities. Or it may be health partnerships with doctors' surgeries, clinics and pharmacies or with children's centres, Sure start or other educational initiatives. Partnerships offer real opportunities for libraries to reach new readers. Look especially at shared reception and waiting areas which are often pleasantly designed in new buildings but lack any activities to engage people. These offer a great chance for libraries to showcase relevant paperbacks to a new audience.

You may find architects, planners and other partners do not respond positively to library suggestions of sharing spaces. In Opening the Book's experience, this is not just about the expected issues of territory; it is because the image of library presence is perceived as bringing grubby products, old-fashioned signage and clutter into clean spaces. To counter this, libraries need to raise their game in terms of how they approach the environments they manage.

The hard truth about physical environments is that there is no opting out of responsibility for impact. Doing nothing will influence the experience customers have just as much as taking action. It is not easy for financially hard-pressed institutions like libraries to consider shifting gear to improve library spaces. However, implementing a reader-friendly approach to introduce small changes in the management of spaces can have a significant impact. A shift in priority from managing products and services to managing how the customer can access and use them is the way forward.

Chapter 4

Reader-centred stock management

The book offer is at the core of the library service. Even when public libraries successfully reposition themselves as discovery centres, idea stores, learning centres or one stop shops, more customers still come for the books than for any other service. The perception of library book stock, accurate or not, is also significant among non-users. In MORI surveys, the second most common reason for not using libraries, after lack of time, is 'they don't have the books I want'.

Managing book stock is also at the heart of the library profession. Getting it right for readers has always been important but in a time when book funds are under pressure and performance is ever more closely examined, choosing the right balance of titles becomes ever more critical. Libraries need to make each title work harder to deliver more loans and more satisfied customers.

Users cannot usually engage directly with major stock management decisions, though it's always good practice to create a route through which readers can make suggestions. To understand the readers' point of view it is necessary to see the effect of local delivery; the readers' experience is determined by what is on the shelf in the branch they use. Of course, not all readers want the same thing. The biggest difference is between those who are focussed, looking for a particular author and/or title, and those who are browsers, looking to be tempted to take something on impulse. You can test what you have for the first category by sample title checks on the catalogue without having to visit specific libraries but testing what you have for the impulse borrower is more complex.

If a stock manager stands in front of the library shelves in the branch it is immediately apparent how minimal is the impact of new book selection. Viewed from the centre, selection seems by far the biggest part of stock management, taking the most energy, time and resources. At the shelf level, the overall impression is given by the libraries' back stock more than the new books. It's not what was bought in the last three months that is visible, it is what was bought in the last five, or ten, or more years.

Stock managers are playing a long game. It is easy and worthwhile to get a quick hit by dropping in an extra promotional display but it will take a long time for change to be visible through a whole library space. This is as much a matter of what is weeded as what is bought. This is an important issue for staff training. Where stock editing is delegated effectively, collections are much fresher.

The impact of stock editing is borne out by the experience of a town centre library moving temporarily into a smaller space. Scunthorpe Central Library closed for the removal of asbestos in 2003-2004 and the library was temporarily relocated to a unit in the nearby shopping precinct. The stock capacity in the temporary space was approximately a quarter of the central library space and only an edited selection of the stock could be transferred. The response from the borrowers was astonishing. Almost everyone that came in commented that these were much better books than had been available in the main library and assumed the library had bought new stocks. In fact, no extra budget provision had been made, it was simply that the newer books could be better seen because all the old ones were not there. The lesson was applied when the library was refurbished in 2005 and the display space was increased to accommodate Quick Choice selections.

Who chooses what to buy for readers?

Selection is the most enjoyable and satisfying part of stock management for most library staff and, traditionally, has the highest status. It also occupies the most staff time. As services have become more customer-centred over the last ten years, it has been realised that lots of librarians sitting in a room choosing from nice, new books is clearly a pleasant experience for library staff but the benefit for the customer is not so obvious. The customer experience is not linked with the librarian who has chosen the books; library readers have no means of accessing the debate that was held at selection, however interesting it might have been. In many cases, there was no time for debate anyway and decisions were simply made with a show of hands and a simple yes/no to purchase for each service point. This tended to reinforce buying of recognised names and strong group behaviour - it was a brave soul who chose differently from everyone else in the room.

The decade from 1995-2005 saw very big changes in book selection in UK libraries where most authorities streamlined and centralised their selection processes in order to save staff time and resources which could be better used elsewhere. This was often a painful process as many professional librarians perceived it as an erosion of their skills and responsibilities. However, there is clear evidence that the choice available to users was improved by streamlining selection processes. The range widened and the speed in getting new titles to the shelves increased. The rise of reader development in the same period helped to ease this transition by demonstrating that there were other areas where professional expertise could be applied which would have a substantial impact on borrowers.

WAKE-UP CALLS

Misunderstandings, however well-intentioned, undermine reader-centred practice. If you recognise the views below, use the arguments in this chapter to challenge them.

❝ *It's good to involve your staff in stock selection to make sure they build up stock knowledge.* ❞

❝ *Your staff learn about stock as they work on the counter, they don't need any special training.* ❞

❝ *Local community profiling shows how different the stock in each branch needs to be.* ❞

The 33 English library services involved in the Branching Out project 1998-2001 were leaders and catalysts in this process. They recognised that the balance of spend on acquiring a book and promoting it was wrong. The time involved in getting a book to the shelf was substantial; the time spent doing anything to promote it once it was there was minimal. In particular, selection processes had become very staff-intensive with large numbers involved in decision making. Budgets were mostly delegated to smaller areas, no-one had the capacity to take risks and staff chose conservatively. It was quite easy to prove that although each group thought it was buying for its own local community, in practice they were all buying mostly the same titles.

Many librarians believe that involving a large number of staff in book selection is a good idea because it increases book knowledge. However, this is another perception which turns out not to hold up under examination. Taking your turn at book selection meetings to see what happens to be on offer that month is not a very effective way to acquire balanced stock knowledge. There is a massive need for greater stock awareness at all levels of the UK library service but involvement in book selection did not deliver this. Attending book selection meetings is not a substitute for properly planned stock awareness training. Staff could learn more about a genre (crime, for example) or a reading audience (20s-30s, for example) in a short planned session which covered classics, bestsellers, minority interests and new trends, than they would learn from attending six months' of book selection meetings on an ad hoc basis. Most selection is now done through electronic means rather than through collections of books on approval and this has increased the separation between selection and stock training. Stock awareness training is best done with the physical books as they arrive at the library. (See Chapter Six pages 195-198 for examples of how to do this.)

Centralised stock selection has not proved to be the professional disaster that some librarians had predicted. In fact, it is quite easy to prove across authorities in England that small teams of selectors have done a better job in keeping up to date with selecting contemporary paperbacks than large groups using the old approvals system. There can be occasional changes in the team so it does not become stale, as long as each member stays long enough to see the bigger picture.

Buying for the service as a whole instead of for particular branches leads to a better balance in catering for a range of readers. Staff buying for their own branch are inevitably influenced by their perception of who their borrowers are and this, as discussed in Chapter One, is not always accurate. Staff can't help but be more aware of the 'dominant' borrowers, the ones who chat and the ones who make demands. The needs of the full range of readers, including that large number of invisible borrowers who don't want to interact with staff, are more easily seen and met when looking at the service as a whole.

New trends in stock management

Evidence-based stock management* has been successfully trialled in UK libraries but not yet widely adopted. The evidence-based approach seeks to replace intuitive subjective judgements with hard information, basing decisions on evidence derived from loan data. This includes highlighting books which have not been borrowed for six months, highlighting books which have had a specific number of loans and can be assumed to be worn out, and offering formulae to calculate overstocking and understocking in subject areas in relation to their use. Book withdrawal and purchase decisions are driven by what

See Kerr, George, 'The need for evidence-based stock management', CILIP *Update*, Vol. 5 (12), November 2006 and **www.bridgeall.com**

the customers are doing instead of by professional librarians making decisions on their behalf.

This approach is certainly a useful one and establishing automated processes will help to clean out 'dead' and 'grubby' stock much more quickly. Evidence-based management should be one element in any stock policy but it is only just beginning to engage with the reader development agenda and the wider cultural role of libraries in the marketplace by offering options, for example, to track performance of 'experimental' collections. Reader development is about opening up reading choices and helping people find books they didn't know existed, not only about managing the most popular titles.

In recent years library services have also delegated more of their selection decisions to suppliers. This was always the case with standard orders for popular authors but a number of services have now moved the bulk of their selection to the supplier. Just as with centralising selection ten years ago, this has been highly controversial. Alarming predictions were made about loss of quality. In practice, supplier selection has proved much more successful than anticipated and more services are moving that way. Library suppliers have raised their game so that range and choice have improved, order fulfilment is much faster and stock is supplied shelf-ready. In the supplier selection model, the crucial role for librarians is drawing up the specification for the supply contract. They may be no longer responsible for the detailed decisions but they are in control of the overall policy decisions just as much as they ever were and this is where a reader-centred approach can help.

However well resourced a library service is, there will always be selection judgments to be made. Even if the service can afford to buy one copy of every new fiction and poetry title published, decisions will have to be made about how many copies of each are bought. The traditional methods of making these decisions include buying by author, by publisher information, by review, by standing order and for requests. The results vary according to the expertise of the selectors, whether they are librarians or book suppliers, but none of them can claim to meet all reader needs.

Requests are the most reader-centred option available in most libraries (though not usually free). Here a reader can request a title not currently available in the specific branch and it will either be bought, brought from another branch, or borrowed from inter-library loan.

The request service is fundamental to public library service provision. The guarantee to bring any book in print from anywhere in the world to your local branch is extraordinary.

However, when requests are seen as a proportion of total loans, it is apparent that requesters constitute a very small minority of users. In the UK requests are not usually more than 3% of total loans; as this includes multiple requesters, the number of borrowers using requests is actually less. The amount of staff time devoted to the 3% rather than the 97% is hard to justify. Recent government targets to improve the speed of supplying requests have not necessarily helped services to become more reader-centred. They improve the service to the minority but take staff time and resources away from the majority. Inter-library loan is very expensive in terms of staff time across many different services. It is likely that new models will emerge in the next five years which combine central co-ordination and local delivery. National library bodies are looking at these possibilities; a national service could offer a top quality book search and delivery facility and charge a commercial rate.

Understanding audience appeal

Traditional selection methods other than requests, are producer-driven rather than consumer-driven. The new method brought in by reader-centred thinking is buying by audience appeal. It is possible to use more sophisticated customer analysis to check the balance of a collection so that over a 12 month period of buying, for example, it can be seen how well different audience groups have been catered for.

If you are going to use a reader-based approach to stock purchase and management, you will need an understanding of different audience needs. One starting point is segmenting into different age and gender groups. It is important not to confuse this with stereotyping readers. Of course, there will be individual 80 year-olds who wish to read new, young writers and some women who want to read fiction principally aimed at men. But this doesn't prevent checking the balance of your collection for overall appeal.

Some authors have much wider appeal while others attract a niche audience. Major bestsellers - authors such as Patricia Cornwell, Terry Pratchett, J K Rowling and John Grisham - appeal across generations and gender. Classics, by definition, last through time.

Some genres change more than others. The classic romance, for example, will change its setting and period from crinoline heroines to wartime nurses to contemporary divorcées, but the essential values and plot shape remain the same. This means the readership crosses generations and remains more constant; romance is read by teenagers through to pensioners.

Reader preferences cluster round other factors which cross age and gender and genre, for example, how traditional or experimental a book is, or how easy or challenging. A genre such as crime contains a huge range of reading preferences. Those who prefer more traditional crime, the classic country house murder mystery and its recent variants, do not have much in common with those who prefer noir, contemporary crime. Although the basic format of solving a murder is common, everything else is very different. Traditional crime has a straightforward narrative approach, a clear moral scheme in which the reader knows who is the good guy and who is the bad guy, and all the loose ends will be tied up. A more experimental crime novel may change narrative point of view and timescale without much explanation and will evoke an atmosphere which is dark and confusing. The perspective may well be that of an outsider and motivations may be presented as unconscious rather than rational.

Fans of traditional crime have more in common with readers who prefer traditional approaches in other genres, for example, family saga, action/adventure or literary fiction. Readers who like experimental crime have more in common with people who prefer experimental writing in approaches to writing, whether it be about family or adventure or in more literary novels. Checking the balance by genre is not enough to check coverage of different reader preferences.

Generational changes

Reader preferences are shaped not just by the style and genre of the book but by the values it conveys. The role of personal values in reading experience has been explored as part of the reader-centred approach (see *Opening the Book - finding a good read*, Van Riel and Fowler.) Values change across generations and this affects what is written and published.

To understand how to analyse audience appeal, light fiction aimed at female readers offers a good example. This has been the single largest stock area in public libraries for the last

WAKE-UP CALLS

Misunderstandings, however well-intentioned, undermine reader-centred practice. If you recognise the views below, use the arguments in this chapter to challenge them.

" *It's better to have a really tatty copy of something by an author than no titles at all.* "

" *If you take off all the multiple copies of an author no longer going out, the shelves will look too empty and anyway they are in too good condition to throw out.* "

" *We don't have that much money in the book budget so we need to prioritise titles we know will issue.* "

50 years so it is important to understand it. The satisfaction of this type of book, the way it fits in people's lives, remains constant. The reader wants a book which relaxes and doesn't challenge or stretch them, something to give them a break. It has to deliver the same basic experience each time but offer a variation because readers don't want to keep reading the exact same story again. It is well known that saga and romance readers in libraries mark the book with a secret symbol when they've read it. It's difficult to remember from the cover and the title whether they've read it or not and they want to avoid the disappointment of taking something home and then realising they've read it before. (The same is true for many readers of crime and westerns as well.)

If we analyse the values of women's light fiction across the last 30 years, it becomes easier to see how reading tastes change and why. Family saga authors like Catherine Cookson and Josephine Cox have topped the Public Lending Right tables for adult fiction every year since PLR records began (**www.plr.uk.com**). The values of the family saga convey the importance of women in holding the family together as the centres of moral value, stressing hard work, thrift, selflessness and putting other people first. These values appeal to women who want to feel that their family role is important especially when it is not recognised and validated in the external world where housework isn't paid and women's work is invisible. The reward of reading the fiction is that it tells you that you matter. The typical family saga has a working-class heroine who comes through a lot of struggle and pain to a sense of achievement and equilibrium, if not fulfilment.

The 1990s' phenomenon of chick lit has very different values and therefore very different audience appeal. Bridget Jones is single and has no family dependents. Her experiences are all centred on herself rather than others; her needs, desires, satisfactions and pressures. The setting is no longer domestic; the most important events happen through work and social life outside of work. (Family saga heroines often have work outside the home, as many working-class women did, but this is not in any way a career.) Bridget Jones is still subject to the pressures of the external world to conform to the female stereotype; much of the humour of the book is derived from trying and failing to live up to the image of a 1990s' woman, good-looking, slim, with a great job and a successful relationship with a man. The book appeals to all those women who sympathise with the pressure and similarly fail. Though, of course, it also delivers the romantic fantasy that the shy, awkward one will get the man in the end.

For Bridget Jones' readers, the heroines of family sagas represent everything they want to get away from - duty, sacrifice, thrift, endurance and, especially, women as the repository of all moral value. Keen family saga readers trying *Bridget Jones' Diary* are likely to wonder what all the fuss is about - all that agony about numbers of cigarettes or minor incidents at the office, instead of the drama of caring for dying relatives.

To meet the needs of all women readers, an understanding of these different reading preferences and how they change over time is necessary. The stark contrast above does not cover all the role models in light fiction aimed at women in recent years. In the 1980s, coincident with the rise of Margaret Thatcher, there was a sub-genre often called 'glitz and glamour' in libraries, which featured women making it in a man's world at a time when very few did. Understanding audience appeal helps libraries keep up to date with trends. Libraries in the UK were slow to realise how big chick lit was and they continued to buy large numbers of family sagas and glitz and glamour, which were still popular, without realising how the younger generation's reading preferences had changed. Bookshops were much quicker to respond on this.

The shifts in publishing trends are happening all the time and clearly relate to audience appeal. The important thing about Bridget Jones in 1996 is that she has no children. As the first generation of chick lit authors got older, they, of course, started to have children and a new wave of 'mum lit' appeared. (This was mirrored in fiction by male authors where Nick Hornby, Tony Parsons and others moved from 'lad lit' to writing about parenthood.) One generation of readers grew older and moved into the new genre, but a younger generation who didn't want to read about family responsibilities needed new authors who wrote about being young and free. A reader-centred library service knows how much stock it has for these different generations of readers.

A reader-centred approach to quality

From 2000 to 2007 in England the reader-centred approach to evaluating quality was translated into a useful tool for libraries. The methodology of the Stock Quality Health Check will be useful to anyone wishing to assess the quality of a library collection.

Opening the Book was commissioned to develop and test a method of evaluating the quality of the fiction book stock in a public library service for the Audit Commission, the independent body responsible for ensuring that public money is used economically, efficiently and effectively. The Audit Commission wanted a tool which could be used by Best Value inspectors, who were not necessarily book experts, as part of the inspection of library services. Following the success of the initial programme, the Stock Quality Health Check was further developed as a self-evaluation tool for library authorities in England in a three year programme funded by the Audit Commission, the Department of Culture, Media and Sport and Arts Council, England. More than two-thirds of English authorities used the Stock Quality Health Check in 2004 and 2005 and 84% submitted data in 2007. It is the biggest detailed comparison of the state of stock in English libraries ever undertaken. Most Welsh authorities and all services in Northern Ireland also sent in returns in 2007.

The reader-centred approach creates a new definition of quality in a stock collection. Many library stock policies referred to quality without defining it. The most precise definitions referred to what is most easily measurable, for example, the quality of paper and the quality of the binding, while avoiding any engagement with the content between the covers! Some authorities claim to choose on the basis of literary quality but this is hard to defend when they buy large quantities of popular fiction such as Mills and Boon romances and westerns. (A reader-centred approach will support buying of genre romance but not on grounds of literary quality.) A more sophisticated version of the literary quality argument is 'the best of its kind' aiming to buy not just the best literary novel but the best romance, the best thriller, the best fantasy. However, this merely shifts the debate about 'best' to one remove without resolving it, as services with this policy do not articulate the criteria they use for judging the best.

Librarians in the UK have been in an intellectual muddle about quality for years, on the one hand needing to justify their investment in popular fiction and on the other wanting to claim some higher role as custodians of culture. And, of course, what constitutes quality in literature is passionately contested by academics, philosophers, writers and critics. There is no clear agreement on what is 'best'. (The world would be a much more boring place if there was.) Taking a historical view demonstrates this even more sharply. Novels which in their day were banned are now mainstays of exam syllabuses for schools and universities. It is easy to sneer at this retrospectively; the real question is, how do we know, when we judge a contemporary novel as outrageous or shallow or incomprehensible, we are not making the same mistake as those who claimed Hardy and Joyce were not great novelists?

Literary quality is therefore a dangerous card for librarians to play. Those that do are likely to find their argument undermined by inconsistencies in their own service provision. And it's always going to be hard to defend the depth of judgment on a book's quality - whether popular or literary - when dealing with such large numbers of books across such a wide range as librarians do on a daily basis. How can you know that crime novel A is 'better' than crime novel B when all you have to go on is a publisher's blurb?

Testing collection quality by range

A reader-centred definition of quality avoids all these philosophical minefields. Reader development has already defined the best book in the world as simply the one the reader likes best and the role of the library as helping people find it. This is a subjective definition not an objective one. Each reader is able to judge what their 'best' book is. 'Best' is not a quality which resides in the book, it is a judgment made by an individual reader in a particular mood and a particular set of circumstances. One reader's best book may be another reader's worst.

The role of the library can then be seen not as defining what is 'best' as it judges each book but in providing what all those different readers consider 'best'. A quality collection is one which has a range of books for a range of different reading audiences. This definition sits much more comfortably with the service ethic of public libraries and their long history of democratic inclusion. It sets out a cultural role which is different from that of bookshops. It is also much more robust than the muddled claims about literary or popular quality which undermine many collection development policies. Quality defined as range is measurable. The criteria for range can be articulated and challenged.

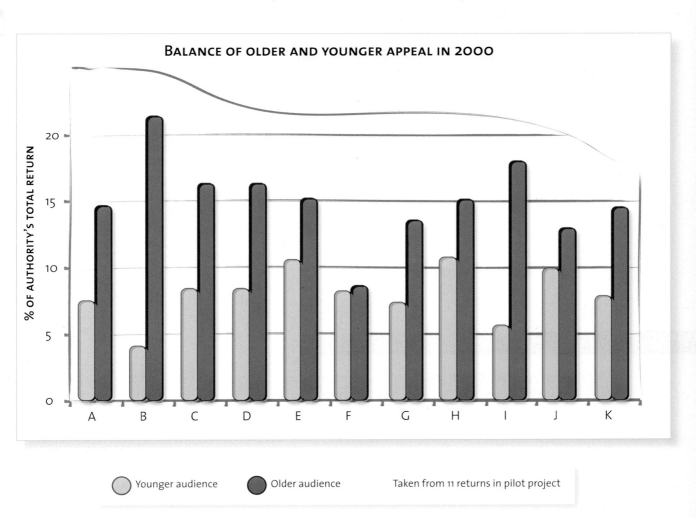

BALANCE OF OLDER AND YOUNGER APPEAL IN 2000

% OF AUTHORITY'S TOTAL RETURN

Younger audience   Older audience   Taken from 11 returns in pilot project

The Stock Quality Health Check tested range by sampling the library catalogue. It is impossible at the moment to interrogate a catalogue to ask for experimental or traditional crime - a representative author and title must be chosen. It is important that these are not seen as a definitive canon of titles a library should have. Individual titles can be selected for what they say about the representative category to which they belong. Titles can be balanced within a category to give a good range of the types of reading experience available within it. The catalogue of a service can then be checked to give an indication of quantities of different categories. This also indicates accessibility to users, irrespective of physical location, as it is reasonable to assume ten copies of a title make it more accessible than one.

This kind of sampling can be used to give very different sorts of information. At the basic level, the question is simply have you got a copy of this title or this author? This will show the overall range available to readers. At a more sophisticated level, the balance between different categories of title can be checked and compared.

In 2000, the first Stock Quality Health Check revealed a shocking imbalance between provision for older and younger readers in a sample of 11 very different library services. Service F (see page 121) is the only one buying roughly equal proportions for a younger and an older audience. (Younger in this context is defined as under 30 and includes *Bridget Jones' Diary* as one of the titles.) The other ten services have up to twice as many for the older generation than the younger. Service B has three times as many. To understand the full impact of this it is necessary to think about what it means translated through to the shelf in any particular library branch. In Library Service B, for every one book visible for under 30s there are three for over 70s. If the one is paperback and the three are hardback the young-appeal title will be even harder to see.

By 2006 the younger adult audience was visibly better catered for in quite a few UK public libraries through the introduction of Quick Choice areas with young-appeal paperbacks. Regular buying of the top 10 bestsellers (as quoted from bookshop sales) has also meant that key titles with younger appeal were more apparent. However, the results from Stock Quality Health Checks across English library services in 2004 and 2005 show that provision for the older audience in popular women's fiction increased its dominance in the first half of the decade. When samples of light women's fiction for four overlapping generations are compared in 2000, 2004, 2005 and 2007 the trend upwards for period saga up to 2005 is immediately visible.

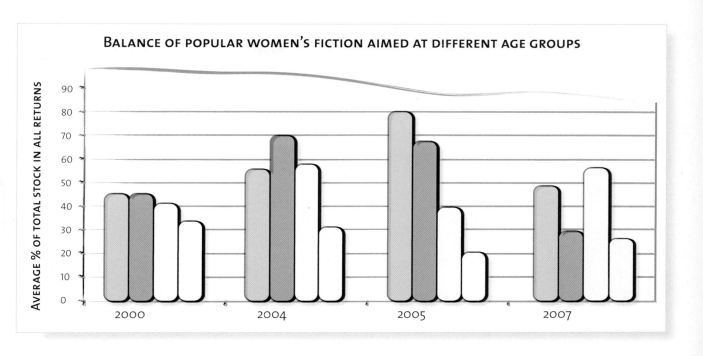

BALANCE OF POPULAR WOMEN'S FICTION AIMED AT DIFFERENT AGE GROUPS

● Period saga   ○ Young saga / romance   Taken from 54 returns in 2000, 138 returns in 2004,
● Saga / romance ○ Chick lit   106 returns in 2005, 126 returns in 2007

This injects some evidence into a debate which is often based on subjective perception. If one member of staff believes 'we need more young-appeal chick lit' while another is convinced 'we've got far too much chick lit already', nobody, including the head of service, knows who is right. A Stock Quality Health Check can give a more accurate picture of the proportions. Services can use this information to inform future buying, for example, consciously choosing to buy three new writers for the younger audience instead of buying extra copies of established writers for the older audience. The Western Education and Library Board in Northern Ireland used the Stock Quality Health Check results to bid for extra funding to buy additional large print and audio titles.

A further check can be made on how titles and whole categories are performing in terms of issues. One service had 20 copies of titles by Catherine Cookson of which two or three of each were on loan. They had only one copy of Boris Akunin's *The Winter Queen*, Karin Fossum's *Don't Look Back* and Hallgrimur Helgason's *101 Reykjavic*. All three of these lesser known titles were on loan. Similarly another service had 26 copies of Maeve Binchy's *The Scarlet Feather* of which four were on loan. It too had one copy of *101 Reykjavic* and, yes, it was out on loan. Comparisons like this help services to perceive how reader preferences are changing. Only one copy of titles perceived as 'minority' interest had been bought - it's easy to imagine conservative staff fears that they would never go out - when potential issues would have justified purchase of at least two or three copies.

Even where the period sagas are justifying their dominance with issues, the upward trend is worrying for a public library service in the context where the audience for period sagas is inevitably reducing. Libraries are investing most in their traditional audience and may not be providing enough for the next generation. Do the books that are missing mirror the audiences that are missing?

Community profiles and purchasing

Library services are concerned to protect the right to buy for specific local audiences and believe their buying reflects the community profile of their area. The approach outlined in the Stock Quality Health Check could be used by library services to regularly assess stock holdings in relation to community profile. One area where it is easy to test this out is the provision of large print. Print magnification improves the reading possibilities for many visual impairments, most of which increase in the population with age. Therefore, provision of large print should relate to the number of elderly people in the community. There are far fewer titles published in large print than in standard print, making it much easier for library services to ensure they are up to date with new titles. Libraries in the UK are the specialist supplier of large print (bookshops do not currently stock it at all, although LP editions are shown on Amazon and priorities may change as the UK demographic does). These factors mean it would be reasonable to expect a high and relatively uniform standard of large print provision across UK library services, with variations able to be correlated to population age. In the last ten years, the look and range of titles published in large print in the UK has also greatly improved, giving new opportunities for purchase.

97 of the 149 authorities in England used the Stock Quality Health Check to compare their holdings in large print with their holdings in standard print in both range and quantity in 2005. In 2007, 126 authorities carried out the same check with a completely different set of titles. The variations between authorities were far higher than expected.

The SQHC uses a list of 500 titles to gather information which can then be analysed in a number of different ways. In 2005, 215 of the 500 titles on the list were available in large print while in 2007, 188 of the titles chosen were available in this format. In terms of range, library services were asked to record if they had at least one copy of the titles on the list. The results varied between 19% and 89% of the 215 titles in 2005 and between 12% and 88% of the 188 titles in 2007. Comparing how many of the total number of items of the 500 titles were large print copies (the totals ranged from 1000 items in very small services to 17,000 in the largest) showed a similar variation from 1% to 16% in both years.

These variations cannot be explained by differing numbers of people in communities with minor visual impairments. The same pattern of wide variation was also shown to be true of holdings in audio formats across England in 2005 and 2007. It seems much more likely differences are caused by other factors such as budget and staff knowledge and expertise. When one library service is offering eight times more large print than its immediate neighbour and they share the same demographic profile (a genuine example) this means the library service is experienced as a postcode lottery by its customers.

The comparison between 2005 and 2007 shows a clear national downward trend in both the range and proportion of large print and audio titles. Some services know they have reduced purchase in these areas. For example, some decided to buy low-cost books as the only way to meet a national stock standard which set targets for titles purchased per head of population. (This standard, no longer used, was part of a national assessment and failing it could drag wider departmental scores down with political consequences for the library service.) Others are aware that new technology is changing how alternative formats might be delivered in the future. However, there has been little debate about the current downward trend and its impact on library readers.

Checking stock for different audiences over a time period is extremely useful to inform policy decisions. Where large print and audio declined in England from 2005 to 2007, the area with the highest percentage increase out of 37 different categories was titles for adults with low reading skills, described in the UK as 'emergent readers'. In 2005, an average of 1.57% of all copies held of the 500 sampled titles were copies of the 20 titles for emergent readers. By 2007, this had leaped to an average of 5.82% of all copies sampled, making it the third highest category after new bestsellers and recent popular fiction. This is likely to be the effect of participating in national initiatives such as the Quick Reads promotion on World Book Day and the BBC's RaW programme. Greater awareness of this audience need has had a substantial impact on the balance of library collections. It would be worth following through to check how these new collections have performed.

Evaluating stock in relation to audience gives library services useful evidence in debating policy priorities and budget allocations. Without this, discussions tend to be subjective and partisan, with supporters of emergent readers, for example, battling with supporters of visually impaired readers. Services can lose control of policy direction while responding on an ad hoc basis to external standards and opportunities; a reader-centred approach to checking stock holdings will provide the evidence on which to base your decisions.

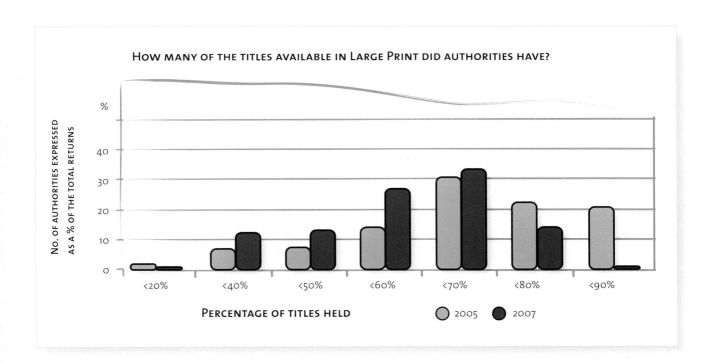

HOW MANY OF THE TITLES AVAILABLE IN LARGE PRINT DID AUTHORITIES HAVE?

No. OF AUTHORITIES EXPRESSED AS A % OF THE TOTAL RETURNS

PERCENTAGE OF TITLES HELD ⬤ 2005 ⬤ 2007

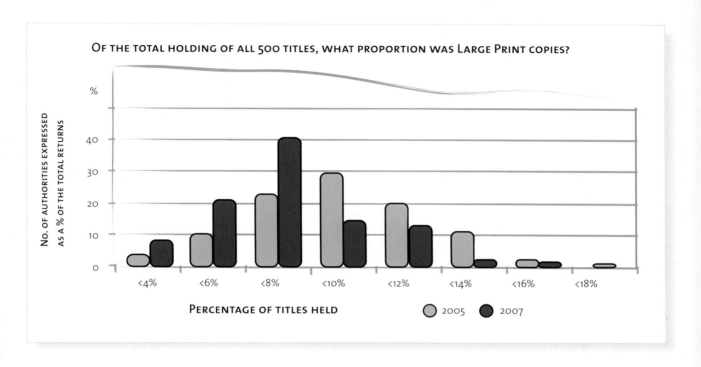

OF THE TOTAL HOLDING OF ALL 500 TITLES, WHAT PROPORTION WAS LARGE PRINT COPIES?

No. OF AUTHORITIES EXPRESSED AS A % OF THE TOTAL RETURNS

PERCENTAGE OF TITLES HELD

2005 2007

Paperbacks or hardbacks?

Another area where libraries have been slow to keep up with changing reader habits is in the purchase of paperbacks. Paperbacks dominate the UK fiction market; a whole generation has grown up using nothing else. Many libraries look as if this revolution never happened. The dominant view on entry is hardback titles arranged in order on the shelves.

Then towards the back there are a couple of spinners, crammed so tightly with overflowing paperbacks that a reader has to fight to pull one out. In one recent library observation, a customer was observed walking up and down the main shelves, clearly not finding what she wanted, and then enquired of a passing member of staff, 'Do you have paperbacks?' This customer was not a 20 year-old; she was around 50 and she was only interested in looking at paperbacks.

Many library staff have noticed that where a title is on the shelves in both hardback and paperback, the paperback issues much better. Reader preference for paperbacks continues even when titles are only available in hardback - rather than take the new hardback, many readers will take a different paperback. When one library service monitored the hardback/paperback issue rate of its one-week loan, multiple copy new bestseller promotions, they found that seven out of ten of the most popular fiction titles in the collections were paperback editions, not hardbacks as they would have predicted*.

The 2005 Stock Quality Health Check enabled library services to compare their holdings of paperback and hardback fiction. Of the 500 titles sampled, 490 were available in paperback and 409 in hardback. The results showed substantial variations across England that could not be correlated with any external factors such as budget or community profile. They were clearly the result of local policy and buying decisions.   Some services had less than one paperback for every hardback; a few services had seven or nine paperbacks for every hardback.   By 2007, the trend to buy paperbacks had clearly increased. Across

WAKE-UP CALLS

Misunderstandings, however well-intentioned, undermine reader-centred practice. If you recognise the views below, use the arguments in this chapter to challenge them.

" Borrowers want new books as soon as they are published, they don't want to wait for the paperback to come out. "

" Buying the hardback is better value for money because it lasts longer. "

" The elderly borrowers prefer hardbacks. "

---

* Bentley, Madeleine, 'Best Practice or Selling Out?', *Public Library Journal*, Vol21 No 3, 2006.

England as a whole, the average moved from 1.84 paperbacks for every hardback to 2.25 paperbacks to every hardback, an increase of almost 25%.

As long ago as 1993, Essex Libraries undertook substantial research which showed that paperbacks were better value on a cost per issue basis than hardbacks. This was tested across adult and children's stock, both fiction and non-fiction, and the cost of reinforcement was included in the paperback cost*. It was therefore no surprise that Essex was the service with the highest ratio - 9.7 paperbacks to every hardback in 2007. Those with higher ratios did better on the other tests in the Health Check than those with lower; Essex had the highest overall score in both 2005 and 2007.

In 2005 the same 500 titles were checked in a mainstream chain bookstore. In the bookshop the proportion of paperback to hardback was 24 to 1. Bookshops clearly do not expect many customers to buy hardback fiction. This leads into some interesting policy questions for libraries. Readers are mostly unwilling to buy the hardback with their own money but some will use and expect library copies to be available. Is supporting these readers at a high-cost per issue an important priority? Is the argument the same whether the title is by a popular writer and in high-demand or by a less well-known writer and no requests have been made for it? Libraries are also offering support to the publishers who bring out novels in hardback only or hardback before paperback. Is this important because it enables a variety of publishers to keep afloat or is it a mistake to use public funding to support publishers who are unwilling to restructure their offer to support lower-cost paperbacks?

The figures for sales of literary hardback novels are absurdly low - only 200 copies of many are subbed into UK retailers nationwide. In November 2007 Picador was the first publisher to officially recognise that the hardback literary novel has become a 'moribund format' (their phrase). Picador plan to release all new titles in 2008 in mass-market paperback with an accompanying short run of high-quality hardbacks for publicity purposes. They hope this will enable them to co-ordinate press coverage for new launches (the media are still lamentably tied to the hardback publication date) with the paperback editions that drive the majority of sales. Libraries will have a choice of which format to buy. Evidence from issues and from the Stock Quality Health Check is clear that the paperbacks will be the most borrowed and the best value.

Matthews, Ian, 'The Issue Life of Bookstock', *Public Library Journal*, Vol 9 No 5, 1994.   *

Streamlining stock management

In 2008, the next decision for many authorities is to delegate more selection to suppliers as leading authorities taking this route have been able to show improvements not just in cost savings but in the range of material available to borrowers.   Delegating the purchase of mainstream titles has the potential to free up staff time to spend on other areas - researching independent presses, training staff in stock awareness, planning stock promotions - all of which are sorely neglected in many services.

One area which is holding back cost-saving on the acquisition process is the adoption of common and minimal servicing standards. The National Acquisitions Group has been recommending this for years and large consortia of services buying together have shown how it can work.

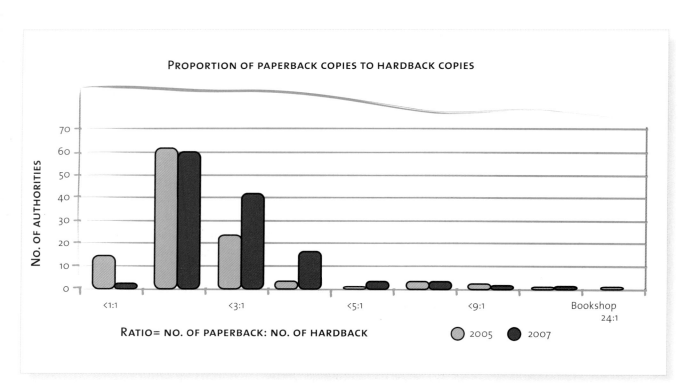

PROPORTION OF PAPERBACK COPIES TO HARDBACK COPIES

No. OF AUTHORITIES

RATIO= NO. OF PAPERBACK: NO. OF HARDBACK

2005   2007

New technology is also enabling better stock management. In fact, the technology has been able to supply quantities of complex data for some time; it's the staff skills and time to analyse the data that have been missing. Small services have managed to increase range in every branch by avoiding duplication when buying centrally and circulating stock efficiently with automated processes. Weeding stock that hasn't issued is also more efficiently managed with automated alerts, though local checks still need to be made on stock condition and a last-copy check should be in place.

Comparative figures on stock turn, circulation and replenishment can be used to inform promotion plans as well as purchase. These have tended to be used as a blunt instrument in the past, especially in relation to national stock standards. The number of issues per title in specific stock areas varies widely, for example, and analysis needs to go into this level of detail to be helpful. Commercial outlets check stock performance and requirements on a weekly and sometimes daily basis, adjusting stock to space ratios, stock positioning and orders as needed. There is no reason why this should not be part of the job of branch library staff in fully automated systems. The opportunities for stock management offered by RFID, which many libraries are investing heavily in for self-service, have yet to be properly exploited.

Demand-led or diversity-led?

The reader-centred approach to stock can help to articulate and define the specific cultural role of libraries. This became very clear in comparisons with major book chains which yielded interesting results. Libraries have a much wider range of backstock and the comparison not only bore this out but revealed that the difference was much higher than those outside libraries would expect. 95% of library services had a better range than a major chain of city bookshops. This should be a much bigger part of library advocacy. When libraries are under pressure to be more like bookshops, this is a factor which should not be overlooked.

Whichever view you take of the best method of stock selection, you face the same problems in how to tell whether you are getting it right. A reader-centred approach will help to check the balance of your collection with greater subtlety and accuracy than previously used methods. It is your key policy decisions, however, which will drive what it is you measure and these will derive from the service's beliefs about the cultural role of public libraries.

How far does the library take an active role in promotion or simply follow the market? Some services purchase at least one copy of all first novels as part of their responsibility to help new authors find an audience. The demand for Black writers and gay writers is lower in most libraries than in bookshops; does this mean libraries should buy less or promote them better? Does a library service have a responsibility to meet needs as well as wants? But who determines what those needs are?

Publishing and bookselling have changed a great deal in the UK in the last few years. Access to books has widened through supermarkets and workplace selling but the range of titles getting the most attention has narrowed, except for online. In 2004, 50% of Waterstone's sales were generated by 3% of the titles offered (*The Observer*, 19.12.04). Libraries need to know which are the 3% most popular titles but should they mirror bookshops' concentration on multiple provision of these? Most UK libraries now buy the

WAKE-UP CALLS

Misunderstandings, however well-intentioned, undermine reader-centred practice. If you recognise the views below, use the arguments in this chapter to challenge them.

" *The more books we have on the shelves the more choice people have.* "

" *Library users pay their council tax, we have to make sure we're giving them what they want.* "

" *We get rid of all the dross really fast in this service; there's no reason to keep out of print titles.* "

top paperback bestsellers as listed in *The Bookseller* automatically. This means every library keeps up to date with the most popular books in a way that they didn't ten years ago. But does there come a point where buying more copies of the most popular titles means that libraries reduce the range of titles available?

Cultural critics are concerned at this narrowing of range and this provides an opening for libraries to make claims for their importance. D J Taylor, for example, wrote an article for *The Guardian,* 12.03.2003, titled '417,000 books, and nothing to read', lamenting the dependence of bookshops on identikit frontlist titles. He trawled the bookshops of his home city of Norwich looking for two less well-known authors, Joel Lane and John Murray. All he could find was one copy of a book by Joel Lane. A check of Norfolk Libraries' web catalogue would have shown four copies of each available.

It is dangerous for those who believe in a free public library service to argue its role is purely to respond to demand because a more commercial model offers a comparable alternative. In the UK a Conservative Green Paper in the 1980s proposed to charge for new fiction while books which had been out for some years would be free. In New Zealand libraries, there is a charge to borrow the most popular genre fiction which is bought in multiple copies to meet demand. Of course, the UK library service is not free - users pay for it through taxes. But it is free at the point of use when many other high-demand local government services are not. Users pay on entry for swimming pools, sports centres and car parking although they have already paid through taxation. Why should libraries be different unless they can claim they provide something extra to what's available commercially?

Communicating your policy to readers

If we leave the bigger political policy debates and come back to readers, it is not always true that buying what readers say they want does meet all of their needs. People don't just want individual titles, they want books they've not heard of, a rich variety and an opportunity to discover something different.

If your library service believes this, it is important that the reasoning for your position is clearly available to your readers, your staff and your elected politicians. Collections policy is not something which is solely a professional concern; your users and stakeholders have a right to debate it with you. This means you need to articulate it in language which is understandable not in library jargon. In the early 1990s Birmingham Libraries produced simple leaflets showing how the purchase budget was spent. Even better, they explained their policy on requests:

> *Each year a relatively small number of titles become very popular. To give an example, three hundred people paid to reserve a copy of Catherine Cookson's novel* House of Women. *We have just over one hundred copies of this title in our libraries. We could buy more copies to satisfy this short term demand but this would seriously damage our ability to offer plenty of choice in our fiction stock - our ultimate objective. To combat this problem we have introduced the Top Titles - a list of very popular titles which will be issued for a short loan period. Titles are added or removed each week according to the number of requests for them.*

The specific numbers really help here. Those in the queue for the Catherine Cookson might have grumbled about how few copies had been bought; when they knew it was 100 copies, this complaint is dissipated. Smaller services can adapt the argument with precise examples from their own service.

Ten years later Kirklees Libraries and Information Service articulates its cultural role with confidence in its Stock Development Policy:

> *Our aim is to provide the widest possible range and choice of stock within our resources, to entertain and educate, to inform and challenge. We value these qualities more than hype or short-term popularity and this means that we will not simply buy more copies of the best sellers many want to read on demand.*
>
> *You will find those best sellers and a good range of other popular books in your library but you will also find the new, the different and, occasionally, the controversial. Newspapers, magazines and television highlight and promote a very narrow range of authors and titles each month, a fraction of those published. The library offers and promotes more.*
>
> *At its core the public library service offers all communities the opportunity*

to access a wide range of human thought and creativity, to choose books to take home and to do this free of charge. One of our unique strengths lies in being able to supply books and other materials that are no longer in print and that, together with free access and borrowing, makes us very different from bookshops.

Our policy is not static and will be reviewed regularly to reflect and take account of changing needs and circumstances. This is your library service and we welcome your comments, questions and suggestions.

Decisions about what to buy get harder, the less money you have. In this context, it is instructive to look at policy development in a small organisation. The National Library for the Blind in the UK (now merged with the Royal National Institute for the Blind) is a charity specialising in production and circulation of Braille books and online services. Production in Braille, online and especially in embossed print, is expensive and the Library can only afford to undertake a small number of new titles each year. The decision of what to Braille is therefore hugely important. From the reader point of view it is even more so; keen Braille readers will be offered only a tiny percentage of what sighted readers have to choose from.

Before engaging with a reader-centred approach as partners in the Branching Out project, the Library concentrated on the most popular titles. There was also a tendency to play even safer than in public libraries and a high danger of patronising readers simply because of their sight problems. Readers who use Braille will have as wide a range of preferences as any other sample group; the only thing they have in common is the means they use to read. The Library undertook user consultation and discovered that some readers found the selection very bland. Readers who wanted anything outside the most popular mainstream titles were not being catered for at all.

The Library undertook a radical overhaul of stock management. Their new policy articulated a strong mission:

We believe that we have a responsibility
- to meet the expressed and unexpressed needs of individual readers
- to attract new readers
- to reflect the culture at large

- to develop reading
- to encourage diversity and equal opportunities
- to meet the special interests of visually impaired people

In acquisition the Library set out three different areas:

- New popular books to meet expressed demand
- Collections development to create quality collections for specific users and to fill gaps retrospectively
- Books that widen choices, including first novels; new non-fiction subjects; books for a male audience; trendy books for young people; gay/lesbian, black British and black US writers; science fiction; foreign literature and translations; poetry; and books from community publishers.

The three areas had different staff teams choosing so that the Widening Choices team, for example, was not distracted by the pressure to keep up with new titles. The policy set out the proportion of titles to be Brailled in each area each year: 50% are New Popular titles, 25% are Collections Development and 25% are Widening Choices. In one year the Library moved from having the most conservative acquisitions policy in the UK to having the most radical. This example now provides a real challenge to mainstream public library provision. Imagine the impact on public library services if 25% of their purchase budget was devoted to Widening Choices defined in this way. Imagine the impact on publishing and the wider literature industry! Libraries really could make a difference.

Reading the future

The next ten years may see big changes in stock procurement in UK libraries. The need for greater efficiency and the pressure on libraries to achieve the same levels of discount from the book trade as booksellers do are shaping very different approaches. Whatever the mechanics of the systems put in place - and the favourite in 2007 was a national e-marketplace - as long as budgets are held by individual services, those services will continue to carry responsibility for specifying requirements for their readers. It will be important that any new system recognises reader-centred approaches to stock procurement instead of simply overlaying old thinking with new organisational structures.

When a service comes to write the specification for book supply, this needs to be more than a list of approved authors. A reader-centred approach would allow a service to specify instead a percentage of materials for particular audiences, for example, action thrillers for audiences aged 15-30, 30-65 and over 70, or literary fiction for readers who are prepared for a bit of a stretch but nothing too taxing. If the supplier is asked to meet an audience need, there is greater opportunity for depth of expertise to be utilised. It would also mean that if a new author with a particular audience appeal is published, the supplier can add that title in to library provision as soon as it becomes available. This speed and depth of response is vital if libraries are to meet customer expectations over the next five years. A reader-centred approach has the capacity to drive a much more powerful stock performance than traditional library methods, resulting in more satisfied customers and more exciting collections.

Chapter 5

READER-CENTRED PROMOTIONS

The success of the reader development approach in UK libraries has seen a transformation in library promotions over the last 15 years. A customer walking into a library in 1990 was likely to find that promotion was confined to a display of face-forward mixed titles under the banner *Recent additions to stock*. Adventurous staff who realised this wording gave away how staff-centred this promotion really was, indicated their modernity by rebranding it more simply as *New Books*. The content was the same, a random mix of whatever the library had acquired recently. The organising principle was when they happened to arrive and the fact that they were new; there was no practice of thinking about who the different titles might appeal to. The *New Books* display was always near the counter so it was convenient for staff to put books on it.

Compare that with the explosion of promotions confronting a library user today. The tradition of using publisher posters all over the walls in children's libraries has passed over into adult spaces. Where posters aren't available, access to colour copiers means that staff can reproduce book covers and put them on walls and shelf-ends. Dumpbins proliferate, tables and window-ledges are pressed into service for displays, shelves are decorated with coloured paper as background for face-out titles. The new emphasis on keeping up with bestsellers means Top 20 lists are prominently displayed everywhere, even if not many of the Top 20 books are visible.

From being virtually non-existent, promotions have become a problem in many libraries. The availability over the last five years of professionally produced promotional packs for libraries, either for purchase from organisations such as The Reading Agency and Opening the Book, or delivered as part of national partnerships like the Orange Prize and the Richard and Judy Book Awards, has caused additional pressure on spaces. Originally conceived to help libraries create small focus areas for temporary promotions and displays, the great number of these printed materials now appearing in libraries adds to the confusion and clutter. Too often promotions become the tail wagging the dog. Each promotion arrives in the library as a self-contained, independent project instead of being the result of a prioritised marketing strategy.

Promotion is just one part of marketing. A full marketing strategy for the library service, or for reader services within that, will involve much more than planning a programme of promotions. A marketing strategy includes careful attention to market research, trend analysis, brand identity and image, audience segmentation, customer profiling and assessing competitors. Which audiences are targeted and which stock is promoted in which library should be planned as the result of this process. Instead, what happens in most libraries is promotions depend on the time available and interests of specific staff on the ground or what it is your turn to have in the circulation timetable.

Changes in promotional practice

To develop a more effective approach to promotion, it is necessary to understand the journey libraries have made from doing too little to doing so much with so little effect. Without a clear analysis, you will be vulnerable to challenge from staff with changing perspectives and will be unable to articulate a strong way forward. This applies equally to the branch manager attempting to curb the enthusiasm of the staple-gun and ribbon brigade, the stock librarian considering which promotions to purchase and the head of service looking for increased performance.

When libraries first started doing promotions, there was resistance from some staff who believed promotion would compromise libraries' neutral stance. Staff felt, rightly, that it was not the job of libraries to tell people what to read. Children's librarians have always seen their role as developmental but library staff serving adults saw their job as providing material and leaving people to find their own way. Staff should be quick to respond if asked, but, unless they were asked, they made no intervention; the service was essentially passive.

Library staff did not want to become cultural legislators or the double-glazing salesmen of literature, using the tactics of the hard sell. But the traditionally passive service was failing. Whether driven by the negative pressure of falling book issues or the positive demand for new added-value services, promotion was the answer. And the new movement of reader development offered a different approach to promotion, one which cut through the old value-systems and felt fresh, imaginative and fun.

The reader-centred approach revealed the large number of people who found it difficult to choose what to read in a library. Readers are grateful for anything which makes one book stand out from another. It wasn't a question of telling people what to read, it was more a need to offer manageable choices. Promotion is the key to helping the majority of

put your nose in a book!

fact, fiction and fantasy

Your library...
explore these worlds and others

WEST LOTHIAN COUNCIL DELIVERS LEARNING OPPORTUNITIES FOR ALL

West Lothian
Council

*Selling the sizzle of reading
with humour in West Lothian*

borrowers, the ones who don't know exactly what they want, discover something they are willing to try. Many readers are looking to be tempted and stimulated; their choice is made on impulse. Faced with the same rows of books they always saw, they gave up and went out.

Staff on the library floor recognised this as the truth of their own experience. Many found it hard to choose what to read themselves and they enjoyed impulse shopping in other environments. At work, they knew the returns trolley was hugely successful but this was never acknowledged or celebrated; reader development brought that success out of the closet and made it respectable. Staff could see that drawing attention to the books always worked as a promotional device, they had just never thought of it that way. Everyone recognised the experience of weeding the stock, going along the shelves to see what's in a bad condition, and then finding that readers suddenly swooped on the pile of discards to borrow them.

In this context, the reader-centred approach to promotion was a glorious liberation for library staff at all levels. Instead of swotting up on prize lists or researching sequels and prequels, staff could brainstorm around reader needs, giving full rein to imagination, humour and that well-known library propensity for terrible puns. These early promotions changed the perception of libraries as stuffy and dusty.

WAKE-UP CALLS

Misunderstandings, however well-intentioned, undermine reader-centred practice. If you recognise the views below, use the arguments in this chapter to challenge them.

" *Libraries are not bookshops. We don't want to pressure readers with lots of offers, we should be neutral.* "

" *We produce a monthly booklist listing our new books alphabetically by author.* "

" *I sent my staff on a course on how to do displays on a budget so they all know what to do with a staple gun.* "

Instead, they came across as lively and irreverent, not taking themselves too seriously. *The Lone Re-arranger*, complete with Stetson and neckerchief, has not become part of library history, unsurprisingly, but the idea was strong enough visually to get a sizeable picture in the Kirklees local paper. *Bookspotting* saw staff in a Buckinghamshire village take a trolley of books onto the station platform for a week to catch early-morning London commuters. Leeds Libraries offered *Spice up your reading* with a choice of Mild, Medium and Hot reads and found the national tabloids wanted to know how *Jane Eyre* would be rated.

Many of these ideas took energy from the realities of how people use reading in their lives. Promotions for readers looking for comfort or risk; books to read in specific situations, in the bath, late at night, on a train; books for different moods - all these carried a recognition that readers have different reading needs at different stages of their lives. They conveyed an acceptance that whatever you read, that's fine, and from that security, they encouraged people to explore a bit wider than they would otherwise have done. The response from readers as well as staff was tremendous; suddenly the real experiences of reading were in the limelight. These had never been visible or discussed before and the release of excitement was palpable as readers discovered that hidden privacies were actually shared experiences.

The language used to describe and discuss books began to change. Mary Cutler, Reader-in-Residence at Birmingham Libraries, broke the mould of the formal book list with an imaginative and humorous series of reader-centred lists under the *Why Read?* programme of 1993. *Why read about love?* included classics and recent novels under the headers 'And they didn't live happily ever after' and 'And they all lived happily ever after: well, sort of'. *Why read when you are ill or waiting to be?* covered situations from hospitals to convalescence to waiting at the dentist.

Reader development encouraged staff to listen to borrowers and use what people said as the starting point for a promotion. Perhaps the most famous example was the response of one reader to a general question about reading habits: 'Well, what I'm really looking for is books about people more miserable than me.' The remark is funny, unexpected and sends powerful messages about the complexity of the reading experience and the motives that drive people towards books. This kind of escapism flies in the face of the generally accepted sense of the word. One library service turned this into a reading promotion as part of the health theme for National Libraries Week 1997, demonstrating the role that books can play in supporting good mental health. Here is a reader who is feeling a bit ground down by her own life and obviously takes great comfort in knowing that things could be worse!

Understanding how books would be used rather than what the book was, led to promotions which aimed to conjure up the situation the book might be read in. Staff set up an ironing board as the centrepiece of an audiobooks promotion, a deckchair with a pile of books for the beach, a sofa with a message to curl up with a good read. These promotions were often ingenious in concept but they took time to set up, occupied a prime space and were hard to make look professional. They also offered too few books; there was a danger of concentrating on the surrounding props and forgetting the real purpose was to get the books borrowed.

This history explains some of the confusions surrounding promotional understanding and practice in UK libraries. In any service, there are staff who do not undertake any promotional work. This may be for very varied reasons - lack of confidence, simple laziness

Traditional spine-on books can be overwhelming

Single author displays restrict choice and squander valuable display space

Too many props obscure the books and covers of the same colour merge into each other

or a principled opposition to the idea of compromising neutrality. There are also staff who continue to promote as they did before the advent of reader development, making displays of books by one author, a seasonal display for Christmas or Halloween and a general new books display. Staff who bought into the reader-centred revolution ten years ago, and haven't moved on, still see promotion as bringing extra props in from home to give the library a different look. Since 2000, there has been a new emphasis on putting books back at the centre of promotions and learning from retail approaches to display and merchandising. Whenever the word 'promotion' is used in a library context, these different meanings will be in play.

Changing the appeal of traditional shelving using face-on display

In the reader-friendly library, promotion should be seen as an integral part of the day-to-day routine, built-in to the job description of every frontline staff member. Very basic promotional techniques - the simple act of turning books face-forward on a shelf, on a table or on a display unit - cost nothing and can have a substantial impact on loans, not to mention the lift they give to the general appearance of the library.

The role of library frontline staff as promoters should be addressed in job descriptions, managing staff rotas and planning staff training. As libraries move more confidently towards self-service, stock promotion and merchandising shelves provide a range of tasks to which frontline staff can be redeployed from counter duties. The library space can be zoned and different staff given responsibility for maintaining specific areas. For example, one member of staff monitors the Quick Choice area to restock and tidy displays; another colleague addresses on-shelf merchandising to highlight a different kind of stock, perhaps thinking about targeting the predominant age group and gender of the browsers expected to use the library at different times of day. If there is an increase in visits by young mothers with school age children around 3.30pm every day, for instance, a selection of young appeal paperback fiction might be turned face forward on the shelves, to catch their eyes as they make their way to the children's section.

The technique of turning individual titles on shelves face-on can also help user-navigation in a library. You can spotlight the Mind, Body, Spirit collection by turning three or four titles with attractive covers face-on in the bay. You could mark out your Biography, Cookery or Travel collections in the same way and these can be very quickly changed at any point of the day to showcase different titles and to signal to your customers the range and diversity of books in any subject area.

In promotion, the basic tool is the book cover. It is well established that most people choose books by the cover. Publishers invest time and money in developing cover designs to appeal to specific readers. They are especially skilled at anticipating and creating design trends; their sales depend on getting this right. It costs libraries nothing extra to draw on the marketing work the publisher has already done to send strong signals to attract the target audience.

In a reader-centred library, the staff need to be able to understand book covers, to analyse the information publishers are using to communicate with the perceived audience for any book, and to use this as a starting point for developing a wider knowledge of stock. There is a tendency to assume that there is one kind of reader for each genre when in reality there is a wide spectrum of writing, and consequently readers, in most genres. Within graphic novels, for instance, a traditional Spiderman or Batman reader would not necessarily find the philosophical, political and cultural nature of the work of Marjane Satrapi appealing. To align these titles within the same category runs the risk of alienating one or both parts of the audience as it shows no recognition of the completely different reading experiences they offer. The reader development objective of opening up reader choices requires more subtle implementation than simply putting very different books together and hoping for the best.

Despite good intentions, library promotions can stereotype readers. For example, a recent display of gay and lesbian books included titles about gay and lesbian issues, fiction featuring gay and lesbian characters, and works by authors identifying as gay or lesbian but which did not address gay and lesbian issues. This resulted in a weird mix of literary prizewinners, poetry and political polemic sitting alongside some sexually explicit material and books which seemed to have nothing to do with gay and lesbian culture, unless you knew something about the author's background. There is an underlying misapprehension here that the only audience for this material will be gay and that their sexuality and nothing else defines the kind of reader they might be.

Some library staff confess to a lack of confidence in their knowledge of fiction outside the mainstream. Others simply don't believe that an audience exists for these books. It is important to understand the need to highlight titles by new and non-mainstream writers in promotions. £6.99 invested in a first novel published by Canongate has to pay for itself in loans and will only do so if promoted. Borrowers know that bestsellers will have been bought and can be found in the expected sequence on the shelves, unless they are already out on loan. For a new author who isn't benefiting from a high profile launch campaign by a publisher, or who hasn't been taken up by the literary reviewers as the Next Big Thing, it is unlikely that borrowers will know a name to search for so filing the book in the A-Z sequence of 'General Fiction' is effectively a death sentence.

There is a reader for every book and the role of the stock librarian, the reader development librarian and all frontline staff is to tempt that reader to try that book. A fiction manager at one of Waterstone's main stores prided herself on her ability to promote new titles she thought deserved a wide audience. The challenge she set herself on viewing new publishing output and deciding what to take into stock was, 'Will it sell - or can I make it sell?' Promotional understanding enables libraries to move in a similar way from 'Will it issue?' to 'Can we make it issue?' If a library service's selection policy contains a commitment to purchase beyond the mainstream, this has to be linked to promotion. The act of linking a promotional strategy to new titles at the very point of purchase changes the perspective on the book from something that is dormant on a shelf to something that has a dynamic currency.

In 1997, Oxfordshire circulated *Feast on Fiction* collections to 33 small branch libraries to ensure that they got a good, regularly updated, supply of contemporary paperbacks, with the accent on the new and non-mainstream. Each collection contained 40 books which arrived in special display boxes. The collections were circulated between rotation groups of three libraries and stayed for four months in each. Staff could request replacements for any titles that got too dog-eared and if the collections fell below 20 titles, more were added before they were moved on. At the end of each rotation period, the books were offered to the larger libraries. This very simple approach supplied a framework into which stock librarians could slot an impressive number of new titles to ensure as wide a readership as possible. *Feast on Fiction* was a great success with the readers in the small libraries. Staff were initially sceptical that the more unusual titles would find an audience in small communities. They were surprised by the positive reaction, and the issue statistics, and became fully committed to continuing the scheme.

The secret of successful promotion lies in selecting the right stock for a targeted audience and locating it appropriately within the library. Once this is understood, the same theme can be targeted towards a variety of audiences; it is the selection of the books that defines who the promotion will appeal to. For example, a promotion called *Journeys* could be targeted towards an audience of fantasy and science fiction readers, people interested in travel writing, or Mind, Body and Spirit readers. Or a collection of new, contemporary fiction could be displayed under this heading, representing journeys through internal landscapes. The graphic header remains the same, it is the books in the display which speak to the target audience.

Interpreting a reader-centred
theme with different books

Displaying books

One of the main challenges facing library staff creating promotional displays is that libraries are generally working with single copies of each book. Bookshops have the advantage of being able to pile multiple copies of a single title on a table-top, forming an attention-grabbing display. It is a great deal harder to draw together a collection of disparate titles and make these attractive and tempting. Libraries often attempt to replicate the effect of the multi-copy display by bringing together different titles with the same colour cover. This is counter-productive because the titles merge into one mass of colour and it becomes very difficult for the eye to distinguish one from the other.

In recent years, library furniture suppliers have begun to address the need for libraries to raise their game in displaying and merchandising book stock. Purpose-built display furniture is now available which targets the impulse browser in libraries and enables libraries to make a collection of separate titles look good together. Since these new designs started appearing in the marketplace, most library furniture providers are now including items like this in their range.

Money and floor space invested in these units have to pay back in numbers of books borrowed. It is useful to ask staff to view display space in financial terms as they would in a retail store where display space is valued per square metre. The value of the space increases according to its location. In a bookstore, for example, the most valuable space is at the front of the table immediately facing the store entrance. In a library it may well be in the same place, or it may be affected by other factors such as attractive windows or the location of barriers or the helpdesk. It is worth experimenting to find out where the best spot is and, once you know, make sure it is exploited ruthlessly.

Installing a piece of display furniture in a service point will have no impact if the staff do not recognise that this new unit performs a different task in the library from the rest of the shelving and therefore has to be managed differently. A common objection to new promotional furniture from some more traditional library staff is that units take up too much floor space and hold too few books. This is a misunderstanding. Evidence shows that books from displays on well-designed promotional units go out much faster than shelved books and the units will more than pay back their additional floor space in loans.

The real problem with using display units in libraries is not the space they occupy, it's having enough good condition paperbacks to keep them stocked up and looking attractive. A picked-over display presents little interest to a browser and research conducted in the retail sector suggests that if a display is less than 70% full, usage falls steeply (**www.envirosell.com**). A book placed here that doesn't get borrowed is not earning its keep. Maintaining a regular rotation of stock on the display table ensures that the stock and the furniture are working as hard as they can. Well-designed promotional units include space for extra stock to top up gaps when books have been borrowed.

The cardboard dumpbins supplied by library booksellers and publishers can be a good tool if well placed and well managed. Their strong primary colours often detract from the books, however, so choose neutral ones, if you can. A cardboard dumpbin is designed for temporary use only, it is flimsy and quickly gets worn and damaged. Promotional equipment in hard-up libraries is so rare that the dumpbins are lovingly held together with sticky tape well beyond their natural life. This does nothing for the library's image; it is

WAKE-UP CALLS

Misunderstandings, however well-intentioned, undermine reader-centred practice. If you recognise the views below, use the arguments in this chapter to challenge them.

" *Sandra is in charge of displays and we wouldn't dream of interfering.* "

" *We did some lovely book displays - all red books in one, all blue books in the other.* "

" *You need marketing training to do that sort of work, how can I be expected to do it?* "

better to promote good-looking books on-shelf than to place them in display units that look like they have been rescued from a trash heap.

A typical sight in libraries is the empty, or nearly empty, dumpbin. Library managers will sometimes point to this as evidence of success when in fact it should be seen as evidence of failure. Of course, it is a good thing that the books in the promotion have been borrowed but if the stand is left empty the promotional space is being wasted. As well as losing potential loans, this gives a poor first impression to customers that the best books in this library have gone and you don't have any more to offer. Key display units are never left empty in shops; priority is given to keeping them stocked at all times. Once the initial activity of siting and stocking a promotional unit is complete, the work is not finished. If no-one in the branch is briefed as to its role or given the responsibility for its maintenance, it soon merges into the background as just another part of the general clutter, overlooked by staff and borrowers alike.

Locating promotions

People approaching a display start browsing it from as much as five metres away. Your gaze is already travelling over the items looking to see if there's anything that interests you. It is worth bearing in mind this aspect of browsing behaviour when determining where to site promotional displays. Angling displays so that they are visible as a customer approaches, rather than placing them flat against walls or at the end of a shelving bay, will make it more likely that something will catch their eye.

Many libraries use shelf ends for their main displays. Endcaps, as they are called in retail, are widely used in supermarkets, at both ends of shelving bays. There has been a big push recently to adopt retail practice to improve performance in UK libraries, introducing concepts such as the 'power' display - a high-performance, high-impact product display in a prominent position. Power displays are just as important in libraries but not everything about the retail context can be transferred successfully to the library context.

Product displays at aisle ends in shops will typically be single products - a stack of bottles of wine, cans of paint or kitchen roll - and the customer can take in what the product is at a glance. Bookshops can make successful endcap displays with multiple copies of the same book. The problem when it comes to libraries is that instead of stacking one product in multiples, the library needs to show different products, so it's very difficult to absorb them at a glance. Libraries simply do not have multiple copies of the same book on display at any one time; where they do buy multiples, the book is so popular that most copies will be on loan.

A display in an endcap position containing multiples of one product is easy to grab from as you pass. A library book display in the same position requires more time to browse, the customer needs to stop longer to absorb the information. In most library layouts where the shelving is in straight rows any browser standing at the aisle end is in danger of being bumped into by passing traffic. Paco Underhill's research into retail outlets strongly demonstrated that customers are reluctant to linger in places where other people are passing close behind them (**www.envirosell.com**). This means that customers may walk past endcap displays in libraries without stopping long enough to look at the books. The endcap position is not necessarily the best place for a power display in a library; it's

WAKE-UP CALLS

Misunderstandings, however well-intentioned, undermine reader-centred practice. If you recognise the views below, use the arguments in this chapter to challenge them.

" We put a dumpbin on the end of every bay and they're always empty. "

" We scrounge dumpbins from everywhere and we make them last. "

" Mary's husband built us a handy wooden dumpbin that cost us next to nothing. Now everybody wants one. "

a good idea to walk through the space and check out all the options before making this assumption.

One of the most valuable things any staff member can do when planning and implementing promotions in a library is take an overview of the impact a new display will have on the space. This is particularly important when there are now so many national campaigns for libraries to participate in. The starting point for anyone installing a new display should be, 'If I'm adding this, what should I take out?' Less is definitely more. If you are in the position of having a range of promotions to draw from, these can be managed in rotation very easily in a way which will help to overcome empty dumpbin syndrome. When a particular display is beginning to look sparse, replace the graphic header with a generic standby, restock the display with the alternative collection of books and customers will perceive that there is always something happening and that there are lots of new books arriving all the time.

Differentiating audiences in libraries

Libraries have a strong sense of their role in communities as a public service and pride themselves in providing an equal quality service across the board. It is therefore difficult for anyone planning a promotion to design it primarily to benefit only one part of the audience. In contrast, libraries are very comfortable with adapting spaces to accommodate the different demands of particular segments of their audience, for example, providing carrels or study areas for people involved in research or who just need a quiet area to work; differentiating by age to separate children's and teens' sections from the main adult lending area; and differentiating by format for large print and audio books, CDs, DVDs, newspapers and journals, non-fiction, fiction and reference.

In the private sector, it would be unthinkable to design and launch a product without determining the exact market it was to be aimed at. Fortunes are spent by companies deciding which customers a particular product might appeal to and how it might be packaged and advertised to sell it to them. In car advertising, for example, the nippy little number ideal for town and city driving may well be advertised showing a woman driver loading her purchases into the capacious boot. A high-marque, high status model will probably be shown driven by a ruggedly handsome, obviously successful man, revelling

in the pleasures of the open road and the vehicle's road holding, brake horse power and dashboard gadgetry. Such sexism may provoke outrage but it is probably, generally speaking, fair to assume that women value safety, economy and can-I-fit-the-kids-the-dog-and-the-shopping-in more than engine capacity, the gearbox and whether it will do 0 to 60 in 4.7 seconds.

Chocolate advertising is much the same. It is widely accepted that women are the largest consumers of chocolate and therefore it is mainly marketed as an indulgent treat to women seeking time out from the pressures of daily life. Chocolate marketed towards men will be the chunkier, nuttier kind, meant to give an energy boost or will be presented as a romantic gift for the ladies. It is interesting to watch TV commercials objectively and analyse who they are targeting and how they are doing it, then to place this in the context of what type of programme the commercial is interrupting, to see who the programmers think will be watching. The message is clear - for the world of commerce one size does not fit all. Enabling the potential customer to identify with a new product, to see themselves using it and how it can fit into their life is a powerful persuader.

In public libraries, the same principle holds true. A library promotion targeted at 'everyone' will end up appealing to no-one because the inability to define a specific audience impacts on everything else - the books, the structure, the location, the timescale, the print design. With minimal budgets and staff time to allocate to promotions, it becomes more important to target them precisely to ensure that the investment is rewarded in terms of outcomes. Within a library service's promotional programme, it is entirely reasonable to commit money and resources to one target group as long as the balance of the overall programme and service adequately reflects and serves the needs of others.

It is also possible to design promotional projects which appeal primarily to one target group without necessarily alienating the rest of the audience. *Textual Intercourse*, the first reader-centred promotion for 16-19s, did not carry precise age-information. The title, design and the books all appealed to 16-19s but 14 year-olds or 40 year-olds could dip in if they wished. *ImaginAsian*, the most important library promotion to date to seek to raise the profile of Indic writing in the UK, targeted adults from Indic communities in the four participating authorities (Leicester City, Brent, Harrow and Hillingdon) as its principal audience. The key audiences came from different backgrounds in India, Pakistan, Uganda and the UK and the promotion included Indic writing in four languages, Gujarati, Urdu, Punjabi and English.

Working closely with community organisations in each of the partner authorities ensured the promotion met the needs of different Asian communities. The involvement of Book Communications, a professional marketing organisation with library experience, ensured the design of the print materials and the website appealed across and beyond the communities directly involved.

Audiences can be segmented in many different ways, for example, by patterns of use, length of visit, what they use/borrow, whether they are alone or accompanied. You might become aware of an audience need through a remark overheard from a customer or a staff member, or by behaviour observed daily in the library. For example, do you have visitors using the library café, theatre or meeting rooms who never browse or borrow anything? What could you do for readers currently on waiting lists for the latest offering by their favourite writer to introduce them to different titles that might make them feel less frustrated about their wait? What about young adult readers who are in transition - wanting to leave the teen section behind but not sure where to start in the adult section?

Coming up with a quirky title and displaying a varied selection of books beneath it will not be enough to support these customers into moving beyond their existing boundaries. In order to directly address their needs, you need to fully understand what it is that will grab their attention and tempt them into changing their behaviour. You have to select the right books to appeal to the audience you have identified - change the books and you change the audience.

Targeting male readers

As part of the Emrald programme (East Midlands Reading and Libraries Development) a cross-regional staff working group looking at small and mobile libraries, identified a need to improve services to male readers who might not be able to reach the library themselves and who had other people choosing for them. It was clear that this group were not benefiting from the full range of fiction and non-fiction on offer as the people choosing for them would tend to stick to 'safe' choices - the tried and tested, the same kind of read he always has. For the person doing the choosing, there are considerable challenges. 'Has he read this before?' 'Will he like this one?' 'I can't find anything by his favourite authors, what do I take instead?'

Carter Beats the Devil
by Glen David Gold

A magical adventure in many ways - not least in its intricate plot involving assassination, the invention of TV and a 'real-life' illusionist. With an eye for historical detail and a thirst for fast-paced thrills, this novel could never be described as a one-card trick.

YES ☐ NO ☐ MAYBE ☐

Global Village Idiot
by John O'Farrell

The 'village idiot' of the title is George W Bush - whose trip to Europe in June 2001 is given the distinctive O'Farrell treatment in the concluding entry of this collection of journalistic gems. Very sharp and explosively funny, beware of reading this in a public place.

YES ☐ NO ☐ MAYBE ☐

One Step Behind
by Henning Mankell

What is the connection between the mysterious death of three midsummer revellers and the murder of a policeman? Riveting, multi-layered police procedure novel set in Sweden - featuring ageing, and increasingly troubled, Inspector Kurt Wallender.

YES ☐ NO ☐ MAYBE ☐

Danger's Hour
by James Francis

A scarily c submarin with an Throug reader intima into the hear minds of the America sailors awaiti deat at the bottom of the Norwegian Sea.

YES ☐ NO ☐

MALE ORDER

CARTER BEATS THE DEVIL

first delivery

Male Order, pulled together a collection of 75 new and recent titles, fiction and non-fiction, all with male appeal. These collections were placed in branches and mobiles across the region and were promoted by the publication of two booklists. These were not the traditional list of book titles, authors and covers. All the books had reader-centred blurbs written by staff members and each book title was accompanied by a suggestion of a further two titles offering a similar reading experience, to try and counter the problem of what the chooser could take should the original title already be out on loan. Another feature aimed at helping the chooser, but also offering library staff an insight into what readers wanted, was giving tick boxes under each title captioned 'Yes', 'No' and 'Maybe'. The reader could tick to signify which books he would consider reading, which he absolutely would not consider, and which he might consider if his first choices weren't available. This list could then be taken to the library by the chooser as a useful reference.

The design of this promotion was crucial in making sure that middle-aged men would identify with the image at the same time as being attractive to the women who might be choosing for them. The image featured a close-up of a man wearing a shirt and tie. This very specifically branded it as targeting an older man, still most likely to don a shirt and tie for a night out.

An additional element recognising the particular needs of this situation was the production of a *Male Order* carrier bag. The likelihood was that an individual choosing for another reader would also be choosing for themselves and would probably, therefore, end up with a larger number of books to carry home than usual. The bag was a courtesy to make life a bit easier for anyone in this situation as well as an advert for the promotion.

Meeting audience needs

Analysing audience needs and applying reader-centred principles can raise a library promotion from the familiar and predictable to become lively and relevant. Seasonal promotions such as holiday reading and Christmas book displays can be interpreted to include a wider range of stock, appealing to a greater number of readers. Featuring Christmas craft books and extending that to include elderly copies of Christmas-related classics will not make a significant impact on loans. People disposed towards creating their own crackers, cakes and gifts will already be heading for the Crafts section; using display space to address this audience is a waste of resources. Thinking about other reader needs around Christmas will give a better scope to include titles that need the exposure. What about the people who find the Christmas season overly busy and stressful, hate the idea of being trapped with their relatives for several days or who are contemplating the prospect

Staying In

online | borrow

▷ What's New
▷ Blind Date

Today's Poll

Do you ever judge
people by the books
they read?

○ Yes
○ No

[Vote] View Results

put your feet up

Staying in is the new going out! Here are heaps of ideas to keep
the world at bay, if you fancy a night on your own, or stuff to
convince your mates you're the host with the most.

FEELING *self-indulgent?*

Sit down and relax - with these great treats
Cold and dark outside? **Indulge yourself**

FEELING SOCIABLE?

Get some mates round - things to help the good times
roll!
What's your party style? **Try this quiz** to find out
Find your perfect partner - **Book Lovers**

FEELING *fed-up?*

Things to get you through the washing up
Have a laugh at yourself
Kick some butt from the safety of your sofa with
Graphic Reads
Try these **Boredom Busters** to beat the blues

of spending this, of all times, alone? Considering their particular situation gives a different perspective on the role the library, and reading, can play at this time of year. For example, collecting a selection of titles with families at the centre of the narrative gave one library service an inspired promotion: 'This year spend Christmas with a family that's nicer than yours!'

In planning a website aimed at 16-24 year-olds, staff from across all nine authorities of the East Midlands looked at what particular audience needs they could address to draw users to the website. One of the key inspirations behind the site was the awareness that libraries often build promotions to this audience segment by trying to present the library as a 'cool' and 'happening' place to go. But libraries can't compete with other local venues such as clubs and bars for excitement so attempts to go down this road always ended in ridiculous claims which made the library a laughing stock among the target audience. The planning group decided not to compete on these grounds but to look instead at what libraries could really offer to 16-24s and how to make this visible and relevant. The site, www.whatareyouuptotonight.com*, was split into two sections, *Staying In* and *Going Out*. The *Staying In* side was divided into *Feeling self-indulgent*, *Feeling sociable* and *Feeling fed up* - recognising that reasons for staying in could vary and that different books, DVDs, CDs and games could be offered to suit these. The *Going Out* side was structured around *Getaways*, *Getting around* and *Going abroad* and included lots to help plan trips away and gap years as well as suggestions for what to read and listen to on everyday train and bus journeys.

There are often promotional opportunities which libraries can provide that bookshops would not be able to tackle. Libraries remain the main source of books for readers who need large print. As well as those whose choice is restricted to text printed at 14 point size, there are many readers who struggle with some of the smaller print sizes used in publishing. It is not easy to tell from the outside which books are laid out so they are easy to read. It is usually assumed that the larger the book format, the bigger the print size will be but this is not always the case. Some larger hardbacks may have smaller fonts than paperbacks; and traditional large print books are not always easy on the eye as they can be very mean with margins and line spacing. *Clear Choice*, a promotion for libraries which was nationally available in 2000, promoted a collection of new and recent paperbacks which had all been assessed and selected on the basis that the print on the pages was extremely easy to read. To maintain this as a regular promotion would cost libraries nothing except staff time and would provide a useful service to a large number of readers. This kind of thinking about customer care gives a different emphasis to promotions as added value offers rather than pressing customers to borrow more.

Reader-friendly booklists

Before the advent of reader development, photocopied booklists of suggested titles were a common sight in libraries. Usually based on a list of author's works, titles in the same genre or a Who Writes Like idea, they were the main guidance offered to readers looking for help with what to choose. Well Worth Reading, one of the forerunners of The Reading Agency, brought professional design and marketing to the library booklist in the early 1990s, and offered a much more lively approach which included taking readers to less familiar writers in promotions such as *The Empire Writes Back*.

* Developed 2001- 2003 as part of Emrald, funded by the Regional Arts Lottery Programme, supported 2005-2006 by Arts Council England. The site is archived at: **www.openingthebook.com/archive/whatareyouupto**

The problem with a title-centred list is how the list works with the books available to borrow. The list allows space for a limited number of titles to be promoted; once these have been borrowed, the list becomes redundant and merely sets readers up for disappointment when the title that has caught their eye is discovered to be on loan and the only option is to add their name to the already lengthy waiting list. The message to the customers who weren't one of the lucky 20 or so to grab the books in the promotion is clearly a negative one; 'That library never has any of the books I want.' Reader-centred concepts help in this situation as single titles can be used as examples of meeting a reader need and it is easier for staff to suggest alternatives. Oldham Libraries' promotion *Make room in your life for a book* created short leaflets with inventive suggestions of books to read in the bathroom, the kitchen and the bedroom. There were only a few titles in each list but staff were encouraged to top up displays with other titles which fitted the concept.

Printed booklists have given way to promotional graphics which enable libraries to group books together and showcase the covers. After all, it is more important to get the customer to take a book than a booklist. As the example of *Male Order* shows, however, the printed booklist can play a key role in reaching readers who can't get to the library to browse themselves. For these audiences, it can also be a great instrument to open up reading choices.

This was the need identified by staff at the National Library for the Blind who worked in partnership with the Branching Out programme from 1998 to 2001. A blind or partially-sighted reader is unable to browse book covers and may have limited access to reviews. Choosing from lists inevitably meant looking for familiar names. For readers receiving Braille books by post, where the average novel runs to ten Braille volumes, taking a risk on something you might not like is a very different experience from a sighted reader who can read a few pages, flick through the rest, check the ending, discard and pick up the next book. The same problem was identified for those listening in audio formats. The National Library for the Blind, the Royal National Institute for the Blind, and Calibre Audio Library worked with Opening the Book and Branching Out to create samplers in Braille and audio formats which brought ten first sections of books together in single volumes or CDs. This gave readers the chance to have a taster before they decided to commit themselves and order the rest of the book.

To help with opening up reading choices, the samplers were created on reader-centred principles, rather than on more predictable genre or author connections. The titles were selected for their availability in Braille, audio and large print editions, and the promotional materials were made available in the same formats. Ten lists of ten titles were put together, including *A Velvet Touch*, *A Touch of Mischief* and *Touching Infinity*; each book was introduced with a reader's comment and information about the formats they were available in. The lists can be viewed and downloaded for free at **www.openingthebook.com/archive/branchingout**.

A Touch of Mischief

The books chosen for this list all have an element of mischief about them, but that's where the similarity ends. There's mischief that will make you laugh (in spite of your better judgement); mischief that teases and taunts; mischief that plays with your expectations as a reader; and mischief that will create an uncomfortable feeling deep in the pit of your stomach.

Use this list to bring an element of surprise into your reading life. Embrace the unexpected. You might find it's the most exciting thing that's happened to you in ages.

Read the introductions to each book and decide for yourself which to go for. Be generous, be daring – you can always swap the book for something else if it's not your cup of tea. But if you don't try... you'll never know!

The Reader by Bernhard Schlink

Set in post-war Germany, the story opens with a secretive affair between a young boy and an older woman. You've barely got to grips with the complexities of their relationship when the mischief kicks in. The scene changes, time moves swiftly on, and you're plunged into a haunting exploration of the terrible hold the past has on the present. An easy read, but the themes run dark and deep. This is one book readers never forget.

RNIB **NLB** **Calibre** ⌐

The Witch of Exmoor by Margaret Drabble

You'll be aware of a kind of mischief at work from the opening paragraph. The voice of the narrator is sharp, dominant and far from neutral – delighting in the exposure of the thoughts, words and deeds of Frieda Haxby Palmer's 'nearest and dearest'. This is a barbed look at family relationships and middle class values; and it may make you feel uncomfortable about certain aspects of your own life too.

RNIB **Calibre**

Amsterdam by Ian McEwan

This is Ian McEwan's witty and mischievous exploration of morality in a modern world, a must-read for its sheer entertainment value. Consider the dilemmas and decisions facing Vernon Halliday and Clive Lindley. What would you have done in their shoes? Expect the unexpected; and watch out for the deliciously wicked twist to the tale.

RNIB **NLB** **Calibre** ⌐

The Waiting Game by Bernice Rubens

Hollyhocks is an old folks' home for a better class of OAP. But don't kid yourself that the residents are quietly and peacefully awaiting death. Far from it! Mischief abounds, and blackmail, suicide, four-letter words and falling in love are all part of the daily routine. If you're looking for a read that turns your expectation of old age well and truly on its head, then this is it!

NLB **Calibre** ⌐

A Touch of... Get a sneak preview of ten great reads

Stuck for what to read next? Maybe you fancy trying something new but don't know where to start. **A Touch of** is a great way for readers who use large print, Braille or audio books to find that good read everyone is looking for. Whether you're choosing for yourself or for someone else who can't get to the library, **A Touch of** gives you a sneak preview of tempting possibilities. There are ten different booklists in the series, including A Touch of Terror, A Sharp Touch A Ticklish Touch and Touching Infinity.

A Touch of Mischief features books available in large print and tells you which ones you can get in audio and Braille as well. If you prefer to start from what's available in audio or Braille, please ask for the ten **A Touch of** samplers which give you friendly introductions and a short extract from each book to listen to or touch read.

RNIB Available from RNIB Talking Book Service

NLB Available from NLB in Braille

Calibre Available from Calibre Cassette Library

⌐ Available in audio through public libraries

If you would like more information about the services to readers offered by these organisations please ask a member of library staff. If you have internet access, you can check out **www.nlbuk.org**

Opposite: Extract from A Sharp Touch *at actual size*

Disgrace by J M Coetzee

This powerful book, set in contemporary South Africa, raises a whole bunch of prickly issues and will jab away at your conscience, forcing a long hard look at your own value system. It's a fast and accessible read – a good story, sharply delivered, not a word more than is necessary. Be prepared to be shocked; be prepared to be challenged; be prepared for a read that leaves you pondering disturbing questions deep into the night.

RNIB **NLB** **Calibre**

Liar Birds by Lucy Fitzgerald

Life is just a lark for Oonagh, Rose and Teresa – three Irish girls – and gossip (received or just made up) is their daily fix. Oblivious to the warning signals, it is Teresa that takes the brunt of the inevitable impact. The joy ride has to stop and there's no hiding from the consequences of their behaviour. A sharp, but very readable reminder that one person's fun can be another person's pain.

Libraries providing a Quick Choice section near the public entrance are already offering a differentiated service for customers pressured by time constraints. There are, however, many other useful considerations that can be easily implemented for other customers where time is the crucial factor. For example, one branch library recognised that there was a problem with a last minute rush of customers turning up shortly before closing time. These customers were being met by grumpy staff, resentful at being detained from their regular closing down routine. As well as ensuring that the Quick Choice section was restocked with plenty of good condition paperbacks in time for the late arrivals, a designated member of staff was stationed close by to give them exclusive support between 6.40pm and 7.00pm when the library closed.

Looking at the needs of library visitors, and potential visitors, at various times of the day, how many city or town centre branches located close to offices and shops actually offer a welcoming service to workers in their lunch breaks? Creating and advertising a comfortable space to accommodate the workers between 12.00pm and 2.00pm, inviting them to eat their sandwiches and promoting newspapers, magazines and coffee table books, which can be browsed to pass the time would offer a pleasant ambience contrary to the popular perception of 'no eating, no drinking, no mobiles, no dogs'. It could also provide the beginnings of a lunchtime readers' group.

When Oldham Libraries wanted to target workers on their lunch breaks, they produced thousands of paper bags printed with the message 'Get your teeth into this - get the taste of books and reading from Oldham Libraries.' These bags were distributed free to all the bakeries in the town centre where people might be buying their sandwiches. For the duration of the promotion, the sandwiches were served in Oldham Libraries' bags as a way of reminding them that the library was there and open at lunchtime. This was great marketing for the library service at a very low cost. The sandwich bags were cheap to produce in large quantities and they put the library's message into people's hands at a point when they would be in a position to respond positively.

Sandwich bag promotion in Oldham

When planning outreach projects, it is useful to review the services already in place which can be extended or exploited to fulfil new demands or as a profile-raiser. Public libraries have run mobile and housebound services successfully for many years. Many of these have been updated to reflect new needs, for example, using the mobile to visit summer playground schemes, supermarket car parks or residential homes.

The mobile library is a very recognisable aspect of the library brand and it is worth considering how it is perceived. Research by MORI for Kent Libraries in 2004 showed that many potential users were put off by the exterior of the mobile library, assuming it would be cramped inside and would carry a very limited range of books. When Conwy Libraries purchased a new mobile in 2007, they were determined to counter this perception and to celebrate the pleasure of reading. They photographed a young library assistant reading a book in an outdoor location and used this for the artwork on the mobile. They also reproduced Opening the Book's mission statement for reader development in libraries: 'The best book in the world is quite simply the one you like best; that is something you can discover for yourself but we are here to help you find it.'

Brighton Libraries used a mobile library to promote the service during Brighton Gay Pride, the biggest free gay and lesbian outdoor event in the south of England. The aim of the promotion was as a profile-raiser for the library service and for their lesbian, gay, bisexual and transgendered collection and reading groups. The mobile was stocked with a wide range of books, including a large selection from the LGB&T collection. It was set up in a prominent position in the park where the event was held, thousands of visitors were welcomed during the day and lots of new members signed up. Brighton Libraries saw this as an excellent opportunity to tap into an existing, high profile community event, ensuring that libraries had a positive presence there - all they had to do was make sure they had the right books and the right message. The Libraries' participation was so successful that it was repeated for four years.

Of course, some audiences don't come to the library at all. Promotions targeted to reach 'missing' audiences not using the library service will always require a bigger investment of resources and time. Consideration must be given at the outset to what realistically can be achieved with outreach projects. There will be good arguments for offering added value promotions to specific segments of your audience only accessible through outreach, or for advertising an underused part of the service to a potential audience who may not know of its existence. However, it is naïve to assume that short-scale, one-off outreach projects will address declining issues or pay more than lip service to social inclusion targets. It is important to consider the situations in which you would be able to make real connections with the different target groups in a context which makes the library service, and reading in particular, relevant.

In outreach work, it is essential to look for situations where people are likely to have the time and the inclination to pick up a book. The choices offered need to be small and manageable but include a range of reading experiences for very different tastes. A member of library staff visiting a cancer care clinic in North Wales recognised the valuable role the library service could play in supporting day-patients and relatives spending long hours, sometimes whole days, at the centre. The centre was newly built with a pleasant atmosphere and artwork on the walls but the reading material available was limited to the *Reader's Digest* and some out-of-date women's magazines.

Conwy mobile

As part of the Estyn Allan (Branching Out in Wales) programme, a team of librarians devised the project to place small collections of paperbacks in three areas of the centre to offer imaginative and tempting books to entertain readers and help them escape boredom, anxiety, stress or fear while they were awaiting treatment or waiting for friends or relatives. Anyone who started reading one of the books was invited to take it home with them to finish it. Books could be returned on another visit to the clinic or to any library in North Wales. Visitors to the centre didn't have to be members of the library to borrow books, they didn't have to check the book out with anyone or leave any information about who they were or what they had borrowed. The project group decided trust was cheaper and easier than setting up expensive and complicated systems to prevent theft. In the first week a book was returned to a library on Anglesey, the furthest physical distance from the treatment centre.

Just Imagine promotion at the North Wales Cancer Treatment Centre

The comments book left alongside the book display was testament to the success of the project with patients and visitors. An added benefit was the positive feedback from the centre staff who said the books provided a welcome topic of conversation with patients other than their illness. A smaller scale version of the project was piloted in some dentists' waiting rooms in North Wales, using small display stands which held just 12 paperbacks.

Another group of Estyn Allan librarians from the South West of Wales started from the same point of looking for situations where people are ready to engage. At key points in life - birth, marriage, death - everyone experiences huge emotions. Many of us are aware that our power with words on these occasions does not match the strength of our feelings. This awareness offers a great route into poetry.

The promotion was called *All the best* and consisted of a tempting book display of poetry books at the library, together with staff training to help people find poems for specific occasions such as retirement, anniversaries, moving house. The promotion made use of the recent growth in publishing reader-centred poetry anthologies - there are collections of 101 poems to meet every conceivable need. Six poems were selected to be made, with permission, into artist-illustrated postcards and printed in multiples for libraries across the region to use.

Staff were truly inventive in how they used the postcards outside the library. One service collaborated with the Registrar's Office to so that whenever someone was registering a birth or death or planning a marriage ceremony, they could pick up a postcard with a poem. Another service persuaded local florists' shops to take them so that anyone ordering flowers for a ceremony could use the poems. Every postcard carried the offer of more help and more resources to be found at the library. Poetry posters and postcards have been used successfully in many promotions round the country - National Poetry Day in October each year sees a great variety of poetry initiatives. What made *All the best* special is the way it connected poetry into people's lives and marketed the skills and resources of the library as well as the work of individual poets.

Regional and national promotions

Regional networking was at the heart of the Branching Out programme which set up nine networks across England, modelled on the success of the first regional collaborations in Yorkshire and the North West. Estyn Allan (Branching Out in Wales) and the Reader Development Network in Scotland involved all the library services of those countries in national co-operation. The benefits of working together are substantial; sharing ideas and support can be just as important as sharing costs.

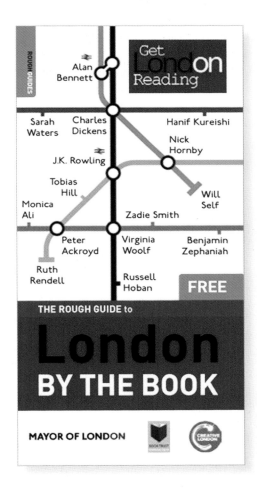

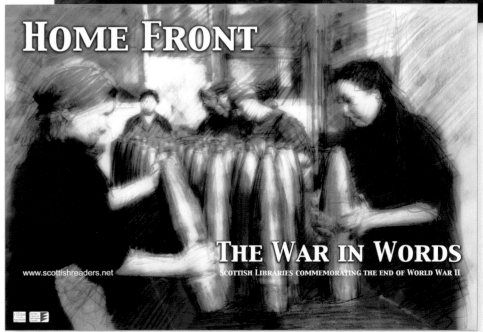

BATTLE FRONT

THE WAR IN WORDS
SCOTTISH LIBRARIES COMMEMORATING THE END OF WORLD WAR II

www.scottishreaders.net

HOME FRONT

THE WAR IN WORDS
SCOTTISH LIBRARIES COMMEMORATING THE END OF WORLD WAR II

www.scottishreaders.net

Working across authorities has enabled higher-quality promotions than services can achieve by themselves. The London Libraries Development Agency ran successful pan-London promotions from *Read Routes* in 2001 to *A Book with a View* in 2007. Time to Read, the North West Libraries Reader Development Partnership, supports the cost of a regional co-ordinator across 22 authorities. This level of collaboration has made larger-scale projects possible. *Everybody's Reading* in 2002 employed 18 outreach workers with youth work and arts skills to work with libraries in the most ambitious and successful initiative to date aiming to reach 16-25 year-olds experiencing social exclusion. In 2007, the region ran the UK's Big Gay Read festival, a tremendous success with both gay and straight readers (**www.biggayread.com**).

With cross-regional or national collaborations it is crucial to determine at the outset who will be responsible for what. A working group or seconded individual is needed to drive the project forward, otherwise the regional momentum is lost as each separate library service feels the pressure of its own concerns taking precedence over the shared initiative. In Scotland, the national Reader Development Network was created in partnership with SLIC/CILIPS (the Scottish Libraries Information Council and the Chartered Institute of Library and Information Professionals in Scotland). SLIC/CILIPS play a crucial co-ordinating role between library authorities, funders and other organisations, enabling an annual programme of national reading promotions to run in all 32 Scottish library services. Sparky collections of books have been put together to enable libraries to tie into major events like the Edinburgh International Book Festival and to explore the meaning of anniversaries such as the end of the second world war.

Smoothing the way for successful promotions

There is a risk, when getting carried along in the enthusiasm of generating ideas for promotions, that the necessary focus on the shape, scale and budget of the activity leaves other areas blurry and overlooked. The best, most exciting promotional idea can only be successful if the context in which it is happening is solid and allows it to flourish. There are many recurring issues that create stumbling blocks for staff involved in marketing and promotion. For example, how easy is it for people to join the library? If you've attracted an audience of first-time visitors into the library for a special event and they're enthused enough to want to become members - are you going to send them home to get their proofs of identification? One library manager reported hearing a staff member telling a customer that they couldn't borrow a book from a new promotion because their ticket was full up. Is it possible to be more flexible about borrowing periods and fines in relation to new promotions? These are some of the issues to consider to ensure that your promotion isn't undermined by rigid enforcement of library rules.

WAKE-UP CALLS

Misunderstandings, however well-intentioned, undermine reader-centred practice. If you recognise the views below, use the arguments in this chapter to challenge them.

" We mostly don't have time but we make a special effort for Christmas. "

" Senior management expect us to do all the promotions - National Poetry Day, World Book Day, all the prizes. "

" Our Trafalgar bi-centenary promotion featured all our books about Nelson. "

Building partnerships

It took a considerable amount of time for libraries to recognise that they occupy a desirable position in terms of their market reach, not just to literature audiences but, more widely, to mass community audiences. Thousands of people come through the doors of libraries every week and a less scrupulous organisation could exploit this to considerable benefit. Libraries would quite rightly regard it as a breach of trust to take commercial advantage of their customers.

The access to the audience, however, is a useful card to play in negotiations with funders and sponsors and in attracting project partners whose involvement offers genuine benefits to the library users. There are now very few publishers who don't recognise the opportunities available in participating in projects such as the *Book of the Month*, originally piloted through Branching Out in partnership with HarperCollins. This project was conceived as an experiment to get new writers' paperback titles in multiples into English libraries at the same time as the bookshops. Participating authorities purchased the books each month and received publicity materials and a free dumpbin from HarperCollins. The response from book borrowers was positive and the books went out quickly. Control copies of the same books which were shelved in the normal A-Z fiction bays didn't do as well. HarperCollins were so pleased with the results that they extended the chance to participate to libraries across the UK and Ireland.

Publishers are also very aware of the huge network of reading groups in libraries and there have been many collaborations which have given the groups free books and author visits and the publishers access to a forum of informed and committed readers/book buyers. Similarly, literary festivals recognise the access to audiences that libraries give them, as well as a range of venues for events. The Reading Agency's Reading Partners project aims to expand the market for books through collaboration between libraries and publishers on promotions and events, with publishers offering authors for tours, visits to Readers' and Writers' Days and reading groups.

Bibliotherapy projects are happening across the UK to promote reading fiction to support mental and emotional health and also using the library as a source for self-help texts. Kirklees Libraries pioneered the use of fiction and poetry to help people suffering from stress, mild depression or feeling isolated and lonely. Starting in 2000, this has grown into a successful partnership with National Health Service Primary Care Trusts in six areas of Kirklees and Calderdale. Since 2005, general practitioners in Wales have been writing prescriptions for patients who they feel would benefit, sending them to the library to borrow books from a specially selected list of titles on subjects such as over-eating, depression, anxiety, and bereavement. Bibliotherapy schemes obviously cannot be seen as a substitute for treatment for patients who urgently need it but they give patients and health staff a different route of support to explore in developing coping strategies.

As key providers of lifelong learning support, there is great potential for libraries to link with local workplaces. Deposit collections in workplace canteens and staff rooms are a useful tool for publicising library services and recruiting new library members. The scheme can be sold to employers on the basis of improved social facilities for staff as well as for supporting literacy and communication skills development amongst the workforce.

In seeking partnerships with outside organisations it is important to recognise where the library service's agenda chimes with that of the potential partner. If you can demonstrate how another organisation's objectives can be achieved by tapping into your audience, it could provide a great deal in helping you achieve your own. However, beware the unequal partnership where libraries do all the work but don't seem to get any real benefit.

WAKE-UP CALLS

Misunderstandings, however well-intentioned, undermine reader-centred practice. If you recognise the views below, use the arguments in this chapter to challenge them.

" *Councillors might be concerned if they saw us promoting gay and lesbian stock so we tend not to risk it.* "

" *We always pull out the stops for anything that comes from the BBC. You are benefiting from all that extra publicity.* "

" *There is a regional network we could join in to do promotions but our own staff can do it better.* "

What next?

There is currently a wide variety of promotional opportunities for libraries in the UK. Many services feel pressured to attempt to exploit them all and would benefit from undertaking fewer promotions with more thought and more impact. Some services would like a future where more sustained outreach work is possible. Others see the future of library promotions in customised services which use technology to tailor recommendations to individual readers.

Whatever form promotion takes in the future, an understanding of reader needs and how to meet them will always be the key to success. Library staff are well placed to explore this as the library is the nexus of so many reader interactions. In the UK in 2008, it is very clear that some library staff have discovered the excitement and stimulus of working with readers in new ways while others, who would probably cite 'working with books and readers' as their reason for joining the service, have no clear understanding or path to doing what they joined for. The user experience in any library will depend more on the staff who create it than on any other factor. Increasing the skills and confidence of the library workforce in reader-centred work is therefore a crucial task for the future. This is the subject of the next chapter.

Chapter 6

STAFF TRAINING IN WORKING WITH READERS

Reader-centred ideas were first disseminated through one-day training sessions run by Opening the Book for individual library services where a mix of library managers and frontline staff participated. These training days gave staff lots of ideas they could implement immediately after the session. They aimed to create an understanding of the approach; participants who went away with a grasp of the principles could then apply them to come up with their own ideas. The new ideas empowered library staff to become more active; the small-scale and low-cost of reader-centred promotions meant that staff could try a promotional idea without risk and without a great investment of time or resources.

From 1998 to 2003 much larger structured programmes of training were run on a national basis in England, Wales and Scotland. Funded by national arts councils who saw libraries as a means to reach a wide reading audience, these programmes invested in a single middle manager from each service to become an agent of change and lead new practice. 2003-2005 saw the development and testing of an online course, designed to reach all those grassroots staff who could not be released for face-to-face training. From 2006 to 2009 this is being rolled out across 85% of English services, many of whom are planning for every member of frontline staff to take it.

Across this 15 years of training staff to work with readers, using different methods and different structures, the feedback from participants has been extremely positive. The spin-offs for library services in terms of staff morale, motivation and confidence have been substantial, especially as these have occurred in difficult years for libraries when they have been losing status, resources and, some critics would say, their way. This is a good point to take stock of reader development training, to analyse just what are the elements which have made it so successful and how is that impact to be maintained in the future? This is relevant for managers who are introducing a reader-centred approach to staff for the first time and for managers already involved in training who need to refresh staff interest each year.

How people learn

Training is managing people's learning. Effective training involves creating a stimulating learning approach and providing environments where trainees can actively learn new things. The purpose of training is to raise participants' skills and confidence and to change staff practice. At its best, training lifts motivation and morale and increases people's enjoyment and satisfaction in their job.

The most important thing for any trainer or teacher to remember is that learning is voluntary. We choose to learn. People go on courses, listen to presentations, read manuals, take part in group exercises - and learn nothing unless they wish to. The trainer cannot make learning happen; only the trainee can do that.

We have all had the experience of tuning out of a training process which didn't interest us, whether this goes back to a particular subject teacher at school or more recent work-related training. Boring delivery, too much information, wrongly pitched in terms of being too easy or too hard, irrelevant to our interests, no opportunity to participate - these are commonly identified as characteristics of training people didn't enjoy. Yet it's extraordinary how when we come to be in the position of trainer ourselves we fall into just the same mistakes. There is something about being put into a position of knowledge 'expert' and thrust to the front of the class which makes many people lose their sense of connection with others and retreat into a recitation of content divorced from context.

WAKE-UP CALLS

Misunderstandings, however well-intentioned, undermine reader-centred practice. If you recognise the views below, use the arguments in this chapter to challenge them.

" We need to get an outside trainer in - they'll say exactly the same things as I do but staff will actually listen to them. "

" Staff love to go on training courses, they get really inspired and have such a good time. "

" We do reader development training - we have an awayday once a year. "

The classroom experience affects participants too. It is likely that a fair proportion of any group of trainees is unconsciously using their school memories to inform their adult behaviour in any formal training situation. That could be good or bad, but it is usually unhelpful in either case because it prompts adults to act in childlike ways and expect to be passive learners. It can lead to back row behaviour. It is hard for people who hated school to be open to learning in any situation that reminds them of the classroom.

The answer is not to use traditional classroom methods. A variety of training approaches are needed to stimulate people to become active learners. A varied approach will also help those who are trained-out - who feel jaded because they feel that they spend too much of their time on training courses. Injecting an element of surprise into a training programme can have a refreshing effect.

When the Branching Out programme introduced the first reader-centred national promotion to English libraries in 1999 (see Chapter One, page eighteen), the training element was crucial. Library staff from every service in England came to regional sessions about *Open Ticket*, a promotion of world literature. When they arrived at the training venue, the first activity was not a lecture or a Powerpoint demonstration. On each table was a selection of fruit and vegetables from different countries. Participants were asked to take each in turn and discuss when they first ate it, did their parents or grandparents eat it and do their children eat it? This led into a discussion of how food availability and preferences have changed enormously in the UK in the last 50 years. It was then a simple jump to make the connection to books. If we have learned to like a lot of flavours in food, why assume that people's reading tastes are restricted to home-grown potatoes and carrots? The staff judgment 'That foreign book will never go out' was completely undermined by the knowledge that chicken tikka masala is now the national dish of the UK, eaten more frequently than fish and chips.

Learning styles

A good learning experience doesn't often happen by accident. The best training creates a situation, an atmosphere and a process which is conducive to learning. It persuades, stimulates and interests trainees so that they are enabled to come up with ideas themselves. Sometimes learning is an uncomfortable experience, especially when the learner feels that their certainties are being challenged. Training shouldn't set out to please, entertain or flatter but rather to encourage trainees to question their established practice.

Good training starts with an understanding that people learn differently, and that their experiences of learning will colour both their learning style and their receptiveness to the training. The way that people learn something differs from person to person and in one person from one week to another. Learning preferences are not generally fixed; many people use a range of styles to learn and are fairly adaptable. However, a good training course will build in tasks that suit a range of learning styles. An effective training strategy will build in different and creative opportunities for learning, not just traditional face-to-face presentation.

There are many descriptions of the ways in which people learn. It may be useful to consider here a brief sketch of some different learning styles. Pragmatists search out new ideas, and see problems as challenges; they enjoy action learning, briefings and work-based projects. Theorists like to know the basic assumptions, the patterns, models and systems. They learn best from Q&A, instructions, seminars and workshops. Reflectors prefer to think, watch and analyse and will take a back seat; they appreciate coaching, appraisal, counselling, open learning and not to be pushed. Activists like immediacy and experiment; they enjoy role play, surprise, job rotation and secondment.

People often lean towards one style but rarely are fixed. Most people react well to variety, even if they get more out of one type of training than another. This means that any training programme - and any individual training session - will work best if it contains a variety of activities to appeal to different learning styles. Some learners like to test new ideas by challenging and questioning them - matching them against their own experience. This can cause disruption to training days, and is often seen as hostile, but can be a successful way for a trainee to learn.

Showing not telling

A one-day session designed as part of the Branching Out programme, working in partnership with the National Library for the Blind (now joined with the Royal National

Institute of Blind People), serves as a good example. It was delivered by staff from Opening the Book, the National Library for the Blind and Branching Out librarians in each of the English regions. A cut-down version was used by many librarians in their own services. Almost all participants were sighted but on a few occasions, the group included a visually impaired member of staff.

The aim of the session was to explore issues involved in working with visually impaired people and to help library staff understand the needs of visually impaired readers. Free reader-centred resources in large print, audio and Braille were provided to all services through a project called *A Touch of* . . . (Chapter Five, page 164) and the training session aimed to help libraries make the most of these.

The programme on the opposite page shows the balance of activity. After 30 minutes of introduction and background, participants were broken into groups and worked on a practical exercise. Following feedback on that, with everyone now fully engaged, the slot before lunch was used to give the key facts and figures, contacts and examples. After lunch there was another short presentation about the project itself - after lunch is often not the best time for presentations but the hooks of free resources and grants available meant people tuned in closely. Keeping the presentations to 30 minutes left most of the afternoon for working in small groups, planning how to apply the knowledge learned and sharing best ideas. All participants left the session with next steps to put in place.

The key to the day lies in the practical activity in the morning. The purpose of the exercise was to get participants thinking about the needs of visually impaired readers. Trainers wanted to challenge and deepen understanding without making participants feel inadequate. It was also important to establish an open attitude in an area where many staff were likely to tiptoe for fear of being politically incorrect.

In preparing the exercise the trainers decided to concentrate on how readers make choices as this is one of the major differences for sighted and visually impaired people. In order to free up expectations and introduce a fun element, it was decided to move the focus away from books entirely. Instead, participants discussed how they choose from a box of chocolates.

BRANCHING OUT
*A Touch Of ...*Regional Training Day

Aims

- To explore what we mean by visual impairment and the issues involved in working with visually impaired people.
- To help library staff understand the reading needs of visually impaired people.
- To use *A Touch Of* as a catalyst to reach VIP readers who may not know of all the services available.
- To share good practice on involving VIP readers in ongoing reader development programmes.

Programme

10.00	Coffee on arrival
10.30	Introduction and welcome
10.40	Project background
11.00	Group work: how VIP readers choose
11.30	Feedback
11.45	Coffee
12.00	Visual impairment and reading - quick statistics, a guide to alternative format providers, some examples of good practice projects
12.30	Lunch
1.30	The *A Touch Of* promotion - a reader development approach to helping people choose
	The *A Touch Of* Festival May 2001 - grants available
2.00	Group work: ideas to bring the promotion alive
2.45	Tea
3.00	Feedback
3.40	Action plan
4.00	Close

Each group was given a box of chocolates of a well-known brand and everyone selected and removed their favourite flavour. (They could eat it if they wished!) They then discussed how they made that choice. What helped them - shape, wrapper colour, familiarity, the selection guide on the box flap? Then the selection guides were removed from the box flaps and each group was asked to tip out the chocolates and wrap each one individually in a square of metal foil before putting them back and passing the box to the next group. Everyone then chose a chocolate from the foil covered selection. They were asked to say what they hoped to have chosen, then unwrap it, eat it if they wished, and say if they made the correct choice and whether they were happy or disappointed with the result. Then they were asked to discuss how this method of choosing felt compared with the first one. Who ate the chocolate and who didn't, who had a good or bad experience, how did they approach it differently, and with what expectations? The parallels with choosing books were obvious and the complexities of individual choices just as rich.

WAKE-UP CALLS

Misunderstandings, however well-intentioned, undermine reader-centred practice. If you recognise the views below, use the arguments in this chapter to challenge them.

" We already do customer care training - we know how to treat people and how to handle complaints properly. "

" Good customer care training is about systems not people. "

" Yes, I get training, my manager goes on courses and tells us about them during staff meetings. "

The last part of the exercise asked everyone to sit close enough to each other to touch the person next to them. They then closed their eyes and passed the box to choose again. They could eat the chocolate if they wished but they must not open their eyes. They then discussed how this felt compared with the first two methods of choosing.

The comparison between choosing chocolates and choosing books enabled lively and thoughtful discussion. If you like what everyone else does, you have a problem choosing because it disappears first - do you make do with your second or third choice? Some people will choose not to eat the chocolate because they are on a diet or have an allergy; others are happy to give anything a go. Then there was the question of the new chocolate in the box. Although traditional chocolate selections vary little over the years, the box contained a chocolate called cappuccino not coffee creme. It's the same with books and readers. How do you approach a new author? If you've never tried it before how can you be sure you won't like it?

The discussion went on to explore the experience of choosing books when you are visually impaired, for example, a lot of participants expected to be disappointed when they couldn't see what they were getting. Does this lead to visually impaired readers having lower expectations than sighted readers? How should staff be aware of the effects of this?

Experiential learning

The practical exercise grounded the discussion in real experience. The gap between sighted and visually impaired readers was narrowed; instead of planning services for people 'out there' different from yourself, the starting point is common ground in exploring risk and preference. This leads into awareness that the biggest problem for visually impaired people in choosing a book is that it is impossible to browse. Choices are made without any visual signals: no covers, no blurbs, no reviews, no chance to read the first few pages or to scan the book.

Instead, what has traditionally been provided for Braille and audio users is a synopsis of the story. Synopsis is the only method of choosing available. Synopsis guides people towards a 'safe' choice and, worse still, you know what's going to happen before you even open the book. So there are no surprises, no shocks, no discoveries, no adventures, just a nice, safe read. For many people this is where they want to be - it's predictable, warm and cosy. But it's not what happens to sighted people. Sighted people can choose safety if they wish but they are also exposed to tantalising glimpses which tempt them to take a chance.

So in meeting the needs of visually impaired readers, staff must be aware of how it is more difficult to take a risk with your reading when you lack access to visual clues. They must respect, as with any other reader, an individual's desire to play safe where that is a free choice. But they must resist the tendency of sighted people to assume that visually impaired readers need any more safety than anyone else - in fact, it's just the opposite, opening up reading choices is even more important for readers who can't access the most common means of choosing.

The final use of the box of chocolates was to move the discussion from how people choose to the choice available. A new box of chocolates was opened and all the contents spread out. The trainer asked participants to consider if the full box represented the number of books published in a year how many did they think were available in alternative formats. Participants could move the chocolates to indicate this. In the UK the total number of books published in large print, audio and Braille is only 5% of what is published overall. In a box of 40 chocolates that's exactly two. Then participants discussed which chocolates, if there were only two, it was likely to be. Would they both be the most popular one - strawberry creme? Or maybe one strawberry creme and one milk chocolate rectangle? It was clear that if you like cappuccino and you're visually impaired you've not much chance. This was a shockingly graphic way of bringing home to library staff the real issue. It's not that visually impaired readers have different needs from those of sighted readers - there is just the same range of idiosyncrasies and preferences as with any other group. It's simply that they have far fewer choices available.

This group exercise underpinned everything else in the training day. It explained why the new promotion *A Touch of* ... focused on offering choices in new ways. It showed why it was important for library staff to have information about every single provider of alternative formats in the country. It encouraged stock buyers to discuss widening range with alternative format suppliers. (The large print market is dominated by libraries so they bear a responsibility for what is published in it.) It gave staff confidence to take on a more active role in opening up choice for visually impaired readers instead of always playing safe. It provided an easy way to explain to colleagues who weren't there what the issues are. Those who took part never forgot it.   Participants' learning was not in a handout or a Powerpoint, it became part of who they were. They might need to look up facts again in future - the number of visually impaired people in the population, the address of a charitable audio library - but their understanding of choice, risk and range was permanently altered.

The exercise took 45 minutes.

The training context

Training of this quality and impact requires careful planning as to purpose, context and relevance. Many library managers attend events that are called training, often without anyone having a clear overview of what is being achieved, how the training will be put into action or what impact it is having. It is important that the quality of training in reader-centred work is maintained as it becomes more mainstreamed in the UK. Reader development courses have been the ones that staff volunteered to attend, where demand often outstripped supply. As libraries look to embed the training in mainstream practice, the approaches which made it successful in the first place must be understood and carried forward.

Planning and organising training in reader-centred work in a library service is likely to fall to those librarians who are keenest to develop reader-centred practice. Many library services do not have a dedicated training officer post and most professional librarians have not received any training as trainers. The national initiatives of Branching Out in England, Estyn Allan in Wales and the Reader Development Network in Scotland emphasised training and support for trainers as part of their programmes. They also built regional networks for sharing training initiatives across services. These have made a good start but particularly in England, where only 33 of 149 services were part of the intensive first phase of the Branching Out programme, there is still a way to go.

One of the most important things to grasp for anyone new to the training role is that training is not a solution to every managerial problem. If you need to tell staff to do something and it is not a matter for discussion, then bite the bullet and tell them. Using training as a substitute for management does not work. A training course which sets out

WAKE-UP CALLS

Misunderstandings, however well-intentioned, undermine reader-centred practice. If you recognise the views below, use the arguments in this chapter to challenge them.

" I ran a training session to explain our new structure. "

" Training is useful - I always send the most difficult staff member to help change their attitude. "

" Training is just telling staff what you want them to do. "

to persuade participants that a particular management decision is a good one will backfire; staff are likely to be antagonised and hostile and the whole programme of training loses their respect.

Training is also not the same as information giving. If you have straightforward information to impart, there is no need to invent complicated groupwork to get the information across. In the example above, it would be foolish to use a training exercise for participants to discover the providers of alternative formats; it's much simpler to give a handout with contact details and a verbal summary of the characteristics of each organisation.

Attitudes to training will be shaped by wider influences in the culture of local government. Some library services have a tradition where senior staff have first call on training and are automatically expected to be the ones to attend a course or awayday. Places on a course can be seen by everyone as a privilege or given as a reward. In other services, all the middle managers are 'trained out' and everyone looks the other way when new opportunities come up. The training programme may be driven by outside targets which don't match what librarians see as the real priorities; all staff must attend corporately provided training in customer care or diversity, for example, and this absorbs all the training time available.

Librarians may or may not be in a position to change any of these aspects of the culture of the workplace but what they can do is set a standard of quality for the training they are involved in. This will build reputation with both participants and managers and may result in increased influence over wider training issues. This is how reader development training, which did not exist in 1994, built its case and centrality to UK library services over the next ten years.

Identifying the most important training needs

Planning effective training starts with analysing the training needs of staff in the service. There will be far more needs than can be met so it is important to concentrate on the most pressing, especially those which will not be tackled by any other programme. A clear-eyed and objective look at the service will also result in an acknowledgement that a lot of time is spent teaching staff traditional practice which is not reader-centred.

Traditional library training focuses on organising and finding books. This is true for library assistants shelving returned books every morning, staff on the counter expecting enquiries and library managers planning the way the collection is laid out in the space. The key professional test at all levels is 'If I'm asked for a book, do I know where it is and can I find it quickly?' It is the height of professional embarrassment to be unable to find something when it has been asked for.

This emphasis ignores basic facts about customer needs. If most people don't ask, libraries need to manage the space so it's easy to find what you want independently. If the majority of users want quick and easy choices, libraries need to display books in ways which help that. The key question library staff need to answer in the 21st century is not simply 'Can I find the book if asked for it?' but 'If the book has already been borrowed, can I suggest an alternative in a way which keeps the customer happy?'

A whole host of additional and different training needs can be seen to arise here. Traditional library practice is very process-driven and traditional training has followed this;

basic training for new frontline staff is equated with learning procedures and routines. It is worth examining these to determine which are absolutely essential to delivering a good service and which are simply the result of custom and practice - 'We've always done it this way.'

Some common practices may not just be inefficient, they may actually have a negative effect on staff learning to do a better job and give a better service. One example is the labelling of books. Library books can carry a multiplicity of labels - a catalogue number, a Dewey code, a genre icon, an initial letter, a category denoted by additional letters or coloured dots. Thus a fantasy book by Terry Pratchett, for example, may have a large P on the spine, plus an F in a different coloured circle or a dragon icon to denote fantasy. If the book is part of a children's or young adult collection it may well have additional labels to denote that. The purpose of all these labels is to help staff shelve the book in the right place. A new member of staff must learn to decode all these signs, separating out those which belong to a previous era and no longer have any meaning, then learning how each of the signs relates to a physical location in the library. This takes some concentration in the first weeks of the job and then quickly becomes a faster, more automatic way of thinking - look at the label, know where to put it. The focus is on the label and the classification system, whether you've been doing it for three weeks or 30 years. At no time is the member of staff asked to look at the book directly.

Compare this with what happens when a book by Terry Pratchett arrives in a good bookshop. Staff decide what it is and where it goes by looking directly at the cover and opening the book. They need to know if this is a new title by Pratchett or a reissue (this could determine its prominence in display); if it is Pratchett writing for an adult, children's or crossover audience (this will determine location and whether all the copies go in the same place); if it is part of a series, whether the series is new or established, where this title fits in the sequence, when the next one in the series is due out (this prepares staff for likely customer enquiries which may arise on the shop floor or by phone). They may also consider if there is an audio or film version available or planned. All of this adds invaluably to the stock knowledge of the staff. Where bookshop staff have an opportunity to increase their knowledge on a daily basis, keeping up with changing trends, library staff are asked to learn a fixed classification system and apply it. If they move job to another service they may have to learn a new iconography - the symbols denoting genre or age group or reference and lending may all be quite different.

This system is often defended on grounds of process; the claim is made that shelving would take far too long if it wasn't in place. For example, although the author's name is already on the book spine, it is argued that it is quicker for staff to look at a large initial letter when shelving than to read the whole name and classify into the right letter themselves. Apart from treating library staff as if they have very low intelligence levels, never the best way to get a good staff performance, this is to prioritise library process over all other aspects of customer service in a way which is ultimately self-defeating. If it takes an extra part-second to register the name Terry Pratchett rather than the P on the spine, this is well worth taking. Staff will become more familiar with author names, they can distinguish established and new authors and develop more awareness of what is available. Given another few seconds they can relate the names to the cover images and start to think about the audience the book is aimed at. If staff take an extra five seconds to shelve each of 120 books, that's a total of ten extra minutes. Is that not ten minutes well spent?

Practical book knowledge

It is worth thinking about how a training programme can tackle issues like these. Library staff in frontline roles in the UK have always been expected to learn about the process more than the product. Product knowledge has traditionally been seen as the province of the qualified librarian. There is an increasing recognition from senior managers that this is not sufficient when the staff most likely to be encountered by customers are library assistants and shelvers. In any customer-facing job in a commercial environment, whether a shop, a restaurant, or an online financial service, staff are expected to know the products.

Of course, some library assistants do take a great interest in books and enjoy regular conversations with customers but this is seen as a matter of personal enthusiasm more than a requirement of their post. It also follows that their knowledge is personal and therefore most likely to be shared with customers who share their reading tastes. Meanwhile many of their colleagues are terrified of being asked for a recommendation by a customer; they fear they will get it wrong, give unintended offence or reveal their own ignorance in a way that's embarrassing for both them and the customer. These fears have been reinforced by traditional hierarchies where the possibility of a reprimand for overstepping the bounds of your role as an unqualified member of staff undermines any confident development. The manager likely to give the reprimand may have retired from the service years before but the memory lingers powerfully in the library culture.

WAKE-UP CALLS

Misunderstandings, however well-intentioned, undermine reader-centred practice. If you recognise the views below, use the arguments in this chapter to challenge them.

" Our training officer has some underspend in her budget and we're looking for a training course to buy in. "

" All we seem to do is go on training courses - it doesn't really affect my job as I never have time to put what I've learnt into practice. "

" The training budget is the first to be cut - I suppose that's inevitable. "

Reader-centred approaches have brought new thinking to stock awareness training in UK libraries. Where training existed, it tended to focus on genre lists and author and title knowledge. This did little for staff confidence as it increased fears of inadequacy in the face of a huge mountain of information to be assimilated. Even where it was successful, the impact on staff confidence was shortlived - without refresher courses, knowledge was always in danger of going out of date. Reader-centred training teaches skills of analysis which can be applied to any books and, once introduced, practised in the midst of everyday tasks. The focus shifts from the book and what it is about to the reader and the target audience.

One approach is to set staff the task of choosing a book for a specific reader. This can be very broad - someone aged 75, for example - and it is up to the trainees to decide on the reader's gender, background and interests.   Or it can become more detailed   - a 40 year-old professional man who likes crime and travel and has only a few moments to choose. Doing a task like this from memory in a training seminar is really challenging and can quickly become unhelpfully competitive. Choosing one title that might fit the need directly from the library shelves is much easier and replicates the customer experience more closely. Discussion of what might appeal and why is made concrete as books are held up and compared. Staff can be encouraged to build their own reader scenarios and swap experiences of reader advice. Exercises like this lead to greater understanding of different reader preferences and greater awareness of the range of titles available. The experience of going out to choose among the shelves can also lead on to further discussion and rethinking of how books are organised and displayed to appeal to different readers.

Judging a book by its cover

Another approach used successfully in reader development training across the UK is book cover analysis. Publishers spend a great deal on jacket design as, despite the old adage, most readers do judge books initially by covers, especially if the author is not well-known. Book jackets are carefully designed to send signals to their target audience and learning to deconstruct these signs is immensely helpful to staff who want to keep up with trends. Exercises can begin with familiar examples which build staff confidence - identifying the styles of genres such as romance and fantasy, for example. From this it is easy to start to explore more subtle signals - what is it that indicates a particular romance is funny, what signs show it is aimed at an older or younger audience, is this a traditional fantasy or a more hybrid genre? Genres and sub-genres can be explored. Even more important, literary fiction which avoids all genre suggestions in its design, can also be analysed and discussed.

Participants are asked to examine one jacket in detail - the size and style of the lettering, the overall colour, the design, any illustration or cover images, any endorsements or reviews, the back cover blurb, the author information. They are also asked to read the first page. Discussion centres on three main questions:

- What kind of book is this?
- Who is the book aimed at?
- Does it have a wider appeal than its target audience or not?

Library staff who thought they knew nothing about books bring their awareness of wider cultural trends in magazines, advertising and television to this exercise and discover they can tell a great deal from the cover design. Running an exercise like this as a weekly 15 minute staff training session increases book knowledge by leaps and bounds. It can be easily adapted to give a more structured learning experience, for example five sessions on different types of crime fiction, followed by five sessions on different types of historical fiction.

Training does not need to be elaborate. It does not always need a special room and special equipment. A simple book exercise like this can achieve important training objectives and meet training needs which have been overlooked or ignored for years. Its impact is not only in the development of book knowledge. The discussion will always reveal hugely different personal tastes - reaction to cover design is very subjective. The design thought dull by one participant will be described as cool and sophisticated by another. This leads into greater awareness of different reader needs and goes to the heart of the blurred boundaries between the personal and the job which are a fundamental weakness of much library culture (See discussion in Chapter Three, page 79). After everyone has had fun pulling faces at the covers they hate, the same exercise can be run again with a new rule that nobody in the room should be able to tell from a participant's description of the cover and analysis of its target audience whether they like or dislike the cover in question.

Achieving training objectives

The reader-centred approach is also changing staff training in display skills. Display is often top of the list when staff are asked to put forward areas of training they think are important; clearly, a lot of staff feel inadequate because they are not as good at display as the one or two regulars who always do it. Display skills training in UK libraries usually translates into window-dressing skills - how to build a good-looking static display using the basic principles of pyramidal design. But how many libraries actually have shop windows that are suitable for this approach? What is replicated instead across UK libraries are table-top displays which use window-dressing techniques inappropriately.

The issue is not just one of skill level. Sending staff on courses to increase the professionalism of producing these displays compounds the problem; there are likely to be more of them as a result. Instead, managers need to address why such displays are not successful in increasing loans and shift the focus from the dressing (the props, the decoration) to the audience and the product. It may well turn out that the staff member who has always thought they were hopeless at display because they couldn't handle pinking shears or a staple gun is actually very creative in displaying books from different parts of the library together to appeal to different audiences.

A training objective can be clarified and reinforced from the very outset. When Renfrewshire Libraries planned a one hour session for frontline staff, they avoided abstractions and management jargon in describing its purpose. The aim expressed on the programme was simply: 'To understand that it is more important to make the books jump off the shelves than to keep them tidy on the shelves.' The reader experience is clearly prioritised over the staff process in that simple objective.

Releasing staff to attend face-to-face training sessions is the most common method in training. A face-to-face course can introduce completely new practice and stimulate new solutions to knotty problems. It can link staff in one place to ideas and good practice in other services. Face-to-face training is very effective at seeding new ideas and introducing new skills but can be weak in cases where staff need more support to put new ideas into practice in their place of work. Face-to-face training can show staff how to go about changing their practice but if they have to defend their experiments from criticism, or have no support in getting them right, then the benefits can dissipate quite quickly.

Libraries may want to buy in outside training if expertise is not available in-house. It is important to have the training needs you are hoping to meet in mind before starting any research into what is on offer. In seeking effective training it is worth looking outside the library field to those who train voluntary organisations or arts administrators. The quality of training can be hard to judge from publicity materials so it's worth contacting other organisations and asking where they source training and whether they know of freelance trainers that they recommend. People with expertise in a parallel field may have more practical training to offer than generic bought-in courses, for example, a design firm can tell a publicity working group about how to write a design brief.

As well as being clear about the needs and objectives, both the library service and the trainer will need to agree the numbers of people who can be trained, because more people on a face-to-face course means that less can be achieved in depth for each participant. The smaller the group, the more intense the learning will be. Consider the optimum balance between size and depth; it will not be the same in each situation.

WAKE-UP CALLS

Misunderstandings, however well-intentioned, undermine reader-centred practice. If you recognise the views below, use the arguments in this chapter to challenge them.

" What's the point of going on courses and getting lots of ideas if my manager won't let us do any of them? "

" Training frontline staff is too expensive - they just need to follow instructions. "

" That was a really inspiring course. It won't work in my library, of course, but I can see how it would work in small branches. "

Whether the course is run internally or externally, there is always the problem that not all staff who need the training can participate. Library services, like everyone else, try to solve this by what is usually referred to as 'cascading'. Too often cascading is a euphemism for saving money by sending one person on a course who then is allowed to give a five minute resumé at a staff meeting. To be successful, a cascade needs to be structured, resourced and supported. Like those huge fountains at Versailles, it takes a lot more than water and a spout. People who are asked to cascade need the skills to know how to do it well and the time to plan how to do it. Don't expect anyone, even a skilled trainer, to cascade a course to others without a structure for doing so - cascade needs content.

Staff may need advice and support before they can even consider attempting new skills. For example, people who are worried about speaking in public, and there are many, will be scared of what they think they will be asked to do as part of presentation skills training and may well go sick on the training day. If managers want to present a high level of challenge to library staff, then they need to offer an equally high level of support. It may be necessary to talk through what you want them to tackle, one-to-one, and listen to their fears. Follow through by arranging support for learning at all stages, either by partnering staff or forming a small group of trainees who support each other. If senior managers recognise the efforts made by trainees, this makes a huge difference to the lasting success of the training.

Hands-on training

The quality of on-the-job training depends on who is leading it and what support is available to them. This can be where staff pick up bad habits and old-fashioned practice or it can be where they try new things safely for the first time. The advantage of on-the-job training in the library, apart from the obvious one of low cost, is that readers and books are right there to work with. Results can be measured and seen in how readers respond and how books issue. Most people learn well by doing so if you can mesh training in new practice with day-to-day tasks this can work really effectively. Learning needs can be broken down into bite-sized sessions and delivered within current staff meetings. Making opportunities within the working day for training points works well; some Branching Out librarians ran a series of themes across the year.

There is little specific feedback on day-to-day work for library staff and no praise culture on the library floor in most services. Feedback and praise help learning and can be very effective in embedding new practice. Managers who employ genuine, specific praise as the trainee leaps some barriers that may not seem high to outsiders but look like Everest to them, will find it has a dramatic effect.

Peer review can put staff together for single tasks or whole courses. Any training objective can be helped by setting up a method of peer review to support and assess it. Staff can be paired at the same or at different levels but it may be best to avoid using the existing management structure. This takes the sting out of criticism, improves communication and gives keen staff opportunities to manage other people's learning without having to manage their work. Peer review is an underused tool in local government because staff lack confidence and understanding of how to make helpful interventions and how to make useful judgments about others' work. This may be a specific training need worth addressing in itself.

E-learning

The UK government is implementing an e-learning strategy and aims to embed e-learning into all education from schools to lifelong learning. The New Opportunities Fund, a lottery stream which funded the creation of the People's Network, also funded training for all library staff in the UK to European Computer Driving Licence standard. This was a massive investment in staff time and, although not always popular with trainees, did succeed in ensuring a base level of computer skills in the staff complement. Now those skills are there, it makes sense to put them to use through further e-learning.

E-learning has a lot of advantages for libraries. It can reach all staff at a low cost. This is especially important in an organisation where a lot of the workforce is part-time and geographically scattered. Trainees can go at their own pace in their own time and the learning can be closely tied in to everyday work practice.

The development of e-learning was the central plank in the third phase of the Branching Out programme from 2003-2006. A structured e-learning course is very different from a website which offers support materials and downloadable toolkits; the Branching Out programme had already developed a very successful website of this kind.

The resulting course, called Frontline, is rooted in practical experience of introducing reader-centred techniques and was tested and modified by feedback from different library services over a two-year development period. Seven modules, taken sequentially, set practical tasks in the trainee's own place of work. They include talking to readers, building book knowledge, understanding promotion and increasing the visual appeal of the library. Because the course is taken from a website, it can be accessed wherever and whenever it is convenient to the trainee. Each trainee has their own online Learning Log in which they record their work.

The impact of any training, including an online course, depends on the quality of implementation and for this reason as much development time went into creating the cascade and support structure for the course as into designing the course content. The Frontline course reframes the job of library staff and asks them to consider a new way of doing their work. Clearly, this requires the support of managers at all levels if it is to be effective. Otherwise, an enthusiastic trainee might go to try out new practice and

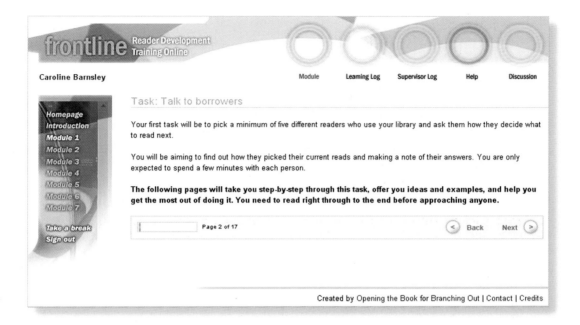

Frontline course module

find their colleagues or line manager totally opposed to the action they have taken - an embarrassing situation for all sides.

The support and assessment structure for Frontline was tested with very different types and sizes of service in England and expanded and modified in the light of their feedback. The support structure enables those who have completed the course to become supervisors of others. The supervisor structure is supported by advice online and clear instruction to help those who are not used to making judgments about the work of their colleagues to practice giving specific feedback and relevant praise. The supervisors are supported by a co-ordinator who is nominated for the role by the service and trained online by Opening the Book.

Library services can use the structure to pair staff from one workplace with those in another or to link staff who do different jobs. Services have used the supervisory role to create opportunities for keen staff to take on new responsibilities. The supervisory structure can be used within an existing management structure but it can also be used very effectively outside it, cutting across boundaries and hierarchies. In two cases, junior staff have supervised heads of service through the course. Each library service has local control of the cascade and is provided with online tools to manage it.

Many English library services plan to take all staff who have contact with readers through the Frontline course between 2007 and 2009. The course has created a benchmark measure for a basic level of knowledge and skills in working with books and readers in a public library which can be recognised, relied upon and built upon. Its widespread adoption is testament to its success, especially as after the initial funding supported piloting costs, libraries must subscribe to use it. The course is also being used in Wales, Scotland and Northern Ireland and a new version for the Republic of Ireland brought in all Irish services in 2008.

Frontline learning log

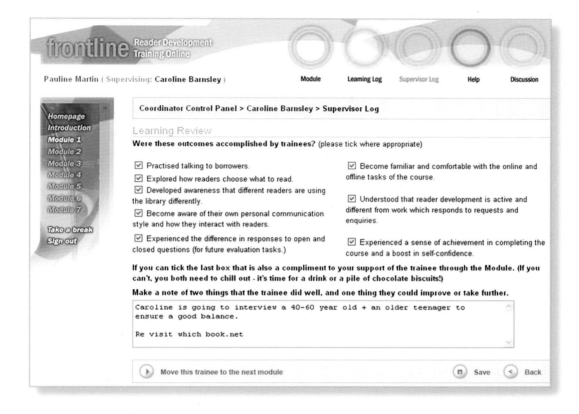

Frontline supervisor log

The discussion boards have been enlivened by individual staff taking the course in Egypt, Australia and Portugal, creating an international forum for reader-centred work in libraries.

By 2009 English libraries will employ a significant majority of frontline staff who are skilled in promotion and display, understand the basics of marketing books to readers and have confidence to talk to readers about their reading and to recommend a wide range of stock. This skilled, motivated workforce at the frontline will be better trained in stock display and promotion and will exploit the introduction of self-service systems and refurbished library space to get more books issued to more borrowers. Staff in most libraries, large and small, will share a common understanding of how to organise stock and space to appeal to readers and how to help borrowers who don't ask questions, as well as ones who do. Library staff moving from one service to another will take these skills with them and fit in easily with new colleagues who have taken the same course. Senior staff will be able to rely on a recognised platform of job-related skills amongst the entire staff body because the quality of learning is shared and can be checked at any time. A shared standard of outward-facing customer skills held by the majority of staff could underpin wider strategic changes to build a more accessible role for the library in the community.

The training support and assessment network that Frontline is creating in library services can be used in future for other learning opportunities, for further change and to discover and meet new learning needs. The workforce is becoming more skilled not just in reader-centred work but in managing tailored training programmes which make a real impact. Skills in supervising, supporting learning, assessing work and giving constructive feedback are being strengthened. And instead of training being something that just a few people go on each year, it is being seen as intrinsically connected to daily work. Many library services aspire to being 'learning organisations' following the business model which argues that a successful organisation must continually adapt and learn in order to respond to changes in its environment and to grow. Looking at how little libraries have changed in the last 20 years, this aspiration seems a long way from achievement. New approaches to training such as the Frontline course could be the first steps in making it a reality.

Co-ordinators are collecting a range of evidence through trainees' work on the course about the impact of the course on readers and on library spaces. Impact on the staff is being measured through staff appraisal procedures. The very large range of customer responses that trainees collect can be exploited to help assess the level of customer satisfaction in the service.

The next stage for librarians with successful training experience in reader-centred work is to take this thinking wider within the organisation. Is reader-centred work taking the service in a new direction while existing training provision is holding it back? Look at how new staff are inducted into their roles. If it's all about library process can you rethink and reorganise to give a better customer focus? Then consider any customer care training that staff attend in-house, cross-departmentally or externally. Staff who are skilled in reader-centred work have learned to give a much higher quality of customer care than answering the phone after so many rings. How could their experience be used to inform better overall customer care training?   Similarly, the reader-centred approach could have a lot to offer in equal opportunities or diversity training.

If you gather evidence of the impact of successful training you can argue for a different allocation of staff time or resources to take the training further. Gathering and analysing evidence is part of evaluation, the subject of Chapter Nine; turn to page 302 for a discussion of how to evaluate training activities.

Chapter 7

READING GROUPS

Readers have been meeting in small, informal groups to talk about their reading experiences for a long time, but it's an activity that, until quite recently, was not particularly discussed. If there was a single point at which reading groups suddenly became sexy, it must have been the National Year of Reading 1998 when celebrities supporting the campaign, like Dawn French and Mariella Frostrup, began talking about the groups they belonged to.

Subsequent years saw national newspapers and magazines set up reading groups and they became a feature in many dramas (wife leaves husband to cook own dinner calling, 'It's book group night,' as she closes the door). Channel 4 built a whole comedy series around a group and even the denizens of Coronation Street have taken over the bar of the Rovers' Return to discuss books. Media figures championing books and reading, such as Richard and Judy, have created significant impact, not only in booksellers' profits, but in the expectations of library users wishing to read recommended titles.

Library-based reading groups have both contributed to and benefited from this wave of interest. Before the growth of reader development in the 1990s, adult reading groups were not seen as part of libraries' remit. Some authorities may have supported private reading groups but the idea that library staff should take the initiative and offer to set up and run reading groups as an added-value service to their borrowers was a new one. To move from a situation where no authorities took on this role to one where almost all library services support groups in the space of just a few years is a remarkable development. It is a testament to the huge energy and enthusiasm generated by reading groups among both borrowers and staff.

Publishers are now very aware of the potential for using reading groups to create whisper books - that is books like *The Divine Secrets of the Ya-Ya Sisterhood* and *Captain Corelli's Mandolin*, which became word-of-mouth bestsellers although they received only small marketing budgets and little attention in the literary press when first published. It is generally acknowledged that it was reader power that brought success to these books - one reader telling another how good they were. Publishers can see that there is a huge opportunity for getting directly to a reading audience via reading groups. Many publishers now have specific reading group areas on their websites and offer support in the form of free or discounted books. Reading group guides are becoming more and more common, appearing on the web or as notes at the back of the relevant title.

Why should libraries support reading groups?

Libraries are an obvious venue for setting up and running reading groups because of the repeat contact with a large number of readers. It is easy for a good branch librarian or library assistant to build a relationship with individual borrowers who come back week after week. The reading habits and borrowing patterns of these familiar faces are well known to the library staff, who may already be providing informal reader development support through talking to them about what they've been reading and passing recommendations from one reader to the next.

Libraries offer a crucial advantage as a venue for reading groups in that they are available to any reader who wishes to participate. Private reading groups usually have restricted membership and they run along friendship or job-related networks. That's fine if you are in a position to find out about them and know someone involved so you have a chance of joining. But there are thousands of readers who don't have that opportunity; they don't know the right people and they're not sure where to start. Libraries offer open access and an equal, quality service across the board; they are the route to reading groups for readers who might not otherwise be able to find one.

Because of this open access, a library-based reading group is also likely to include a broader social mix than a private one. There may well be a big variety of ages and backgrounds; there will certainly be a wide range of reading tastes and preferences. There are not that many places in our culture where people of different backgrounds and beliefs can meet safely to share experience on equal terms. Increasingly individuals move in work, family and friendship networks where they meet mostly others like themselves. The points of crossover are few and where they happen are often associated with tension or conflict. The library-based reading group is a force for community cohesion, a place to explore how people have different views in an atmosphere of mutual respect. As one London reading group member said after joining a group in her seventies, 'It is the only place in a long life where I have experienced amicable disagreement.'

The reader-centred approach ensures that everyone in the group will have something to say, confident in the fact that they are the expert in their own reading experience. It does not attempt to objectively analyse or deconstruct the text, although this may happen as a natural result of discussions. The focus is always on individual experience, what the book felt like to read. The move towards the reader-centred reading group has occasionally led to accusations of dumbing down. This arises from a misunderstanding of the approach and a false assumption that readers who express their response to a book in terms handed down by literature study courses or the literary press are thinking more deeply than those who rely on more ordinary language to convey their experience.

Libraries can also take the reading group offer to people whose situations, for a variety of reasons, make participation more difficult. Libraries have set up groups in hospitals and day-centres; they have started groups for people with poor literacy skills; they include audio formats for those who listen instead of reading print.

Reading groups have become part of the library offer in prisons, though often logistically difficult. The library is an important resource for men and women in prison; many people using prison libraries confirm that they have never visited the public library. The correlation between poor literacy skills and offending is well documented and the role of the prison library in supporting emergent readers and writers is invaluable. Reading, discussing and writing about books in the unpressured, social context of a reader-centred reading group give extra support to existing prison education programmes.

WAKE-UP CALLS

Misunderstandings, however well-intentioned, undermine reader-centred practice. If you recognise the views below, use the arguments in this chapter to challenge them.

" Why should reading groups have the new books first? "

" I'm staying late to lock up after the reading group, I don't see why I should have to make them tea as well. "

" We'd love to run reading groups but we don't have the capacity. "

Too much effort for too few people?

In the minds of some library staff, reader development and reading groups are inextricably linked. Ask some staff to define what reader development is and they will reply, 'It's setting up reading groups.' This can lead to heads of service and senior managers arguing against any reader development activity on the grounds it takes up a lot of staff time and benefits only a small number of readers.

Reader-centred work is much wider than supporting reading groups. It is more important for a library service to meet reader needs in stock management, in the library environment and in reader-centred promotions than it is to run reading groups. It must also be recognised that reading groups are not for everybody - many keen readers hate the very idea. The messianic tone in describing reading group experience should be avoided; there is no especial virtue in being a member.

However, the success of reading groups testifies to the huge importance they have in individual lives. Participants will often go to great lengths to make the session, putting it ahead of other work and family commitments in a way which shows how the experience is valued. The mix of intellectual challenge, emotional depth and social networking in a relaxed atmosphere offered by a reading group is hard to find anywhere else. One couple in Durham had a fire in their kitchen on reading group night but they still made it!

Managed well, reading groups can also bring benefits for the library service. They can help to deliver other management objectives as well as being a pleasure in themselves for participants. Reading group members are library advocates; they are committed and supportive users and provide a ready-made audience for consultation and events. Running reading groups is a proven way to develop staff skills and confidence in areas where traditional practice is weak such as stock knowledge and talking to customers. Staff working in partnership with reading group members can deliver a quality of reader-based promotion which benefits the whole service.

Reading groups can provide an endless resource of reader-to-reader promotions or regularly changing 'reading group choice' book displays in the library. Members should be encouraged to write short reviews or comments about the books they read; this can be made part of the group activity and library staff can support those who are shy of writing

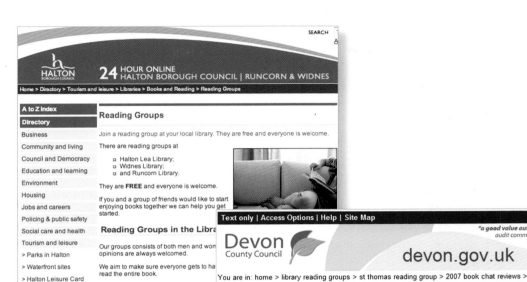

*Reading Group pages
on library websites*

by taking down what they say. Comments can be used on readers' noticeboards in the library and swapped between groups and branches. Reader recommendations are the single most powerful force in promotion and are under-exploited in most services. They can be used to highlight specific titles, to make unusual connections, to draw attention to books which might otherwise be overlooked. Bookshops in the UK have adopted this practice with staff recommendations of specific titles, often presented as handwritten comments to convey personal authenticity.

Reader comments can be stored as a resource to be used by all staff when searching for a particular kind of read for another borrower or when compiling booklists or themed collections. The resource can be made accessible within the library for other readers to browse or published online within the readers' pages of the library website. Several libraries co-operate with the local newspaper to provide book reviews written by members of the reading group every week. This helps make the added value activities being offered by the library service visible within the community.

WAKE-UP CALLS

Misunderstandings, however well-intentioned, undermine reader-centred practice. If you recognise the views below, use the arguments in this chapter to challenge them.

" *Our poetry reading group has written some great poems - we're setting up a display of them in the library.* "

" *I don't think our reading group members would want to write down their comments.* "

" *Our stock librarian is a literature graduate and he provides extensive notes on all the reading group books.* "

In Pontefract Library (Wakefield MDC), the long-established reading group managed readers' noticeboards, the library bookchain and, through applications to outside funding organisations, funded a reader-in-residence post and set up and delivered reader activities in schools and hospices. They have also regularly run sell-out events such as a Spanish themed evening and a Valentine's Day event on 'books we're passionate about'. Events were accompanied by a collection of recommended books and a printed booklist (funded by a small grants tranche of the Lottery). All of these activities were planned and managed by the reader-in-residence and the reading group members themselves.

Involving reading group members as event hosts takes pressure off staff and highlights the role of libraries at the heart of communities. During the Essex Book Festival, the Bishops Park reading group co-hosted Barbara Erskine's visit to their library. As well as providing the refreshments, they cared for visitors and showed off the new library with great pride. One member of the group enthusiastically explained to visitors how the new self-service facility worked so that they could use it when it was unveiled at their own library.

Being involved in reading groups is also of great value in developing the skills and confidence of library staff. There is no question that staff who have reading group experience become more confident in talking about books with a wide range of readers. They also develop better stock awareness. Confidence in talking about books, wide book knowledge and the ability to talk to a range of readers with very different needs - these are invaluable skills for library staff. These skills are often identified as missing in skills audits as they are not part of traditional library training. Involving staff in reading groups is one way of addressing the skills gap.

Birmingham Central Library's science fiction reading group has had an impact on the science fiction stock in the service. Pam Gaffney, who originally set up the group, admits that she had never been a science fiction reader and knew very little about the genre. She relied very much on the expertise of the members when selecting titles for the group. Working with the group has kept science fiction to the fore in stock selection where Pam brings their expertise to make sure new SF titles are looked out for and purchased.

Formally involving reading groups in stock selection has been tried in a number of authorities but with mixed results. While it is useful to draw on the expertise of well-read group members to increase awareness of who are the new authors to look out for, who is on the wane and what titles should be present to constitute a respectable collection in any genre, professional library staff are the ones charged with determining how a stock fund drawn from public money should be spent to maintain a balanced, inclusive range of titles and too much input from a particular reading group could distort this.

Do you need a reading group strategy?

Reading groups have mostly developed in an ad hoc way in UK libraries. If you only have a few groups and the staff involved are happy to make the commitment, this is fine. But what happens if your reading group gets too large for the space you can provide? Or if you have a request to start another group on a different evening from the existing one? Or if you have two groups both demanding the same title at the same time? As reading groups have burgeoned, the need to manage them has increased.

In many library services, reading groups are run on an almost grace and favour basis by committed staff members who are interested. The danger here is that either the group becomes very cosy, a nice evening with the same few people every time, or conversely the staff member gets overstretched, runs out of steam and the group collapses. It is worth planning the targeting, staffing and resourcing of reading groups to make more impact than this.

In developing a reading groups' programme as part of a reader development strategy, expectations have to be clearly defined in relation to staff and users. Will there be training offered to staff members? Will the time spent by staff in the meetings themselves (if outside normal operating hours) be a voluntary commitment - how will this be represented in staff contracts? Will there be an allocated budget to purchase multiple copies of books for the group(s)?

For users, the library service must be clear as to what they can justifiably expect. Will this group be permanently supervised/organised by a member of library staff or are they expected to build towards a self-management model? If the group is to be self-managing, what can they expect from the library service? Space? Books? Refreshments? Cambridgeshire Libraries provide a leaflet which spells out exactly what reading groups can expect from the service, whether meeting in libraries, in private homes or in workplaces:

Every reading group can:

- Register at a chosen library
- Borrow up to ten books
- Place a free hold for multiple copies
- Borrow books for a six week period
- Receive advice and guidance about Reading Group management and what to read.

Cambridgeshire Library Service leaflet

As with every other activity, the audience you get will depend on the context you establish, the tone you set and what you're offering. A reading group running during the day can be accessible to retired and unemployed people but those in full-time work would not be able to come. The offer of childcare would tempt many parents and carers, so establishing a children's storytime alongside a reading group session would make the session much more accessible. Evening sessions will attract full-time workers but may deter elderly readers who don't want to be in town centres late in the evening, particularly during the winter months.

It may be that, in order to give people fair access to this activity, more than one reading group, running at different times of the day on different days of the week, is the way forward. It may not be possible to attach the staff time and resources to a series of groups, however, and this makes it important to decide which is the priority target audience. Being clear about the target audience makes subsequent decisions around appropriate time of day, venue, publicity strategy and reading programme much easier. Focusing resources on a narrow part of the audience can be justified by limiting the run of this reading group for so many months and then establishing another one for a different audience. Be prepared to allow the group enough time to settle and become established, however. If the first group wishes to continue it can do so with limited support from the library service - for example venue and books but no staff supervision.

There is no shame in allowing a group which has run its course to die. West Sussex Libraries found that teenage groups worked best if it was clear from the start that the group would only run for a limited time. Girls were happy to make a short-term fixed commitment, they then brought all their friends and some boys would come because the girls were there. Open-ended teenage groups did not generate the same interest.

Oldham Libraries reading groups leaflet

the company of readers

Share your love of reading at Uppermill library

Some formal staff training is valuable when supporting a reading group programme. The ability to get a good discussion going; to keep the peace even if opposing viewpoints are being aggressively expressed; to make sure everybody gets the chance to speak and, at the end of the session, have people wanting to come back next time - all these are skills which can be learned. Understanding a little about group dynamics, appreciating that people read primarily for pleasure, and are coming because they want to share that pleasure with others, and simply putting the kettle on are more important skills for the reading group facilitator than a degree in literature or, indeed, librarianship!

The Reading Group Toolbox, jointly published by Waterstone's and Opening the Book in 2000, contains many useful resources for people with no previous experience in running groups to spark entertaining and stimulating discussions about reading. The Toolbox was funded by an Arts for Everyone lottery grant and 1,000 copies were distributed free to all English library authorities, including one to each prison library.

The Reading Group Toolbox

Reading groups in the community

The perception of the typical reading group member is a middle-aged female. Library services and others (especially the media) sometimes treat the prospect of male reading groups as nirvana. The ambition of attracting more male readers to reading groups is fine as long as we don't forget to celebrate and value the female readers we're already attracting. A non-fiction focus may be of greater interest to male readers. In Northern Ireland, more men came to a reading group called *Reading our histories* as it was clear it wouldn't be fiction-based.

Where a 'missing' audience has been identified, libraries sometimes divert attention and resources towards it, using the already existing battery of products, services and activities. If libraries are failing to reach a particular audience, this will be because of bigger issues - the poor image of the service, competition from online and offline booksellers, competing demands on leisure time, for example - which setting up a group reading only sports biographies, for example, cannot hope to solve. Using a reading group in a bid to attract non-users into libraries is an unrealistic goal; there are other routes which will be more successful and less time-intensive.

One library authority attempted to address social inclusion targets by tasking a staff member to establish reading groups in a branch library in one of the worst sink estates in the district. Library use was already very low so an approach which is more suitable for adding value for existing borrowers and deepening their engagement with books was doomed. It takes time to establish an understanding, a willingness and then, hopefully, an expectation of additional activities around reading and libraries, beyond the basic provision of the book and the individual's relationship with it. Approaching borrowers to join a reading group when they have no former experience of sharing their reading is likely to be met with suspicion and/or mirth. A reading group is not a response for all circumstances.

There are times when specific pockets of funding are available for reading group projects targeting a particular audience group, or supporting their role in community development. It may be possible to establish groups for refugees, teenagers, visually impaired readers, looked-after children or prisoners using funds obtained from organisations such as the Paul Hamlyn Trust, the Community Investment Fund or regional regeneration budgets. All funding organisations have their own priorities for projects/audiences to be supported and

WAKE-UP CALLS

Misunderstandings, however well-intentioned, undermine reader-centred practice. If you recognise the views below, use the arguments in this chapter to challenge them.

" If you're not doing reading groups, you're not doing reader development. "

" Reading groups are a waste of time, why should a dozen people get all that attention? "

" Our head of service expects a reading group in every branch by the end of the year. "

these may well change year on year. In any funding approach, it is advisable to beware of claiming more than you can deliver. If your group is likely to be made up largely of middle-class women, that is well worth doing and it may be a very significant part of their lives but you can't get extra funding support on the grounds of social inclusion.

Supporting workplace reading groups could help to open up some 'missing' audiences for public libraries. People working unsocial hours, or who are isolated economically or geographically, may well be reachable via their place of work. Essex Libraries supports workplace reading groups in venues as diverse as a tractor plant, council offices and an educational publishing house. Making links with local employers for projects like this raises libraries' profile as a community resource. Public libraries help to create the healthy communities that employers draw on for their workforces.

Barnsley Libraries have supported reading group programmes in several of their branch libraries through local and regional grants by stressing the impact on local people. As an ex-mining area, funding exists to support projects which encourage social interaction, lifelong learning and citizenship in deprived communities. Amounts up to £10,000 have been received (from the South Yorkshire Key Fund) to support reading groups and associated reader development activity. These bids have been made by the reading groups, not by the library service. Barnsley's reading groups are set up with constitutions so that they are in a position to make funding applications where this formality is required, although there are sources which don't demand this. The Co-op Dividend Fund, for example, distributes grants of up to £500 to groups which don't have a formal constitution or a bank account. Books purchased with these grants are made available to all the reading groups in the libraries and in the community but don't go into library stock for at least two years after the grant has been awarded.

Essex Libraries reading groups' programme celebrates and promotes its role as a community arts activity. Essex launched a Booktalk Group of the Year competition in 2006, as a way of looking at the impact of reading groups on the wider community. Groups entering are asked to say how they promote the joy of reading beyond the group. Staff and reading group members have also worked hard to develop a good relationship with their local BBC radio station and a different reading group each week participates in a 15-minute books' slot which had previously featured publishers promoting their latest output. It is a good technique when trying to interest local media in libraries to put local people centre stage and involving a reading group provides a ready-made way of doing this.

Where a library service has insufficient resources or no suitable venues for reading groups, support can be offered to groups meeting privately in their own homes. Many library services are now holding a collection of books in multiples to supply to reading groups. Warwickshire offers a special reading group membership card which is issued to one member of the group and gives access to the multiple collections. Each set of books is issued with a review sheet which the group has to return with the books.

Managing stock for reading groups

Successful reading group sessions can be run without having multiple copies of single titles. With access to library shelves, readers can explore how they choose, compare known and unknown titles, and discussions can be based on themes, genres or different reading situations. (The Reading Group Toolbox contains ideas like this which have been tried and tested by many different groups.) However, many groups choose to read the same title for an in-depth discussion and this poses problems for library stock managers in supplying the books.

Many library authorities find it hard to justify investing in multiples of individual titles to feed the demands of library-based and independent reading groups. There is plenty of evidence, however, to suggest that the most popular titles will more than earn their keep, only being discarded when they drop to bits. Titles still in good condition when they have done the rounds of the groups get put into stock, either as single titles or, often, displayed as multiples. Some authorities do ring-fence small amounts in stock budgets to support the purchase of reading group titles and in a few authorities the money is provided via a little creative accounting:

> 'The bulk of titles are purchased from the local Ottaker's bookshop, where I have built up an excellent relationship with the staff. I try to cover as wide a range of genres as possible, including classics, travel, current fiction, biography and crime, and the shop's main fiction buyer is always happy to help with personal recommendations (I have never met anyone who has read so much!). We fund this through a small reader development budget, which was created by a couple of thousand pounds from our binding budget as we bind very little nowadays. In an emergency it's usually possible to dip into the (inadequate) main book fund, especially as the reading group sets are returned to general library stock when we're finished with them.'
>
> Librarian, Scotland

In Stirling Libraries, reading group collections do the rounds of all the reading groups, library-based and private, and then get sent as sets around the community libraries as 'reading group recommendation of the month' accompanied by a reader-centred blurb, printed onto a speech bubble and displayed with the collection. The feedback from the libraries involved in this promotion attests that the books fly off the shelves. Keeping the books together as multiples also allows them to be recalled if other reading groups come on board.

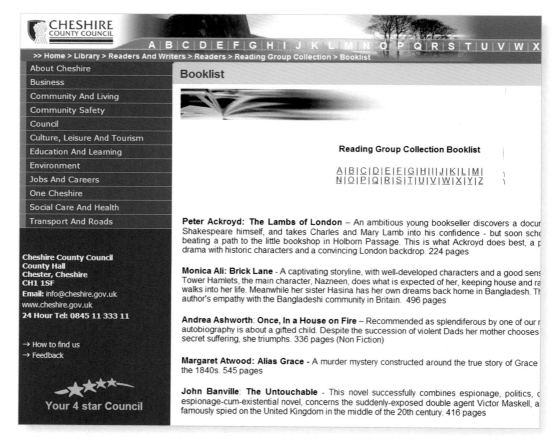

Cheshire Libraries' online list of books available to reading groups

The multiple copies purchased as part of the *Book of the Month* scheme offered by HarperCollins and Penguin are utilised as reading group titles by many services. In Oldham, for example, the HarperCollins titles are circulated around all the reading groups before being allocated to libraries.

Neath Port Talbot's reading group programme, *Hooked on Books*, is a collaboration with Swansea, Rhondda Cynon Taff and Bridgend. At the start of the project, each service purchased four to five titles which went into a communal collection. Each service keeps the books it bought and sends them out to groups in any of the participating authorities on request. Paul Doyle of Neath Port Talbot has led the expansion of reading group provision from one group to 12 over a period of 14 months, including establishing groups in a sheltered home and a health club:

> *'The health club group has been running for about five months and not one of the members was a regular library user. At the sheltered home, the audience of readers was there but what we needed to do was reach the staff, and that's been done.'*
>
> Paul Doyle, Neath Port Talbot

Kirklees Libraries buy multiples in paperback for reading groups but supplement this by providing themed boxes of books with a linking idea or subject. These have proved very popular with the groups and have generated some of the liveliest discussions. Another tried and tested approach has been to use single titles by the same author, or by authors who treat similar subjects in different or contrasting ways.

In the West Midlands, five neighbouring library authorities, Sandwell, Shropshire, Walsall and Wolverhampton, with Dudley acting as co-ordinator, agreed to share information about reading group resources co-operatively via the inter-library loan system. This ensures that the same titles aren't purchased by all. Each authority sends a list of holdings to Central Services in Dudley and these are collated giving author, title and holding authority details. A brief synopsis is added and the complete list is sent to each authority. Many more authorities co-operate on sharing multiple collections on an informal basis.

Coventry Libraries run eight readers' groups within libraries and also support a group meeting in the BBC Open Centre and two in city centre café bars (one of which has 24 regular members). They are also supporting a group in a Borders bookstore and are helping the local chain bookstore to establish its reading group. Members of the bookstore reading group generally buy their own copies of books (with 15% discount) but those who don't want to buy the book have a copy bought for them by the library service. This book is then absorbed into the general library stock. Multiple sets of books purchased for specific promotions such as the Orange Prize and Man Booker are taken into the readers' group collections at the end of the promotional period.

It is clear that any book purchased specifically for reading group use will pass through a great number of hands. In authorities like Essex, where there are 360 groups within its ambitious Booktalk programme, reading group multiple titles are well used. Essex also runs a number of groups for readers requiring different formats, supporting visually impaired readers meeting to discuss audio books and mixed groups of sighted readers and visually impaired readers who discuss books chosen on the basis of availability in the different formats, audio and print. Another group from a local mental health day centre meets in a nearby library and uses Quick Reads audio titles for its discussions.

Providing titles in different formats presents a further challenge as large print and audio books are more expensive. Services providing mother tongue texts for readers whose first language is not English also find acquisition a problem. In Greenwich, for example, their Chinese reading group is the most expensive to support because the stock is pricey but providing added value service to this audience of readers deserves the extra investment.

Many authorities have been fortunate to receive free copies of titles direct from publishers who recognise the importance of the role of reading groups in making books successful. Some publishers even provide pre-publication copies of new titles to groups and value the feedback the readers offer. Library services subscribing to *newBooks*, a magazine for reading groups developed out of work with libraries, take advantage of the free books offered.

Bookchains

For authorities where the skills, resources and time are not available to invest in reading group activity, or for small libraries lacking the space to accommodate reading groups, the bookchain offers a valuable alternative. For readers who want to share their reading experiences but don't have the time or the inclination to attend a regular reading group, the bookchain provides an opportunity to express opinions, find out what other readers think and discover new authors and genres which may have passed them by. Starting bookchains is a good way of testing the water to see if there is sufficient interest in forming a reading group. If you run three or four bookchains and then invite all the members to a social event, there will often be demand to start a reading group as well.

WAKE-UP CALLS

Misunderstandings, however well-intentioned, undermine reader-centred practice. If you recognise the views below, use the arguments in this chapter to challenge them.

" We can't afford to buy multiple copies for reading groups. "

" What's the point of supplying books to reading groups meeting in private homes? Surely we want them to come to the library, don't we? "

" If a borrower requests a title that's in the bookchain we'd break the chain to provide it. "

A bookchain can most simply be described as a reading group that doesn't meet. Readers are grouped together - three or four people per bookchain is typical - and they choose, write about and pass on books to the other members of their chain in a process managed by the library staff.

Bookchains are unique to public libraries. This is a classic reader development project which requires no money, no authors, no external support and which exploits the basic library mechanism which already exists where books are passed from person to person. It meets the objectives of introducing readers to new writers and gives them a chance to share their opinions. It also provides for the library a large resource of book comments which can be used to promote the books to a wider audience.

Many library services run both reading groups and bookchains. This enables readers to make choices about belonging to either or both and to change when it suits their circumstances.

Cutting the umbilical

When a group is well-established, confident and keen, it may be time for library staff supporting it to move out and for the group to assume control of their own programme and meetings. This leaves staff free to direct their energies and time elsewhere. Not every group will reach this ideal position and for a group which is heavily dependent on one member of staff to keep it going, the decision may well have to be sink or swim. The balance of time invested has to be calculated within a strategic framework - are the stated goals and priorities of the reader development plan really being met by continuing to support this group?

Staff working with reading groups can identify keen, confident members who may be willing to work towards becoming the chair/facilitator of the group, taking over the staff member's role when it is no longer viable for her/him to attend. This can be done gradually by the reading group member actively observing how the staff member manages the group, discussing with them how to handle tricky situations and how to ensure everyone gets a say and has a nice time. They can then gradually begin to lead parts of sessions and then a full session, under the supervision of the staff member. Any formal training sessions being provided for staff in running reading groups could also include existing group members who are suitable and who show an interest in growing into this role.

Where one member does not feel comfortable carrying full responsibility for managing the group, two or three members could share roles, taking turns to lead discussions, act as a greeter and organise refreshments. The Waterstone's/Opening the Book Reading Group Toolbox, is an ideal resource for supporting reading group members into independence.

Keeping it reader-centred

There are now many books, websites and other resources which are intended to support individuals wishing to set up new reading groups. Many of these use a book-centred approach which can be quite formal, even scholarly. Some of the earliest reading group guides resembled English Literature exam papers which must have served to turn off any reader who craved a more sociable, less demanding approach. One reading group guide, for example, asks groups discussing Sara Gruen's *Water for Elephants* to consider:

How does the epigraph apply to the novel? What are the roles and importance of faithfulness and loyalty in Water for Elephants? *In what ways does Gruen contrast the antagonisms and cruelties of circus life with the equally impressive loyalties and instances of caring?*

These guides are written by people who are very experienced in literary criticism but probably not that experienced in engaging and motivating a group of disparate individuals on a wet Thursday night! There is a danger that anyone inexperienced in organising reading groups may feel that the approach advocated in the reading group guides is written in stone as 'the correct one' - coming, as they do, mainly from respected publishers and media pundits. The friendly group chatting over a cuppa in a corner of the library may seem lightweight by comparison but a key principle for the reader-centred, library-based reading group is that it is inclusive. These groups are intellectually and socially accessible and provide an alternative to a literature class for people who want less formal, directed discussion.

It is important for library staff, or anyone else running reading groups, not to be thrown by these guides. There are often questions in each of the guides which give easier starting points for discussion - they don't need to be followed zealously, ticking off each question in turn. Readers' own starting points will be every bit as good and may provide a more comfortable way in for a lot of people in the group. As a facilitator gets to know a group, it will become obvious which questions will inspire lively discussion and which will have members staring longingly at the kettle.

Libraries have played a huge role in increasing the numbers, availability and significance of reading groups in the UK and this is a testament to the energy and enthusiasm among both borrowers and staff. The libraries' responsibility to participants increases, as in any situation where value is being added to a service, but this has to be balanced against the enormous benefits to staff and the wider readership using the library. If staff resources and time are reduced in a future library service, the pressure may be great to abandon the reading groups programme in order to focus on other priorities. It would be a great mistake, however, to throw the baby out with the bath water. The next stage of development, which some library services are already working towards, is nurturing library-based reading groups into independence. The wide implementation of reading group programmes represents a major shift in culture from libraries as passive providers to initiators of creative and inclusive events within local communities.

Chapter 8

READERS ONLINE

It's ironic that when pundits foretell the dire changes that the internet will bring, it is the book whose grisly end they predict. And yet some of the most interesting, popular and successful sites in terms of interest and profit on the net have been aimed at book readers. It is true that e-books and the Sony reader will offer readers different ways to acquire their texts - but this won't change the essential thrill of the reading experience, or the reasons that readers want to read. The method of delivery is a matter of individual choice - the lure of the reading experience is the same. So it is publishers and booksellers who are worrying about a reduction in booksales - and libraries who are free to look at different ways of offering the reading experience to the reader.

The world wide web is developing so fast that aspects of this chapter will be out of date between proofreading and publication. However, that is no excuse for not attempting an analysis of such an important area, crucial for both readers and libraries. The picture explored here will be a snapshot in time from early 2008 and will reflect the social, technological and political trends of that moment but the potential of a reader-centred approach as libraries develop online services is long-term.

In 2008, most library websites, like most library buildings, are built from the inside looking out. They reflect the organisations behind them, their needs and structures. Like traditional library collections they are full of riches for those who know what's there and will take the time to look. But they are ignored by a large number of people who simply walk straight past. Glance in and move on is even easier on the web than on the high street. The accepted web mantra is 'three clicks and you're dead', meaning if it takes the user more than three clicks to start getting some interesting information, they will get bored and give up.

This isn't just about speed, it is about how you organise information so that people can find what they want and get to it by as direct a route as possible. The danger of website design is that it is so easy to put quantities of information online that we reproduce what we have offline without thinking whether or not it is suitable for a web audience. In the early days of library website design everyone had an alphabetical list of their branch libraries, as if the only purpose for which people would go online was to find a physical location. The worst example of this was a local authority website which took three clicks to reach the alphabetical list of service points, three more to get to a particular branch and then, when you clicked for details, gave the message 'Please refer to a phone book!' Nobody is quite as bad as this any more but you will find A-Z lists on most local council websites. In an age where Google and keyword searching dominate the internet, reliance on A-Z lists looks inefficient and old-fashioned to frequent web users.

Council websites

The library web pages sit within the larger structure of the council website. Every council in the UK now has a web presence so it is important to understand this wider context before exploring the particular contribution a reader-centred approach might make.

Local council websites share a common challenge. They need to organise a large amount of detailed information about their disparate services and make it easily available to all local people. The organisation of information varies from council to council, and some have more online facilities available to the user, but the overall approach is universally shared. Local authorities use their website to tell people about the procedures, actions and services of the council. In many cases they offer an online route for an enquiry or complaint. For many councils, the website is the place to show the world how good they are and to promote to a wider audience the locations and communities that they serve.

All local council websites aim to make their information user-friendly but it is a lot harder for them to be user-centred. The information is built from the department to the user, from the service to the recipient, from the inside looking out. This is not to decry their achievement, as many work very hard to make decision-making transparent and information accessible, some offering users the chance to view minutes of council and cabinet meetings online. But users must negotiate their route on the council's terms in order to find what they want. In many ways this is the antithesis of the online experience of commercial sites, where the aim is to offer the user many personalised ways to discover, use and create content.

However smart the organisation of a local authority site, the structure still feels a bit like online filing. Typically, information is offered to the user behind gateways that either simply name the service - education, culture, waste management - or describe its essential role in the user's life - live, learn, enjoy, work. The latter option may seem to offer a user-centred route to the information but the choices turn out to be quite shallow, simply leading to the same departmental service offers at the next level.   Whatever the navigational terms, the information is still differentiated into the separate services.

Although most of these sites are very similar in look and feel, they are built in isolation. Each authority offers its own services, with little reference to the fact that the local user may need to consult a range of other organisations to find what they are looking for. Each local council site is an island unto itself. Other local organisations and services are often indicated by formal links in a separate section but not often integrated into the warp and weft of the site. The lack of acknowledgement of other relevant sites has a real impact for the user.   65% of the UK population lives in areas with two tier government; users could be accessing services and information from a district council as well as a county council, for example. These two sites rarely acknowledge each other or link to each other or mediate for the user. The way they are organised is invariably different, leading to confusion about where to find information on each, and which council has responsibility in which areas of provision. Design conventions are often different and so are opportunities to feed back.

WAKE-UP CALLS

Misunderstandings, however well-intentioned, undermine reader-centred practice. If you recognise the views below, use the arguments in this chapter to challenge them.

" The library service web pages are accessed through a link from the Education section on the council website. "

" We don't usually introduce users to readers' sites when we're doing the web awareness sessions. "

" The firewall blocks access to lots of sites, it's words like Scunthorpe that cause the problem. "

Local authority sites are conspicuous on the web for their lack of opportunities for users to interact with the information. The web offers unique opportunities for users of a site to explore and select content to answer personal needs. Many other sites, equally information-heavy, consider these functions to be key to their success. On a site like Amazon, for example, people have many ways to record their own preferences, to pick up and refer to their past uses of the site, to share their views and influence the content of the site, to feed back to the site administrators and to post their own views. The information given on a local authority website, and the way it is organised, comes across to the user as fixed; the website often has the tone of an announcement.

The web involves people in an intimate, unique environment of their own creation. In this context, your customers are usually no more than two feet from the screen, so there's no need to shout. The communication is one-to-one, casual and informal - people want to feel as if they are involved in a conversation. The recipient of the message is in control, they are in their own physical space and can decide to end their engagement with your site at any moment they choose. In the wider world of the web, users are organising information for themselves and cherry-picking items according to their own needs and interests. The web thrives by users sharing information they discover between them, creating new content, discovering new ways to inform, support and help each other.

Perhaps local councils will develop this better in the future. There are excellent opportunities for councils to meet people's needs by putting local users of services in touch with each other to share experiences and help each other through the maze of provision. Plenty of council sites offer opportunities to complain to providers but not to seek out and hear the experience of other users of the service. A confident local council might provide a prominent place where users could report a brilliant aspect of the service to others, recommend a shortcut they had discovered or commend another way of accessing a service locally.

The mission statements, logos and claims with which councils decorate their homepage refer to real world delivery not web service delivery. A web presence offers the council many opportunities to serve local people and improve real world services. A website should be an integral part of the organisation not just a representation of it.

DIFFERENCES BETWEEN LOCAL COUNCIL SITES AND THE BEST COMMERCIAL/ INDEPENDENT SITES

LOCAL COUNCIL SITES	COMMERCIAL SITES
Tell	Ask
Announce	Listen
Give information	Share information
Logos and mission statements	Use style, voice, branding
Focus on council priorities	Focus on customer or user priorities
Key message is how good they are	Key message is what they offer
One site for all	Separate sites for different audiences
Filtered communications	Users exchange information
Users unseen by others	Users visible to each other
Statements, closed language	Questions, open language
One voice	Many voices
Information organised in the same way as the real world service organisation	User functions often lead the site
Authoritative	Enabling, questioning, amusing
Explaining existing procedures	Making new procedures for the web
Static	Changing
Not much time sensitive material	Daily changes where appropriate
No user content	Often mainly user content
A large range of information for all	Specific information for you
Geographically based appeal	Language/interest based appeal
Late with common web innovations	Cutting edge uses of the web
Photos of smiling elders and cute kids	Images of products and users - often users' own
No adverts (usually)	Pop ups and flashing ads
Text heavy content	Lots of white space
Few personal named contacts	Often named people on site
Blogs by prominent members or officers	Postings by customers and users
No way of owning/personalising a space	My X Site, my favourites, my account

The council service that most often employs a user-centred approach online is the library service. The reader-centred work that has taken place over the last ten years in libraries has informed their web offer and often shows in particular features of their web presence. There is an irony in the fact that finding the library service is not always straightforward for the web user. The gateway to the library online presence lives under different categories online because libraries are managed under different departments depending on the council. Where the website attempts to become more user-centred in offering options in terms which relate to people's lives rather than departmental titles, it is no easier to navigate. A library can be seen to contribute to 'live', 'learn' and 'enjoy', for example, but will typically only be found under one category and the user must guess which.

Getting it right online

Going online offers libraries an opportunity to escape inadequate buildings, poor marketing and limited book budgets. Here is the place where a library can be truly reader-centred and can start with the readers' needs, not the stock or the staff or the building. There are a few library services in the UK who see this, and some who have led the whole council in terms of interactivity and user-centred content on the web. They have learned what works by experience and have trained staff who write and update content as part of their job. They have webmasters who oversee design and make sure that the site is moderated and refreshed, and invite and answer requests and feedback from readers. Often access to the online services is determinate on being a library member, but there is also content for a web visitor to use, and plenty of temptations to join the library (online, of course!). These library services have trialled and tested editing software, can add content themselves instantly, gather web statistics and change the emphasis on the homepage in response to use.

Gateshead Libraries' online presence is built and managed by a team of trained library staff; crisply designed and regularly updated, it offers a reader-centred gateway to all aspects of the service. There is a range of interactivity for web visitors and a real draw for the user to get involved, follow trails and join a community of readers.

The key design features running in the columns on Gateshead's pages are about sharing, discussion, feeding back and hearing new opinions. There is absolutely no sense here that feedback actually means complaint, as in so many local council sites. Staff have the confidence to present themselves as real readers and to divert any user's prejudices about librarians with humour.

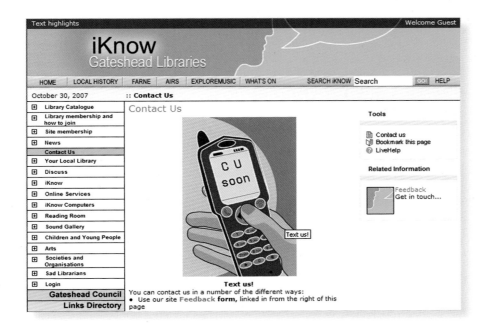

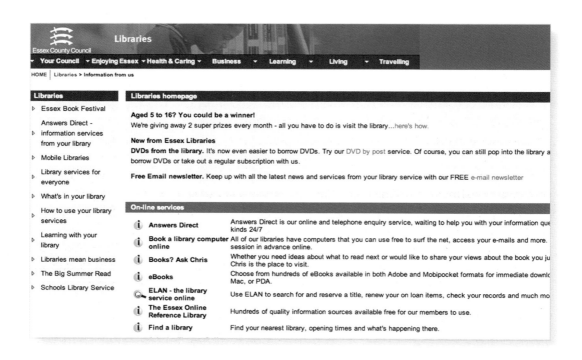

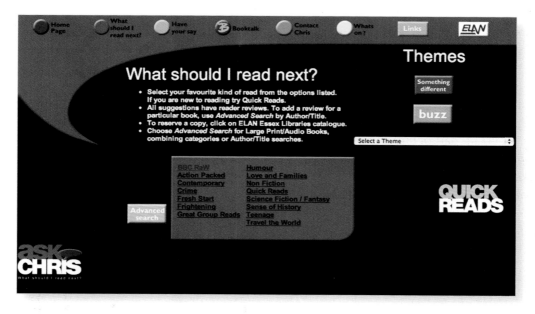

Essex Libraries' web pages show a strong reader focus. However, the *Ask Chris* section is offered as one option for readers from a home page that conforms to the more conventional web offer. The contrast for the user is evident and the approach very different. The problem is that the interesting reader-centred pages will take quite a lot of persistence by a reader to reach. This is the most common use of reader-centred approaches on library websites in 2008; they are presented as one feature of a site, an option among many for the user, rather than used to shape the whole approach of the site.

The strength of the Essex online offer lies in its integrated approach to marketing. Building on a long investment in offline marketing, Essex was quick to perceive the value of marketing services online. The web offers the opportunity to reach audiences for events, to make personal contacts between staff and readers, to increase the number of visitors to libraries and to widen use of a range of services both offline and online. Essex Libraries run a very successful email newsletter. Visitors to the library website are invited to actively subscribe, so that a personal link is made between staff and online users. The newsletter acts as a guide to new stock and highlights online services. It has a good success in attracting new audiences to offline library events as well as to online subscription services. Many libraries offer a newsletter online, but if it is offered as part of the website, visitors need to remember to visit it regularly. In contrast, the approach in Essex gives the newsletter delivery an interactive feel, where readers elect to create a personal connection with the libraries online. This is one way in which a community is built online without venturing into social networking on site or hosting discussion boards.

Both Gateshead and Essex Libraries recognise that an investment of staff time in building and maintaining online resources pays dividends. The responsibilities to create web content are shared amongst a range of staff and seen very much as a marketing function. An important part of both strategies is to make sure that results can be clearly evaluated and then acted upon. A well-run web offer will have a quantifiable impact on loans, take up of online services and attendance at library events. The fear of some services is that a successful online offer will work to the detriment of offline visits - that the online visitors will get what they want online and cease coming to the library - has been proved unfounded where a successful online offer has led to increased take-up of both online services and attendance at events.

Barriers to good online services

Everyone knows the web is important, and will be even more so in future, but it requires courage to make the management decisions that are necessary to develop online if it means transferring resources from face-to-face delivery to virtual delivery. Convincing politicians that future votes lie in successful online services is easy if it costs nothing but much more difficult if it means closing a local branch library (even if it has underperformed for years) with all the emotion and bad publicity that entails.

In this context, online developments are growing in a piecemeal and uncoordinated fashion, rather than as part of a coherent strategy. Where there is external funding, as with the investment in the People's Network to give everyone free internet access through libraries with trained staff in support, change has been fast and successful. Where development relies on local initiatives, the library service is dependent on the council's wider online provision which will vary according to local policy and circumstance.

For most libraries, the problem is the same as for the council as a whole, to find ways to offer their complex service to users online. The catalogue and all its riches, online membership procedures and renewal of books, free access to subscription-only information resources - these are just a few of the things that the library has to map for the online user. Most offer a scattering of links to other readers' sites as well.

One library homepage that succeeds well in showing routes through this complexity is Kent County Council's. The offers are simple and unambiguous: the minimal text gives clear pointers to the depth to be found on site. There is a sense here that each user will have specific needs and that the site will meet them. Help and feedback features, although conventional, are offered prominently and the whole page feels efficiently organised. Salford's site offers clear navigation and lively language and includes opportunities for users to link into Web 2.0 social bookmarking sites such as Facebook and Stumbleupon.

It is not surprising that most libraries find it hard to transfer their reader development expertise to their web approach. In some authorities where web services are outsourced, content decisions can be left in the hands of staff who have no contact at all with libraries. In some cases content written by libraries is drastically changed, and subsequent corrections are impossible to effect. Whether the IT is outsourced or internal,

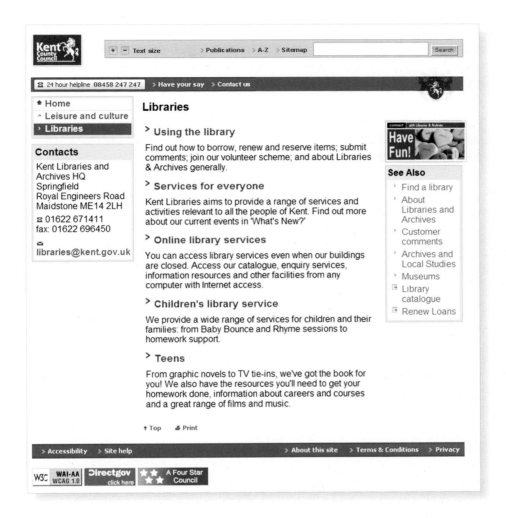

communication is not always good. Many librarians experience such bad communication with their webmasters that they no longer submit notices of upcoming events for their website, knowing that by the time the material appears on site, the event is long past.

The bottleneck caused by a tiny IT department trying to control the web output of a whole council has given way in the last few years to investment in better content management systems. These should make it possible for key staff to manage updating their own departmental sections. However, some of the systems are overly complicated or over-rigid and often library staff don't get time or training to use them properly.

Where a library service has taken a pioneering approach and built an innovative, user-friendly online presence, they can find they are constantly fighting a battle with the corporate website to retain the very online independence that has gained them such popularity. Independence in creating content, in policy and design decisions and in interactivity with users, is hard won and takes assertiveness to keep. Instead of being

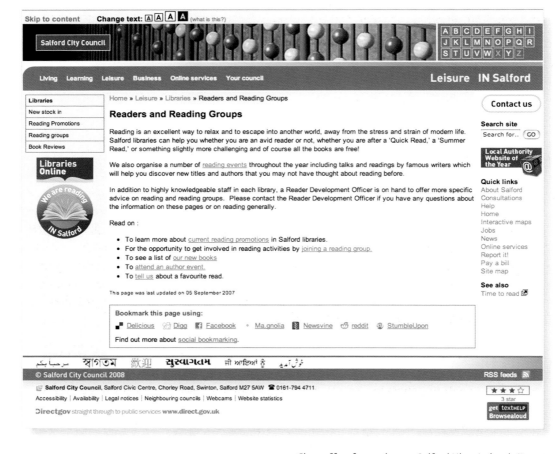

Clear offers for readers on Salford Libraries' website

able to influence the council's approach to creating a successful online presence, library experience online tends to be swept aside in favour of a top-down, uniform and static web presence. There seems to be a lack of confidence amongst council web policy decision makers to trust their library services to lead their online presence, either in their role as information professionals or where they have cast-iron experience in building popular web features for users.

All library staff responsible for creating content for the web, however near or far they are from designing, uploading and editing material on the site, have little time in which to do it. In many authorities it is the function of one person to collect and write information and submit it. In others, trained staff write pages for the website. In a few, staff edit their own material directly online which is then overseen by a library webmaster. Time spent on discussing policy, design and then writing content is difficult to identify and separate from other functions. Web work tends to be part of a range of work in most authorities and fitted in when the staff responsible have time.

Few libraries have a clear timetable for creating and updating material for the web. There is a sense that the web material is extra to the work in the real library, and not all contributors have a say or feel they can express a view about the overall web policy. This tends to demotivate staff from trying to push forward new ideas for the library web presence and leads many to see web work as a thankless chore with few evident outcomes. Library staff involved in web services are aware that the library pages could do more to reach readers but there is an even stronger perception of the difficulties caused by lack of direction and clear ideas, lack of staff time and organisational problems in working with IT departments who have power over design and content. Web decisions seem often to be made elsewhere, somewhere beyond the library, and there doesn't seem to be a coherent argument being made by library staff in those spheres for change. Maybe it's just that nobody is listening and librarians don't often shout.

Few library staff with a responsibility for writing or managing web content can access detailed statistical information on who is visiting or how the site is used. It is therefore not possible for content generators to use this information to plan changes in what appears on site and how it is organised. In most cases there is no visitor information posted on site and no way of finding out what is most used, what works and what does not. The main concern in most councils seems to be in keeping information up to date. Whether the information is relevant, appropriate or visited is secondary.

This is a top-down passive approach to providing an online service which mirrors the traditionally passive provision of adult lending services before the advent of reader development. Just as with the face-to-face service, it excludes many potential users and limits the role of the library in the community. Reader-centred work is active and can widen the reach of the library service. A user-centred web presence is also an active one and offers similar opportunities to widen the reach of the service online.

Beyond the catalogue

By 2007 all but three of UK library services had made their catalogues available online. This is a great step forward in providing virtual services. It is likely that catalogue searching remotely will become more important than catalogue searching in the physical library. Once you're in the building, most people will look on the shelves to see what's actually

WAKE-UP CALLS

Misunderstandings, however well-intentioned, undermine reader-centred practice. If you recognise the views below, use the arguments in this chapter to challenge them.

" I've noticed a factual error on our website but I'm not sure who is responsible for correcting it. "

" All the online content for readers that we write has to be sent to IT for uploading. "

" We don't know how popular our readers' pages are because it's impossible to extract the statistics just for those pages. "

there in preference to using the catalogue. But if you can check from home, before making the journey, having a look first becomes much more useful.

Systems suppliers are all looking at ways of enriching catalogue entries with extra information - cover illustrations, author biographies and photos, lists of other works, extracts from published reviews, links to publisher sites. Some are more ambitious in offering mixed media approaches with author interviews in video rather than print.

All these offers start from the book rather than the reader. But library system suppliers are exploring customisation too. Talis, for example, has a vision of being able to aggregate information from different library services to provide better quality content for readers, accessible through one central site and not limited to use by Talis customers. Talis is hoping to offer ways for site users to customise the way they access the information available through user-generated tags, for example being able to filter the reader comments to only those submitted by specific readers. There may also be the possibility of introducing Amazon-style features such as 'readers who borrowed this also borrowed....'

There is already web research showing that impulse buying is just as common on the web as it is offline. Work by Jared Spool and User Interface Engineering has shown that the major driver of impulse purchases is use of the category links and other aspects of site design instead of the use of the site's search engine[*]. Enjoying the experience of shopping is as important as finding the best price. The length of time many people spend on sites depends on how much they enjoy using them. And the longer they stay the more likely they are to buy. Enjoyment relates to how the offer is structured not just what it is.

Libraries need to find ways to engage impulse users over the web. Putting the catalogue online is essential but not enough by itself. We need new routes into the information, new ways of making the experience of finding a book interesting as well as easy. If the experience is tempting in itself, people who would never bother with a catalogue search are pulled in to try it out.

This is the origin of the most successful reader-centred website built in partnership with libraries. Whichbook.net began life as part of the first phase of the Branching Out programme to train librarians in reader-centred work. Piloted as Book Forager in 2000, it was an immediate success, and was then expanded and developed with support from

'What causes customers to buy on impulse?' **www.uie.com** [*]

the New Opportunities Fund, part of the People's Network initiative, and launched as whichbook in 2002. It attracts around 30,000 individual users every month and has done so consistently for seven years.

Instead of starting from book titles or author names, whichbook starts from the reader, and enables each individual to build the elements of that elusive 'good read' we are all looking for but don't quite know how to define. Users can play with choices, changing the balance between different elements such as happy/sad or safe/disturbing and getting immediate suggestions of books which match what they asked for. The choices are not binary alternatives but are offered on a continuum where the user controls how much or how little of any element is included. The site is simple and intuitive to use but it allows for complex and sophisticated mixes of reading preferences. For instance, you could look for a book which was very funny at the same time as being quite bleak and a little unpredictable.

All of the books have comments written by trained whichbook readers which are designed to describe the reading experience offered by the book instead of evaluating its critical worth. The readers are all library staff, working in different services, and brought together for shared training. All 90 librarians involved in the major national training programmes in reader development - Branching Out in England, Estyn Allan in Wales and the Reader Development Network in Scotland - have been whichbook readers.

Whichbook concentrates on offering choices which are not available elsewhere. You can choose the gender, age, race and sexual orientation of the main character in a book; you can select a plot shape such as lots of twists and turns or success against the odds; you can spin a globe and choose where in the world the book is set. Whichbook does not seek to replace traditional author and title searches, genre classifications or bibliographies of national literatures; it offers a completely different reader-centred approach to choosing what to read next.

Whichbook is the product of a creative synergy between the disciplines of reader development, psychology and computing. (Daniel Brown, one of the creators of the original software, is a clinical psychologist.) It answers complex demands which catalogue searches cannot begin to address. The site was also the first to link from individual book titles directly to online library catalogues so that any reader finding a book they want to read can click through to their local library catalogue to see if it is available to borrow. Users

whichbook.net

happy	sad
funny	serious
safe	disturbing
expected	unpredictable
larger than life	down to earth
beautiful	disgusting
gentle	violent
easy	demanding
no sex	sex
conventional	unusual
optimistic	bleak
short	long

reset   go!

change to character, plot, setting

audio books   large print

Welcome to whichbook.net - a completely new way of choosing what to read

Text only version

Large text version

How to use whichbook.net - click here for a demo

About whichbook.net

Customise your screen

Get Flash

Feedback

Supported by

BIG
LOTTERY
FUND

are taken not to the catalogue home page but directly into the specific book entry in the catalogue.

Whichbook is an astonishing library success - a beacon for the reader-centred approach and for libraries online. After eight years, a long time in the dotcom world, it has no real competition in user-centred choosing. When whichbook first launched in 2000, the software was cutting-edge and way in front. In 2008 the basic algorithm for fuzzy searching is still sharp and simple but many sites use similar software now. The real value of whichbook turns out to lie in its understanding of audience and the accumulation of data. No commercial firm can afford to invest in the training and editing process which ensures consistency on site while involving readers with quite different tastes. No reader-enthusiast site can afford to do this either. Librarians working collaboratively with many different reading preferences but a shared set of values in respecting reading experience can do it. Yet almost every library web page that mentions whichbook cites it as just one of a group of diverse websites that readers might like to sample, as an outside site of interest to readers. Here is a library resource, built for and with libraries, that is rarely used as it is designed to be used - as an alternative gateway to the catalogue and for a reader to discover a good read for free.

Whichbook is unique to UK libraries - no bookshop has it, no online bookseller either. Blogs, commercial websites, professional chatgroups and commercial web operations all over the world have praised whichbook. Yet it is largely unexploited by the very library services who helped build it. It could be as successful in raising performance online as the Quick Choice

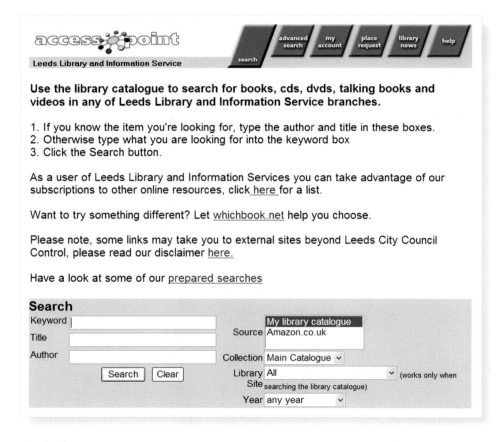

Leeds Libraries promote Whichbook prominently on their catalogue homepage

concept has been successful in increasing loans from library buildings because it is built on the same principles. The database of books is not comprehensive - but just as a Quick Choice collection will represent the range of a library's holdings, so whichbook offers a range of intriguing titles as a showcase.

Libraries could exploit their reader development strengths further in creating partnerships online. One example shows the potential. In 2004, Colman Getty, the public relations agency, sought a relationship with libraries to promote the Man Booker Prize, the most important fiction prize in the English language. Book Communications, the library marketing agency, brokered agreements in which public libraries could access print promotional materials. Book Communications also saw the potential for online connections and contacted Opening the Book to connect to the team of whichbook readers. The result was MyManBookerFavourites, a new reader section on the Man Booker website which received 150,000 page views in the two months between longlisting and announcing the winner. The site used the successful principles of the whichbook approach adapted to the new context.

The trained whichbook readers were crucial to this process - they each had a maximum of three days to read a longlisted title and return their scores on the agreed sliders, plus a longer piece of writing describing the reading experience.

Involving readers online

Most active reader-centred work on council websites takes the form of giving readers the option of posting reviews of books they have read or putting reviews from readers' group members online. Libraries are often the only council service to invite people to post their opinion and share it with others in this way. Surrey has a good example of this kind of offer to readers which works well (see page 256).

Readers' reviews exist in quite separate web space from library catalogues and the prospect of greater connection seems some way off in the UK. Even without structural integration, one aspect which all services could improve is in presenting different online services as part of a coherent whole. A library user will encounter the catalogue screen, the library pages on the council website, the self-issue and return screens, the procedure for booking computer time, the access to online reference resources and the home screen of a library computer in entirely separate ways. Because these services have developed separately, and often through different providers, they may look entirely unconnected; it would help if they shared a common branding and navigational structure. Further opportunities to join them up are missed. Online pages for readers are not linked with promotions in the physical library. The catalogue does not link to readers' reviews. Websites for readers on the web don't appear in the library and their resources are not exploited online. These are all areas that could link the online and offline library service and increase the use of both.

Understanding readers, both inside and outside the library, is the key to developing an attractive web offer. Thinking about who needs what and why is crucial rather than rushing into writing web content which nobody will ever visit. An email bookchain project at Copenhagen Central Library offers an example of how to get the most out of both virtual and physical promotion.

The bookchain concept was developed by Opening the Book to exploit the fact that library books are passed from one reader to another. It is designed to appeal to those who would

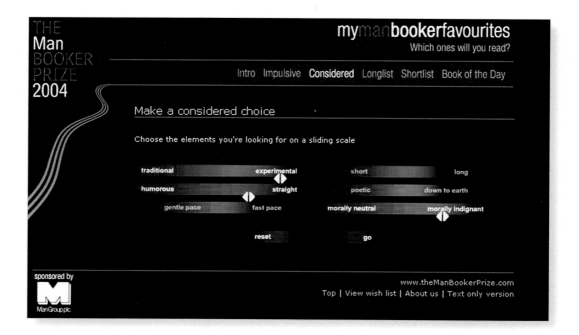

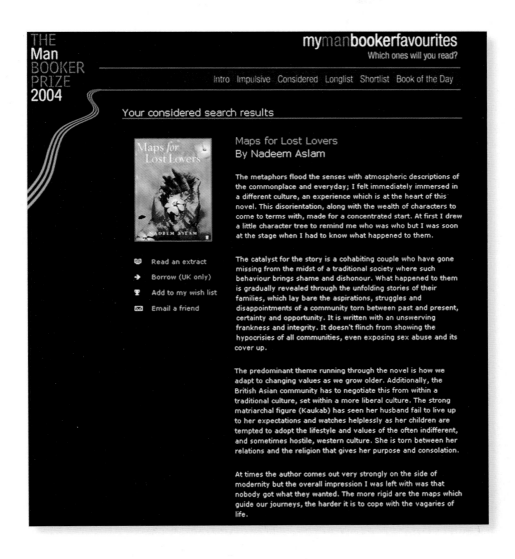

THE Man BOOKER PRIZE 2004

myman**bookerfavourites**
Which ones will you read?

Intro Impulsive Considered Longlist Shortlist Book of the Day

Your considered search results

Maps for Lost Lovers
By Nadeem Aslam

The metaphors flood the senses with atmospheric descriptions of the commonplace and everyday; I felt immediately immersed in a different culture, an experience which is at the heart of this novel. This disorientation, along with the wealth of characters to come to terms with, made for a concentrated start. At first I drew a little character tree to remind me who was who but I was soon at the stage when I had to know what happened to them.

The catalyst for the story is a cohabiting couple who have gone missing from the midst of a traditional society where such behaviour brings shame and dishonour. What happened to them is gradually revealed through the unfolding stories of their families, which lay bare the aspirations, struggles and disappointments of a community torn between past and present, certainty and opportunity. It is written with an unswerving frankness and integrity. It doesn't flinch from showing the hypocrisies of all communities, even exposing sex abuse and its cover up.

The predominant theme running through the novel is how we adapt to changing values as we grow older. Additionally, the British Asian community has to negotiate this from within a traditional culture, set within a more liberal culture. The strong matriarchal figure (Kaukab) has seen her husband fail to live up to her expectations and watches helplessly as her children are tempted to adopt the lifestyle and values of the often indifferent, and sometimes hostile, western culture. She is torn between her relations and the religion that gives her purpose and consolation.

At times the author comes out very strongly on the side of modernity but the overall impression I was left with was that nobody got what they wanted. The more rigid are the maps which guide our journeys, the harder it is to cope with the vagaries of life.

- Read an extract
- Borrow (UK only)
- Add to my wish list
- Email a friend

like a stimulus to their reading and a sense of connection to other readers without the complications of actually having to meet people you're not sure you're going to like. The library acts as go-between, enabling individual readers to swap books and exchange views anonymously. Many libraries have run bookchains in the UK but very few have moved this concept into the digital age. Bringing readers together through email is a natural development; it extends the convenience and privacy for bookchain participants. Books are still collected from the library building but all the communication about them is online.

Copenhagen Central Library set up a virtual forum on the library website to advertise the Reader to Reader email bookchain and to publish the readers' comments on the books that were swapped. They also made a display of the Reader to Reader books in the library, with the comment sheet inside each book. The loans from the Reader to Reader display quickly made it the most successful promotion ever undertaken by the library, generating great interest in what the books were and what had been written about them. What started as a virtual project became, unexpectedly, a route to promoting the range of the library's backstock. Susanne Balslev, the librarian, commented, 'I learned that any title, no matter how forgotten, can be revived by sheer recommendation.' Joining up the physical and digital services in this way clearly benefits both.

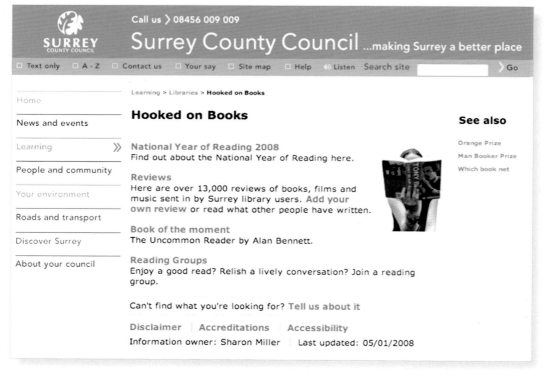

Readers' reviews on Surrey Libraries' website

WAKE-UP CALLS

Misunderstandings, however well-intentioned, undermine reader-centred practice. If you recognise the views below, use the arguments in this chapter to challenge them.

" *We can't tie up a whole PC just to run readers' sites.* "

" *We encourage borrowers to submit reviews to our website readers' pages but we only use the really well-written ones.* "

" *We highlight each month's most borrowed books on our homepage.* "

Connecting not competing

Library websites compete for attention with all the other book and reader sites available. Books have always done well on the web with bookselling sites leading e-commerce and publisher sites investing in design. In the first phase of web growth, the reader was secondary to much of this organisation-driven activity, apart from a few well-known examples such as **www.bookcrossing.com** and **www.whichbook.net**. But the recent explosion of user-generated and social networking sites has seen a growth in connections for readers too. In 2008, there are more opportunities to interact on commercial sites and many new sites for enthusiasts, often run by individual readers.

www.librarything.com offers readers the chance to create their own personal catalogue of books and then interact with hundreds of thousands of other readers who have done the same thing. **www.lovereading.co.uk** offers personalised email newsletters with recommendations and free downloads of first chapters. In this context, it may make more sense for librarians to keep up with new reader sites and look to promote them before trying to create fresh web content of their own. If the library site is a poor imitation of what is already available, it is not going to be able to compete. A site with a few book covers and a message saying 'Most borrowed books' is the equivalent online of the old-fashioned branch library display. It will do nothing to increase loans and it will convey a poor impression of the quality of your service.

Not all new reader sites are successful, of course. **www.mybookyourbook.co.uk**, an online library where readers donated ten paperbacks and then selected titles which would be mailed to them for a subscription fee, launched in 2005. Two years later the notice on its home page said, revealingly, it has closed down 'for lack of support and ongoing interest'. Those librarians who commented when the site first launched that libraries already offer this service for free might have a point. **www.storycode.co.uk**, a more schematic and less intuitive version of whichbook, appears to have stalled after ten years in development; the blog stops in August 2006. Storycode concentrates on elements in the story and lacks the understanding of reading experience and reader psychology which underpins whichbook.

It is in the nature of the web that for every reader site that fails, new sites are started from a different point all the time. Web space, design and technology are now so accessible that anyone can try out an idea without much risk. If the library service is unable to give resources to compete with whatever new sites are created every week, it may be better to develop a linking role instead of an originating one.

Linking up what is there already can meet the particular needs of a targeted audience very well. Tailored information online aimed at older people could bring a range of resources together to a specially designed page - links to a catalogue search for particular formats, links to reading lists for visually impaired readers, news about reading aids, easy audio e-book downloads, live chat for visually impaired readers on the web, news snippets and links to local organisations. Once an audience of readers is targeted, and their reading needs considered, many opportunities exist to engage them and widen their choices. The pages for older people, for example, could carry links to what their grandchildren might be reading.

The stock knowledge of library staff could be easily used to help readers on the web. Members of the public often say that they trust library staff to recommend a book to them.

A MORI survey in 2005 found that 89% of people trusted online information from libraries compared with 84% for the BBC, 73% for the National Health Service and 59% for a local council. (Reported in CILIP *Update* 4 (3) March 2005.) Staff could post short, snappy guides for readers on the library website. A reader-centred approach is much more engaging than a title list and will build an audience of interested users who like and trust the advice. Libraries could use their reader development expertise to identify common questions, for example, 'How do I make a start with science fiction?' 'What's the latest thing in crime fiction?' Once the feature is up and running, the site could ask web visitors to submit their own guides as well.

The blog is a phenomenon that allows individuals to speak to the world and there are plenty of readers' blogs to be found on the net. Some council websites host blogs by the Mayor or the leader of the council. A library service looking for a new voice could consider running a library blog and invite comment by library users. It could be a single voice or staff at all levels could be invited to contribute in turn. There are quite a number of online magazines and newsletters run by staff on library pages but they replicate the offline newsletter format; they are more like announcements and so don't really make use of the potential for informality, interactivity, feedback and the human factor that makes the blog form attractive.

A readers' group could undertake to run a blog on the library website and add comments as part of their regular meetings. This could begin to exploit the readers' group as a sounding board for library users and would reflect the real pleasures of meeting in a group, rather than limiting the appeal to asking contributors to write book reviews. After all, a huge attraction of readers' groups is meeting other people and not everything that gets discussed is about reading. A blog tends to reflect real life. An online presence for a readers' group would enable the realities of reading group experience to animate a formal website.

Delivering quality through partnerships

From 2001 to 2006 Opening the Book pioneered new websites for readers, working with libraries across Scotland, England and Wales. The models developed are interesting to examine because they used the web to offer reader-centred content in new ways and because they were built on cross-authority collaborations. External expertise in site design and reader development supported a regional network of key staff, each of whom recruited other staff and members of the target audience to test the site as it developed.

Each site began by identifying the target audience and analysing their needs. In the case of 4ureaders[*], a site for 11-16 year-olds in Scotland, the importance of differentiating between potential users was immediately apparent. 11 year-old girls and 15 year-old girls are into different things, and a website they want to visit must start by recognising this. It is not just a question of taking different audiences to different books and DVDs but of designing a whole environment with the right look and feel - the language, the style, the colours, the visuals. And to attract 12 year-old boys, a quite different approach is needed. It was decided it was better to hit some of these target audiences strongly, even if that meant the site wouldn't hit them all.

Library staff recruited groups of young people to operate as focus groups to sound out ideas for content and style, and to test different versions. The site was built from their responses and feedback. The site had three distinct areas; E-claire, Girls with Attitude and The Lads - all names chosen by the focus groups. None of the sections specified what gender or age group it was targeted to - it was left to the user to determine which of the areas suited them best.

One of the biggest advantages that the web can offer is interactivity. Online quizzes, questionnaires, voting, message boards all give the user the chance to have their say and 4ureaders made good use of all of these. Visual devices which require a mouse-click deepen engagement and offer fun. One popular feature showed an interactive horoscope wheel - spin to your birth sign and view a selected book that fits your personality. This was fun to use and appealed to teenage girls' natural curiosity about their image and identity. Books were regularly changed and library staff used the facility for all sorts of reader development purposes - getting new authors noticed, persuading readers who stuck to a favourite author or genre to try something different, using the site in small groups where opinions on both the books and the personality characteristics could be shared. The Lads' site used the same approach with more mocking humour - horridscopes instead of horoscopes.

[*] 4ureaders.net - site originally developed by East Ayrshire Libraries, working with Opening the Book, with the support of the Scottish Arts Council through the Local Authorities Partnership Project. The site is archived at: **www.openingthebook.com/archive/4ureaders**

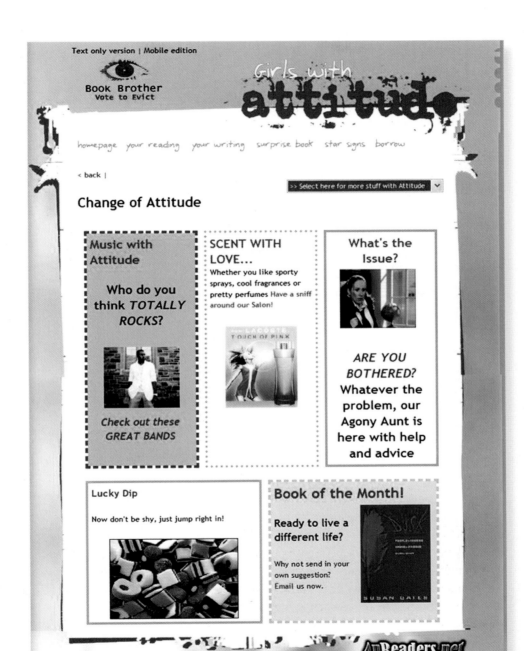

Text only version | Mobile edition

Book Brother
Vote to Evict

Girls with
attitude

homepage   your reading   your writing   surprise book   star signs   borrow

< back |

>> Select here for more stuff with Attitude

Change of Attitude

Music with Attitude

Who do you think *TOTALLY ROCKS*?

Check out these GREAT BANDS

SCENT WITH LOVE...

Whether you like sporty sprays, cool fragrances or pretty perfumes Have a sniff around our Salon!

LACOSTE
TOUCH OF PINK

What's the Issue?

ARE YOU BOTHERED? Whatever the problem, our Agony Aunt is here with help and advice

Lucky Dip

Now don't be shy, just jump right in!

Book of the Month!

Ready to live a different life?

Why not send in your own suggestion? Email us now.

SUSAN GATES

4nReaders.net
◀◀ Homepage

A more ambitious interactive feature reached all three audiences on 4ureaders. Exploiting the popularity of Channel 4's *Big Brother* with the site's target audience, Book Brother gave readers the chance to vote to evict a title every week until one book remained as the winner.

People coming across an independent website won't necessarily know anything about public libraries so this is a great opportunity to sell the service. It is possible to tackle directly any prejudices and assumptions which put people off using libraries, for example, 'They won't have any books I like' or 'I'll never remember to take them back.' As well as linking all the books featured to the library catalogue so a reader could borrow or request them, 4ureaders linked online and offline through a surprise book service. A reader could order a surprise book to be delivered for collection at the service point of their choice. This worked particularly well to encourage links between public and school libraries when the site was used in school and the book collected from the public library.

The temptation on a website aimed at 16-25s took the form of a Blind Date with a book. Whatareyouuptotonight* offered a menu of ten types of date, from 'Funny, witty, sharp, engaging' to 'Dark, mysterious, unpredictable, moody, sinister'. The user was then given

Developed 2001- 2003 as part of Emrald, funded by the Regional Arts Lottery Programme, supported 2005-2006 by Arts Council England. The site is archived at: **www.openingthebook.com/archive/whatareyouupto**

a choice of three possible dates. Choosing, 'Hot, steamy, passionate, one-night stand', for example, the next screen reads:

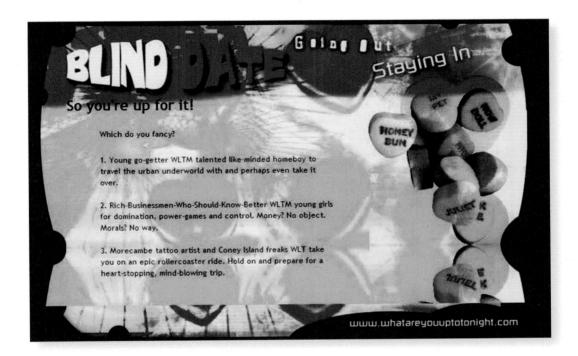

When you select one, the two titles you turned down are revealed and if you wish, you can click to borrow one of these titles instead. If you are still up for the Blind Date, you can only find out what it is by visiting a library.   The message containing this information continues the Blind Date metaphor: 'Your date will be waiting for you five days from now and will wait for you for three weeks. All we need now are a few details from you and we'll fix you up.' Blind Date was a way of hooking non-library users and drawing them in to using the service. It is more elaborate than a simple surprise book option but as a user is engaged by the playful element and their curiosity is piqued as to what the books might be, their time has already been invested and they are more likely to follow-through with a visit to the library. Their first experience of the library service through this feature was sophisticated, friendly and funny, rather than formal and impersonal. Often users did not go through to the final offline link, they simply played around to explore what was visible but this in itself acted as a great advertisement for library services - offering an experience which was very different from the average web user's perception of what libraries offer.

Local creation, global audience

The structure to deliver and update 4ureaders and whatareyouuptotonight was similar though quite different groups of library services took part. Opening the Book ran training sessions on creating reader-centred websites and getting users involved. Each library service set up a small group of staff to develop content and recruit individuals from the target audience to test and feed back on content and design. Ideas were brainstormed in shared sessions and then each service worked on specific site areas. Each authority nominated one person to be site editor; editors were trained to use the easy content management system and then took responsibility for inputting and updating specific areas. Opening the Book managed overall site design, editing and the more complex technical features.

This sharing of the workload had enormous benefits. The efforts of nine library services went into creating one quality site instead of nine separate ones. This improved the quality at all stages of building and maintenance from user-testing and feedback to keeping sections regularly updated. Each editor was asked to work for three hours per month. What each library service could achieve with three hours on a solo site would be limited but 27 hours per month of total library staff time ensured the site was constantly lively, topical and refreshed. The stimulus of working with other services and the creation of cross-service support networks were also greatly appreciated.

4ureaders was developed with one authority, expanded to two the following year and grew to involve nine at the high point of its five-year history. Whatareyouuptotonight was conceived and funded as a regional project involving nine authorities in one region, though it too recruited some additional services as it expanded. Of course, the sites were free to users and this meant library services anywhere in the world, as well as individuals, could benefit from the work done in one region. Specific connections to local services such as catalogue links and surprise books were available only in the participating services but 95% of the site could be enjoyed from any location. This enabled the sites' success but also ultimately caused their downfall.

Switch to high contrast

Scottish Readers.net

Read mòr...

...landscapes

...on the edge

...on the move

...to relax

...together

Read any good books lately?

Whether you loved it or hated it, click here to share your latest reading experience with other Scottish readers.

Scottish readers recommend

Popular Tags

provoking moving
exciting chilling
informative gripping
different educational reflective
challenging captivating
entertaining absorbing
thought romantic

About | Copyright | Contact details

One of the major challenges to locally-delivered library services is that, from the user point of view, the web has no boundaries. Online content is freely accessible from anywhere. This does not fit with the priorities and accountability structures of locally elected councils. Work done by one service will inevitably benefit its neighbours who have not contributed to its costs either through contracting external expertise or releasing staff time. While sites such as 4ureaders and whatareyouuptotonight had external funding from regional and national bodies to cover the costs, the participating services were willing to carry this burden as the work not only benefited their localities, it put the council at the forefront of web developments and raised its profile. When the development funding stage was complete, however, services became increasingly reluctant to continue the same level of support. Sites had been deliberately created to be easily refreshed with low-level maintenance but even three hours per month was hard to justify for some services. The result was that within the nine participating services, greater inequalities of contribution became apparent as the burden fell more heavily on those who were keenest.

The national reader site created and managed through Estyn Allan (Branching Out in Wales) - givemeabreak (see Chapter One, page ten) - followed the same model of shared content creation with 22 librarians from different services contributing. The site was very successful, especially in the number of users on the Welsh language side. Some keen librarians continued to refresh content after the Estyn Allan programme concluded but after 18 months it was decided the site could not continue. In Scotland, the continued

Read the Festival

Scottish Libraries working with Edinburgh International Book Festival

Cafe
Food for thought -
menus of reading...

Designed and hosted by Opening the Book

involvement of the national bodies CILIPS (Chartered Institute of Library and Information Professionals, Scotland) and SLIC (Scottish Library and Information Commission) has secured the continuation of **www.scottishreaders.net**. All 32 library services in Scotland market the site and participate in an annual offline book promotion. The site design has been successfully adapted to support different national themes each year from the Read the Festival promotion in 2004 (in collaboration with the Edinburgh International Book Festival) to Read Mòr for Highland 2007, celebrating the culture, people and landscape of the Scottish highlands.

Building in user-generated content

One way forward out of the local web dilemma is to identify what all libraries might want to offer to a wider online audience of readers and to create and share that content nationally, allowing individual libraries' web strategy to focus on local adaptations. This is the intention behind the Museums, Libraries and Archives Council sites designed to deliver the content for the People's Network Service. However, often individual library sites don't feature links to these sites, or where they do, cite them as outside links rather than core offers. The national sites - Enquire, Discover and Read - tend to exist in isolation on the library site, and don't seem to take advantage of the national offer to focus the local one, nor use the content of the national site to enrich their own.

Opening the Book won the contract to deliver the *Read* part of the People's Network service. Learning from the problems of involving library staff in content creation, the new site **www.reader2reader.net** was built on the principle of readers recommending directly to each other, a fundamental tenet of reader-centred thinking long before it was tried on the web.

Reader2reader is targeted towards the 45-65 age group, the rising retired, who were identified as a key library audience in the 2005 marketing strategy developed as part of Framework for the Future, the government's vision for libraries. This is nowhere stated, of course, so the site does not alienate users from other age groups, but the visual design and language can clearly be seen to target an older age group than whatareyouuptotonight or givemeabreak. Reader2reader is designed to create different levels of engagement for whatever length of time the viewer might have to spend. For the reader who wants an immediate, quick hit recommendation, the homepage features the covers of the most

WAKE-UP CALLS

Misunderstandings, however well-intentioned, undermine reader-centred practice. If you recognise the views below, use the arguments in this chapter to challenge them.

" Our staff aren't allowed to explore the internet at work. "

" Library assistants do not need their own email addresses. "

" None of the staff visited amazon.co.uk during ECDL training - the course concentrated on information sites as examples. "

viewed books on the site and three books recommended by another site user. These features are automated so the site is always changing. Reader2reader was also the first public library site to make use of the new technology of user-generated tags which sum up different kinds of reading experience, such as charming, compulsive and thrilling - clicking on any of these produces a list of all the books on the site which have been tagged with this word.

For users with more time to spend, the Browse section offers a number of routes into choosing what to read next. Users can view the reading recommendations from other site users and add their responses, or they can share their own recent reading experiences by inputting new titles. There are playful features such as Bin-a-Book, to which disappointed readers can despatch books which failed to live up to expectations. This feature has the more serious purpose of reassuring readers that it is okay not to have liked a book. And, of course, it shows how reader opinions vary as there is also an option to rescue a binned book if you disagree with the reader who binned it.

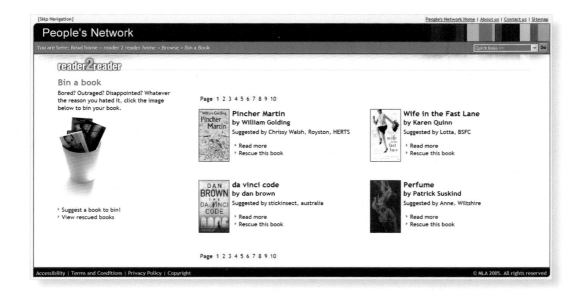

The site is moderated by users who are invited to contact the web master directly with alerts to any offensive content. Following library traditions of open access to all legal information without filtering, the Museums, Libraries and Archives Council, who funded the site, took the brave decision to risk the possibility of occasional misuse in favour of site users being able to instantly see their content appear on screen. This has proved an undoubted success with only one instance of undesirable hacking (which was promptly removed) in the two years since the site launch.

Reader2reader offered a regular, monthly live chat session for readers to share reading experiences online with other readers. Interestingly, this proved to be the least popular

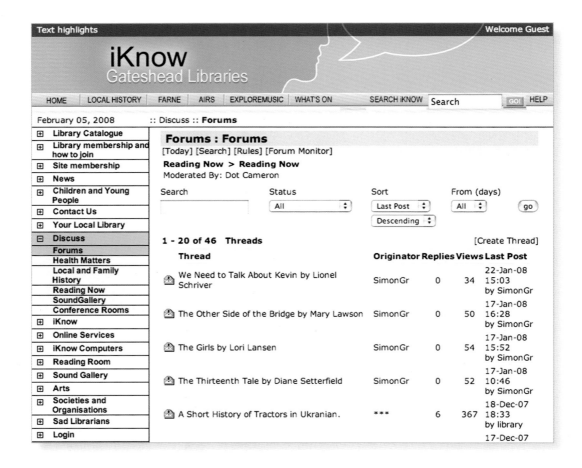

feature of the site and has been removed for this reason. All other pages on the site are well-visited but users simply did not wish to engage with online chat, even when intriguing questions for debate were trailed in advance. This may reflect the older target audience, of course, but it is also worth thinking further about what readers want and how the web delivers it. The chat room format is instant and informal; it can be lots of fun but it isn't the place for in-depth discussion. Staff involved in reader development know that many readers are looking for something deeper, they want to share opinions but not in 20-second soundbites. Live chat also requires readers to go online at a particular time when the advantage of a web reading offer is that it is available 24/7 whenever the user wishes to access it. Librarians who believe if only they could provide live chat facilities, users would flock to their sites, should find this sobering.

Online chat on library sites is most successful where it is more targeted to specific purposes. Gateshead Libraries, for example, use a discussion board and a forum area for live conferences and discussions. These are moderated by library staff and have been actively used to bring readers from groups in Europe together with those in Gateshead.

Word-of-mouse

Marketing strategies which work well offline may have little impact in the virtual world. The web has its own forms of publicity; it is a medium where the users are in control and referrals from one site to another are its life-blood. Word-of-mouse is the only way to get sites used. Word-of-mouse will recommend the innovative, the quirky, the niche - not usually characteristics of council sites. Even if libraries had the finances to mount a full web advertising campaign, this might well backfire as scepticism of hype is a characteristic of the web community.

The history of the usage of Opening the Book's most popular and long-established site will illustrate this. Press releases were sent out to all the national media and all the computer magazines when whichbook.net was launched in 2000 and received not a flicker of attention. It was the online community which built the interest. All the features in the media were from web users not general journalists. Three years after the launch, whichbook generated excellent media coverage - Literary Website of the Year 2003 on Radio 2's Steve Wright Show, features in *The New York Times* and *The Wall Street Journal*, a 5-star rating and a Silver Award in *Webuser*, the most popular UK computer magazine.

WAKE-UP CALLS

Misunderstandings, however well-intentioned, undermine reader-centred practice. If you recognise the views below, use the arguments in this chapter to challenge them.

" There's a great site for readers that we really like so we're going to try and set up the same thing on our web pages. "

" It's most important that people can find library locations and opening times on the web so we make that the most prominent thing. "

" The website isn't really a part of our service. It's just a shop window. "

This acclaim was unsolicited and entirely the result of users recommending to each other. Tracking back the online referrals to the site is a fascinating process. Postings on weblogs are crucial. One posting on the respected US weblog, Metafilter, resulted in some of the best compliments for the site and more than 2000 people jumping to whichbook from the blog to check it out. The web is definitely a community where personal opinions are shared freely. Yahoo sent an unsolicited email to say the site was 'absolutely wonderful, everyone in editorial and directory at Yahoo! is passing it around' before listing it in their Directory.

Whichbook is the only public library site to have made this sort of impact outside the library world. In every case articles mentioned the link to library catalogues - most were previously unaware these existed online - making this coverage a tremendous advert for public libraries in general.

What next?

At the time of writing, the web is growing many opportunities to influence sites, to form new communities of interest and to get directly involved in the creation of all kinds of online and offline commodities and services. The creation of virtual environments offers individuals, businesses, artists, academic institutions and public bodies opportunities to create and collaborate which are geographically, spatially or financially impossible in the 'real' world. New art forms and new fiction are constantly evolving on the web. The principal development is the way that web users are invited into creative processes, content decisions and product and service delivery. User-centred websites are rapidly becoming the norm; MySpace, YouTube, all the current web phenomena have grown by users creating their own content. The web has empowered citizen reporters, bloggers, film-makers and collaborative writers. Successful sites are ones that solve a range of problems by bringing people together. Wikipedia, the online encyclopedia that invites contributors' definitions, is a prime example. Social networking has exploded as an online phenomenon in sites such as Facebook.

Business is trying hard to find profit in these developments. Public services, however, seem entirely absent at the moment. They are stuck pretty firmly in Web 1.0 where information is posted from the inside out and consumed without any question or moderation by users. This is not surprising, as government tends to lag behind new trends, and perhaps rightly so, because often the technology is untested and the experience somewhat too raw and unreliable for officialdom. However, if local authorities and libraries are serious about belonging to the online community, it is a change they will eventually embrace.

In its user focus, reader development was ahead of the Web 2.0 trend and in the 1990s, it helped to prepare library staff for the next century. From 2000-2007, reader-centred sites created by or with public libraries were among the freshest and liveliest of any council pages. Senior library managers did not build on this advantage and missed a chance to position libraries as experts to lead councils into the user-generated age.

Now sites like **readitswapit.co.uk** offer the equivalent of a library in a much more personalised way. **www.goodreads.com** exploits social networking for readers and moves ahead of the random book review approach by enabling users to easily see what their friends are reading and to limit recommendations to those from people they know. In true

Web 2.0 fashion, goodreads.com not only allows you to create your own bookshelves of what you have read or might read, it provides a widget to add what you're reading to your MySpace profile, blog or website and the capacity to export to a spreadsheet if you wish. The prospect of library websites and library catalogues using widgets like this is some way off.

Librarians putting their hopes in Web 2.0 services may need to look first at some basic Web 1.0 delivery. Firewalls still block simple external web functionality in some councils. Reader records are not yet developing to offer customised recommendations for individual readers, alerting them to new books they may be interested in. And traditional library practice is still there on the frontline. One retired librarian in a rural location started to use the mobile service and assumed that reservations could be made online to be delivered on the mobile. But no, there was no alternative to physically going to the mobile, filling in the request card and hoping the book would come on the next visit. Staff would not even accept print-outs from their own catalogue, the information had to be laboriously copied onto the correct card!

In the future, the predictions are for a more 'semantic' web that allows the user to search more precisely and gather relevant information and personal preferences in highly customised ways. A 'convergence' of the web that welds together currently diverse media. A web that becomes accessible in different ways and many locations. A unified web that comes to the users, rather than the other way around. Future gazers talk about the web achieving a kind of hive intelligence, where the individual contributions of its users are much more available to all. The development of the web is in the direction of co-operation and equality. It will be even more important for those organisations with a presence in this environment to know how to be outward-facing.

In this context libraries need to be realistic about what they can offer online. The desire to create communities of readers is laudable but sometimes naïve. If the aim is to reach local communities, then the site needs to make very strong links with offline services, as in Essex. If regional, then ways need to be found to work together with other services in the region and possibly other regional bodies to create a unique offer. In either case it requires the dedication of staff time in the long term in writing, editing, training and support.

Libraries might consider a national effort to create and share a social networking site for readers, but why aspire to create what goodreads.com is already doing very well? In attempting to reach young people through social networking, libraries must realise they are in competition with MySpace, Facebook and whatever the new hit site with young people is in the next few years. Why should a 16 year-old use the library site to share opinions with others if they are already doing this on sites of their own choice? It is a certainty that anything that libraries build in imitation of a popular site will look out of date to young web users once it is launched. Libraries long ago faced up to the fact that, however distressing it may be, they are part of the establishment, and therefore simply not cool. Useful, serviceable, friendly they can be - and perhaps they command more respect with target audiences if they are more honest about this. Sites which offer routes to real library services, whether online or offline, will be more successful than vague promises of interaction.

Some web forecasters believe the drive to community-created sites will wear itself out. As more and more opportunities to participate are offered, users may become not only more selective but more disenchanted. Sites which can create trust in their information will be the winners in this situation. It is interesting that one of the most successful commercial sites for readers in the UK - **www.lovereading.co.uk** - has taken this line. The site offers lots of different ways into its book information but posting reader reviews is not one of them. Instead, the site relies on the expertise of a leading book trade figure for selection, organisation and introduction to the titles featured. Is there a lesson for librarians here? Is there still a place for the traditional role of 'honest guide' and are librarians missing this possibility in the desire to create imitations of famous social networking sites? Thinking hard about audiences and reading needs is the basis for offering successful services online just as it is offline. Librarians looking to web developments to take the public library service into the future should pin this mantra over their desks next to the Web 2.0 conference invitation.

Chapter 9

EVALUATING READER-CENTRED WORK

It's the last question on any form. You suspect no-one ever reads evaluation reports. Evaluation is often given lip service and is the bit tagged on at the end of the project that everyone dreads and nobody feels is useful. Evaluation can also be the staff meeting full of praise for the project when you know everyone hated every minute of it. Or there's the scenario of the key political figure who is swayed by one lone powerful voice despite the evidence of a battery of painstakingly collected statistics. Or the readers' suggestions box with only two comments in, one of them illegible. Everyone is tempted to treat evaluation cynically; why bother to evaluate?

Evaluation can be vital and powerful if you build it in right from the start and are clear on what you want to know and why you want to know it. You need to be in control of what evidence is collected and how to collect it if you want a useful tool at the end of the activity. Evaluation is the process that helps you know whether you have achieved what you set out to do and to discover what else you could do to develop your work.

Often we know intuitively whether something is working or not but subjective impressions are not enough; we need evidence to prove it to others whether they be colleagues, senior managers or external funders. And if something isn't working, we need to understand why not in order to plan a different course of action.

Evaluation is often imposed from outside. Funders and partners quite reasonably expect to find out not just if their money has been well-spent but if the project delivered the results they hoped for. Under this pressure it is tempting to resort to a blow-by-blow account of every action taken in a frenzy of self-justification! This is both time-consuming and pointless; it is much more helpful to write a short analytical report. Weigh up what it would be useful to others to know. Being clear about went wrong or what failed to work can be as valuable to others as recounting success stories.

Who will read it?

It helps to be clear from the start who the evaluation is for - the end users, the staff directly involved or managers and stakeholders with a wider agenda. All of these are worth doing but the evaluation may be shaped differently according to which is more important. For example, an evaluation of a reading group programme for the participants will check out their reactions to what is being provided, what they like and don't like, what could be changed to improve the experience. The example below and overleaf from Fife considers frequency and length of meetings, group size, the range of books and how they are chosen as well as the format and organisation of the sessions.

Reading Group Questionnaire

In order for us to provide the best service for you, we would appreciate your comments about your Reading Group. We would be grateful if you could complete the attached questionnaire and return it by (date) in the stamped addressed envelope.

Personal details
1. Which age group do you belong to?

Under 20 ☐   21-30 ☐   21-40 ☐   41-50 ☐   51-60 ☐   60+ ☐

2. Are you?   Male ☐   Female ☐

3. Which library are you a member of?..

4. Which is the closest library to your home?...

5. Were you a member of a Fife library before joining a reading group?   Yes ☐   No ☐

6. Do you borrow library books other than the reading group books?   Yes ☐   No ☐

7. Which reading group do you attend? ....

8. How often do you attend?   Every month ☐   More than 6 times per year ☐   Less than 6 times per year ☐

Your Group
9. Your reading group meets once a month. Is this?

Too often ☐   Not often enough ☐   Just right ☐   If not just right, how often would you like the group to meet?........................

10. Your reading group meets for 1.5 hours. Is this?

Too long ☐   Not long enough ☐   Just right ☐   If not just right, how long should the meetings last?..........................

11. What do you think about the type of refreshments on offer?
....
....

the venue your group meets in?

14. What do you generally think of the books chosen for you to read in the group?
....
....

15. How do you want the books to be chosen for the group?

By staff ☐   By group members ☐   A mixture of both ☐

16. Which of these would be your preferred format for the group?

All members read the same book every month ☐

All members read different books every month ☐

All members read more than one book per month ☐

Half the members read one book, half another ☐

Staffing and organisation

17. Library staff organise and facilitate your group. Would you prefer the group to run without staff being present?

Yes ☐   No ☐   If yes, would you like to help organise a reading group?..........................

18. How well do you think library staff ensure that everyone in the group gets a chance to speak?

Very well ☐   Adequately ☐   Not very well ☐

19. Are their any improvements you would like to see made to the organisation of your group?
....
....
....

Value

20. What do you get out of being part of a reading group?
....
....
....

21. Have your reading tastes changed at all since joining the group?
....
....

.... you were introduced to in the group?..................................

If the focus of the evaluation is on staff involved in reading groups rather than participants, a different set of questions will need to be asked. Midlothian Libraries formulated these as:

- *Have you read books for the reading group you would not normally have chosen to read for yourself? If yes, please give examples.*

- *Has being involved in the reading group affected the books you select for your library? If yes, please say how.*

- *Has being involved in the reading group affected the books you display in the library? If yes, please say how.*

- *Has there been any change in your confidence in the following skills areas:*

  - talking about books with customers - less confident / about the same / more confident

  - presentation skills - less confident / about the same / more confident

  - group management skills - less confident / about the same / more confident

Evaluation with group members can have immediate practical consequences for how groups are best organised to meet participants' needs. Evaluation with staff can have the effect of raising awareness of skills developed through running reading groups, development that can be invisible even to the staff involved. If the purpose of the evaluation is to gain management commitment or more resources to maintain or expand a reading groups programme, then specific aspects are the most useful, for example, the answers to the question on what people get out of being part of a reading group.

Essex Libraries undertook evaluation with Ongar Booktalk Group, a group that had been in existence for five years with two sessions in the same week, one in the afternoon in the library and one in the evening in the pub next door (both read the same book so people can swap between them as convenient). Essex wanted to test how reading groups could be shown to contribute to the Generic Social Outcomes developed by the Museums, Libraries and Archives Council to connect with the shared priorities of local and national government and social outcomes defined in health, social care, quality of life, community capacity building and the cross-departmental framework *Every Child Matters**.

Comments were gathered in discussion at the meetings and through phone interviews. Many of the opinions and emotions expressed will be recognisable to those involved with reading groups - 'You can meet a diverse range of people and hear a diverse range

Mears, Sarah, Regional Learning Network Research, 2008, Essex Libraries. *

of opinion'; 'A good opportunity for older people to meet younger people'; 'The first time I came I didn't dare say anything but after two meetings I felt confident to speak and not feel stupid.' Relating comments like these clearly to the language and concerns of wider social agendas, as Essex have done in the table below, makes it much easier for policy-makers who are unfamiliar with the concept of a reading group to understand the social role they can play in a community such as Ongar. Of course, the language of Generic Social Outcomes was not used to get participants volunteering their opinion. Questions were simple and concrete - What's special about the group? If the group wasn't running, what would you miss? It was up to the library staff to relate the answers to the policy, for example, when a young mum talked about how she 'wanted something for me, it got me out and gave me something to open my world up' this was related to the outcome of *Encouraging healthy lifestyles, contributing to mental and physical wellbeing.*

1   STRONGER AND SAFER COMMUNITIES

The Booktalk group has a role to play in *Improving inter-group dialogue and understanding.* 19 of the comments provided evidence for this. The social aspect of the group is really important for people who are lonely - young mothers or older people or people new to the area. 13 of the comments could also be categorised as *Encouraging familial ties and relationships* where individuals have not just met others at the group but made friends of group members.

2   HEALTH AND WELL-BEING

Two members' comments could be categorised as *Encouraging healthy lifestyles, particularly contributing to mental well being*, whilst at least one of the group members felt that the Booktalk group contributed to her ability to continue to *Lead a more independent life.*

3   STRENGTHENING PUBLIC LIFE

The reading group has an influence in the town. The group is visible - it meets both in the library and the pub so that non-library users are aware of it and participate. The group maintains a display in the library where non-members can read reviews and borrow books; they also publish reviews in the local press. The group organises a monthly book walk - rambling through the countryside talking books. Six comments demonstrate *Encouraging and supporting awareness and participation in local decision-making and wider civic and political engagement* and five mention links to other groups in the town, contributing to *Building the capacity of community and voluntary groups.* The reading group has hosted an author visit to the largest community public space in the town for which tickets sold out. Six comments demonstrate *Providing safe, inclusive and trusted spaces* - the afternoon group welcomes parents with small children and several members mentioned feeling safe in being able to participate and not feel stupid.

There is a great sense of pride in what the group as a whole has achieved - they won the Brains of Ongar quiz and they scored 18 out of a possible 20 in the Essex Booktalk Group of the Year Award, winning in 2007. The four criteria were openness, sharing reading via written reviews, community involvement and media involvement. Judges were particularly impressed with the way Ongar actively recruits new members.

These reading group examples show very clearly the importance of clarifying your purpose at the start. Some of the same territory will be covered in each but in very different ways. The example from Fife is of most direct use to the participants, the example from Midlothian may encourage other staff or managers to support reading groups while the example from Essex is likely to have the most strategic potential. Each is appropriate to its purpose. These examples also show the importance of interpretation and presentation of the results of evaluation. The question - What do you get out of being in the group? - may be asked in all three and may elicit similar answers. The presentation of the answers, however, will be very different in relation to the purpose.

Timing it right

Evaluation is nearly always undertaken immediately after a project finishes but this isn't the only time an evaluation is worth doing. If you want to learn immediate lessons while the project is fresh in everyone's minds, then evaluating straight away is a good idea. Evaluating six months after a project finishes, however, will give a much more accurate picture of its long-term impact. How has all that enthusiasm and satisfaction translated into continued work? What aspects of policy or everyday practice have been changed by it? This is a much tougher test - and much more useful - than a hundred completed questionnaires all saying how great it was. It is also important to test beyond the honeymoon period. When Gateshead Central Library introduced *unclassified*, a collection of on-the-edge paperbacks displayed in a separately branded browsing area, there was an increase in issues of 57%. This was a wonderful result; it could be used to demonstrate the immediate impact of the approach but not its sustainability.

Trainees who complete the Frontline course (see Chapter Six, page 202) record their immediate reaction as they finish and this is displayed on the course website as live feedback. This demonstrates openness, allows the course authors to pick up any problems and boosts the confidence of new users, as well as evidencing the success of the course and the pleasure which trainees get from doing it. But the real evaluation happens when the trainee receives an email three months later which asks in more depth how they have used the learning they did on the course and if they have been able to put it into practice.   This completed questionnaire is delivered automatically to the authority's Frontline Co-ordinator and allows them to see where the course is having an effect, where implementation may need support and what further training needs have been discovered.

Evaluating part-way through a project is also worth considering as it may throw up useful lessons which help to shape later parts of it. For example, towards the end of Year 1 of the three-year Branching Out programme, participant librarians completed a self-evaluation questionnaire on skills competency.   The section on skills, not yet addressed in the training programme, revealed very clearly the areas in which training was felt to be most needed. This had a direct influence on the training programme where sessions on fundraising, working with designers and working with reading groups were developed as the first training days in Year 2.

Who will carry out the evaluation is an important decision. Most often we evaluate ourselves; undertaken honestly this can be the most important evaluation for personal development. Articulating the lessons you have learned for yourself, clarifying what you'd do differently in the future, understanding where you could improve or change - this is likely to have the most direct effect on your practice.

Self-evaluation - Skills not yet addressed in Branching Out training

	very competent	quite competent	adequate for task	undeveloped	total no of respondents
Writing about books in a reader-centred way	0	10	10	12	32
Working with reading groups	4	6	8	15	33
Publicity and media skills	2	10	11	10	33
Designing training sessions	3	10	9	11	33
Delivering training sessions	6	10	8	9	33
Fundraising skills	0	3	7	23	33
Working with designers	0	6	5	22	33
Project management skills	5	11	7	10	33
Evaluation skills	2	10	12	9	33
Total number of responses at each level of competency	22	76	77	121	

Greater objectivity, however, is provided where someone external to a project evaluates it. The Branching Out project sought an academic partner at the outset so that the attempt to change library culture could be fully monitored through a longitudinal study from 2001 - 2004*. The University of Central England attended every training session and carried out learning reviews and skills audits with the participants. In order to evaluate the wider impact of the project, the researcher also undertook interviews with project partners and with heads of service in the participating library services in both the second and third years of the project.

This detailed external evaluation meant that claims about the impact of the project could be made with confidence and backed up with evidence. This was important in seeking further funding support from Arts Council England and in winning commitment from more heads of service who wanted to replicate the effect of Branching Out in their own services. Detailed lessons learned were also applied to the national reader development training schemes in Wales and Scotland where more of the training was delivered regionally than nationally in response to feedback on the success of working in smaller groups and negative views about the amount of time and money spent on travel to national training days.

If you decide to use external evaluators, make sure they have sufficient contact with the project and don't simply attend an evaluation meeting at the end. Consider the specific expertise you need them to bring; there is little point paying a firm of professional researchers to point out the obvious mistakes you've worked out for yourself. It is worth building a relationship with key departments at local academic institutions where there may well be students looking for dissertation topics. The library offers a wide range of possibilities for research for students taking courses in marketing or cultural studies to those involved in town centre planning or early years learning.

Peer review is an extremely valuable and underused form of evaluation. Asking staff from another library or members of another reading group to assess a similar activity to their own can be hugely productive. Just seeing how similar work is done differently in another place is a valuable lesson in itself. It can lead to skill-sharing, activity-swapping and greater co-operation in planning and working together. When the first national reader-centred promotion was set up through Estyn Allan (Branching Out in Wales), peer review was built in as an evaluation method. Estyn Allan librarians were paired together and each was asked to visit anonymously a library running the *Give me a Break* promotion (see Chapter

---

* Train & Elkin, *Branching Out - Overview of evaluation findings*, Centre for Information Research, University of Central England, 2001.

One, page ten) in their partner's service. They then met at a training day to feed back their observations to each other. The purpose of the exercise was not to score promotional success competitively but to offer an outsider's objective viewpoint of what was working well and less well, and to offer suggestions and support for any improvements. The form to record the observation was agreed as part of the training and included these questions:

- *Where is the promotion sited? Does this work? Could it be improved? Draw a sketch floorplan if this helps.*
- *Where is additional display material sited?*
- *Is any display material in sight line of the entrance?*
- *Is any of it visible on the counter?*
- *Is the display angled well in the space?*
- *Is the display kept topped up?*
- *Note any titles which you don't think should be in the display and why (wrong age group / poor condition / hardback etc).*
- *Do borrowers notice / interact with the display?*
- *Do you observe any staff interaction with borrowers in relation to the promotion - talking about it, gesturing to it, offering anything else - eg evaluation forms, surprise breaks?*
- *What do you pick up about staff knowledge / skills / attitude to the promotion?*
- *Pick something positive that can be fed back to the staff at the library.*
- *Pick something you think they could improve on and make suggestions for how this might be done.*

Tracking change

You cannot evaluate every aspect of a project or evaluation becomes the focus and not delivery. Selecting what to evaluate and structuring an evaluation process is crucial. Even a simple meeting of those involved benefits from a clear structure - otherwise people can end up simply chatting about what a good time they had or moaning about what went wrong. There are lots of templates offered by different schools of management thinking on how best to structure evaluation. To be of most use, evaluation should be bound up with what you are trying to achieve. This can be short-term in relation to the specific aims of the project or longer-term in relation to wider development.

Checking against the aims of the project is basic and always effective. How far did you achieve the aims you set out with? Were some aims achieved more than others and, if so, why? Have your aims changed in any way as a consequence? Checking against wider development is harder but has more impact in revealing the underlying trends and issues which your project is contributing to. The self-evaluation at the end of the first year of the Branching Out programme is a good example here. Branching Out set out to create agents of change in the library service. The 33 participating librarians came from very different services, they had different levels of experience and positions in the organisational structure and different levels of support from their management and colleagues. But they were all expected to make change happen. At the end of the first 12 months, the self-evaluation asked participants to list changes they were seeking to make, name the people involved, describe their own contribution and estimate how far through the change process they were at that particular point in time.

The value of this evaluation lay as much in the process as in the results. Each librarian was required to analyse specific changes, to articulate accurately what they were and who was involved, and then to honestly assess their own role and overall progress in their service in achieving these changes. How often do any of us sit down and assess wider progress in this way? Evaluation is too often treated as a quick tick box done in a hurry before moving on to meet the pressures of the next task. Branching Out did not ask participants how many projects they had undertaken or how many meetings or training sessions had been run. It required participants to assess the bigger picture; how were they affecting much wider change in the library service? In itself, this reinforced the emphasis on the aims of the project in achieving change and the responsibility of each Branching Out librarian to become an active agent in making it happen.

The results were useful in that they showed both common themes and individual situations very clearly. For example, changing book selection to ensure a wider choice for readers was cited by more than two-thirds of participants with progress towards implementation varying from 10% to 95%. Networks of support for reader development were well on the way to being established, both within services and regionally, while cascading of training in reader-centred work had hardly begun.

This evaluation acted as a benchmark to look back to assess progress at the end of Year 2 and Year 3 when it could be clearly seen how reader development had become much more centrally embedded across whole services. This benchmark was useful for individual participants, for their library services and for the project as a whole and its Board.

Self-evaluation

Branching Out is about fundamental change at a series of levels. What changes do you feel you have contributed to in Year One? Think about who you meet with/influence/network with, both inside and outside your department and authority.

What is the change you/your authority is seeking?	Who are the people involved?	What is your contribution?	How far through the change process are you? (10%,40%, 60%....)
① North Yorkshire involvement in a National Project	Self	Library & Info Show helped prove this to Director of Education	100%
② Build on existing OTB-started initiatives in order to: a) widen availability of modern fiction	Self and other Group librarians	Some source provision	60-65%
b) far from alienating traditional audience, widen their experience of fiction	"	Share Branching Out suggestions Other authority initiatives Establish readers' groups Supported Readers' Day	60-65%
c) Empower staff with custom...			
③ Ensure readi... 'Arts Experien... as important...			

Self-evaluation

Branching Out is about fundamental change at a series of levels. What changes do you feel you have contributed to in Year One? Think about who you meet with/influence/network with, both inside and outside your department and authority.

What is the change you/your authority is seeking?	Who are the people involved?	What is your contribution?	How far through the change process are you? (10%,40%, 60%....)
→ To persuade Senior Mgmnt that 'Reader Development' is an important part of our service.	Head of Culture&Tourism Head of Libraries	Canvassing during regular update meetings re: Branching Out plus proposals on paper.	90%.
→ To change books stocked to represent wider range of publishers & attract more 18-40 year olds.	Stock & IT. Manager Myself	I am solely responsible for fiction buying in West Berks. I have amassed a collection of catalogues from independent publishers, but have yet to order material not on library suppliers' lists.	50%.

continue over..../

Asking the right questions

Evaluation tends to be a numbers game. In the early days of promotions in libraries, establishing the success of new approaches in terms of numbers of books borrowed was essential. Library staff looked at the number of times a book was borrowed over a fixed period; the number of books in a promotion on loan at any one time; the number of titles in a promotion which had not been borrowed. To be meaningful, these numbers must be compared with the average performance of titles not in the promotion. In North Yorkshire, for example, the top titles in Branching Out's *Loud and Proud* promotion of gay and lesbian writing were borrowed once every three weeks. This compared very well with the best of other fiction issues and proved there was an audience for gay and lesbian fiction in libraries. In Herefordshire, the *Book of the Month* promotion with HarperCollins, which promoted multiple copies of a new book by an unknown writer in a special display, achieved an average of 2.4 issues per copy every month. All the books in *The Mind's Eye* promotion of narrative non-fiction paperbacks were borrowed in the first three days at North Tyneside Central Library and the promotion continued to have 85% of all titles on loan at any one time as it circulated to other libraries over the next year. These figures were crucial in changing staff perceptions of what books could be popular in libraries.

Librarians were also encouraged to set up simple control comparisons. In Doncaster, the titles in *The Mind's Eye* promotion were also available in the standard shelving sequence; books in the display went out twice as often. Gloucestershire placed one set of *Loud and Proud* books in a display bin and a second set on the shelves. Comparison after three months showed:

GLOUCESTER LOUD AND PROUD AFTER THREE MONTHS:

	From display bin	From shelves
No of loans	139	61
Currently on loan	23 (out of 50)	7 (out of 50)
Books which have not been borrowed	3 (out of 50)	14 (out of 50)

However, numbers aren't everything. A story told by a participant in an early reader development workshop in the south of England became a byword on this. One library assistant in the group, now in his 50s, had joined a library service as a young man where the practice was to give new staff a book to read which was not of their own choice as a part of their induction. He had found the book given to him - an adventure story - very hard going and struggled to finish it. Despite this, he stuck with the library job and worked in a variety of libraries over the next 30 years. He took a personal interest in the fate of the title he had had such a bad experience with. It seemed to be popular and was kept continually in print; every library he worked in had a copy and it was regularly borrowed. So he took to asking every borrower he came across with the book, what they thought of it. In 30 years of asking, he had never found one person who said they liked the book or had finished it! This book would have shown up in any numerical analysis as a popular title - repeatedly borrowed and repurchased.

Evaluation of the first surprise project in Birmingham Libraries revealed different complexities. This was a project to open up choices for readers who were housebound and had their books chosen and delivered by others. It originated in a training session where a member of staff told of their experience in delivering the wrong books to the customer. When the customer phoned up to report this, the staff member was full of apologies only to be interrupted with 'No, no, I'm ringing to thank you. I have just had the best read I've had in years. You delivered me someone else's books by mistake!'

From the kernel of truth about reading preferences at the centre of this story, a new project was devised called *A Surprise*. Everyone on the housebound delivery service usually received six books. Under the new scheme, they received five books, based on their previous choices as usual, but the sixth one was a surprise - something quite different from what they had had before. After the scheme had run for 12 months, an evaluation was undertaken with all the participants. Some people had liked their surprises and some had discovered new authors but there was no question that a clear majority - almost 70% - had not. But when asked 'Would you like the *Surprise* scheme to continue?' the answer was 100% in the affirmative. Everyone enjoyed the idea of a surprise and anticipated it with delight. And even when they'd had four bad surprises in a row, there was always the possibility that the next one would be just what they were looking for.

The *Surprise* evaluation shows the danger of evaluating the wrong thing. If judged on how many people liked their surprises, the scheme would have been deemed a failure. But if judged on how many people liked this way of books being presented, the scheme was a tremendous success. This is an important lesson for reader-centred promotion. It is the job of the promoter to make the choice of books tempting and enjoyable - it is always up to the individual reader to judge whether any particular title is right for them. The library can bring the book and the reader together - how they get on with each other is up to them.

On a much larger scale, the Best Value Performance Indicators used in England to evaluate local authority performance changed the measure of user satisfaction as a direct consequence of the impact of the reader-centred approach. Performance was measured through CIPFA (Chartered Institute of Public Finance and Accountancy) PLUS (Public Library Users Survey). The question in 2000 was 'If you were seeking a particular book(s) during today's visit please show if you were able to obtain it/them.' Once libraries could prove that many people were not looking for a specific book, this question was changed in 2003 to 'If you came to the library today without a particular book in mind, did you find any to borrow?'

This change gave a much more accurate measure of user satisfaction and had wide-ranging consequences. A library service which made sure that all users found what they were looking for would need to concentrate on having sufficient copies of the most popular books. (That would have a greater impact on the percentage who were satisfied than trying to have single copies of the more esoteric titles which might be asked for by single individuals.) A library service which made sure that all users found a book that satisfied them could concentrate on range, promotional techniques and staff skills as well as judging which titles must be held in greatest quantities.

Measuring quality

Evaluation based on numbers must be supported by qualitative evaluation. In evaluating reader-centred promotions, it's not just the numbers of books borrowed that count. If your aim is to open up reading choices, it is worth finding out if readers have chosen books that are new to them. This can be done by looking at the loans of new books by unknown writers. In the North Yorkshire *Loud and Proud* example above, for instance, the average of one loan per three weeks applied not just to popular writers like Val McDermid or Armistead Maupin, the same performance was achieved by a first novel by a New Zealand writer unknown in the UK, *50 Ways of Saying Fabulous* by Graeme Aitken. Comments gathered on cards in the *Book of the Month* promotion in North Tyneside emphasised over and over that readers had chosen books they would not usually take:

> *'The promotion brought this to my attention and I may well have never selected it from the shelf otherwise.'*
>
> *'Enjoyable read - very different from my usual choice of book.'*
>
> *'I would never have chosen this book as the cover put me off.'*
>
> *'I don't think I would have chosen this book from the shelf but I found it a rewarding read.'*

Kerry Wilson and Briony Train of the Department of Information Studies at Sheffield University helped Estyn Allan librarians evaluate *Give me a Break*, the first national public library book promotion in Wales. Short questionnaires were given by staff to individual borrowers who took books from the promotion. 264 questionnaires were returned across 12 Welsh library services. The results on the next page show that the promotion was very effective in opening up readers' choices.

The librarian in Merthyr Tydfil posted out questionnaires to readers who borrowed from the promotion and included a pre-paid return envelope. 48 borrowers responded. 85% of them had not read a book by that particular *Give me a Break* author before and 79% had been encouraged by the display to try something new. Individual comments showed that readers valued the display's role in helping them find something new, especially when they had limited time:

> *'It encourages me to read different topics and authors, because I never really know what I am looking for in a book so these displays really help.'*
>
> *'I like the idea of the display as I can look for new books and authors easily. I am a heavy reader and a serious science fiction reader so it was good to find something new.'*
>
> *'I have used the displays in the past as I like to see suggested authors. I wouldn't know where to look and I don't have the time to enjoy a browse.'*

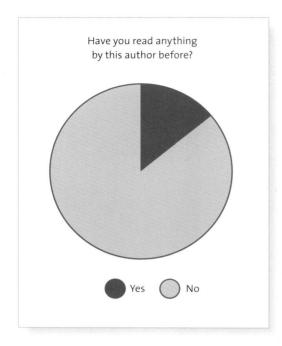

Have you read anything
by this author before?

Yes   No

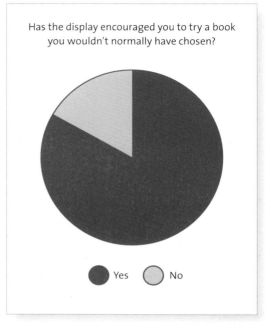

Has the display encouraged you to try a book
you wouldn't normally have chosen?

Yes   No

Analysis of 264 Give me a Break *questionnaires*

We need to be aware that any questionnaire will be filled in by a self-selected group and that those who feel positive are more likely to respond. This can be balanced by focus group research with a wider range of people or more objective observation (see Chapter Two for more information). Another objective technique is the use of a mystery shopper. Mystery shopping is used in retail and other customer services where an anonymous tester is asked to visit and report back on the treatment they receive.

It is especially useful to evaluate the quality of customer care but can also be used to evaluate a wide range of service aspects from the effect of the overall environment to joining procedures.

If you are going to use mystery shoppers, the process needs to be understood and supported by frontline staff. Everyone should know it's happening, and that the point is to improve the service as a whole and not to spy on, catch out or blame individuals.

Mystery Shopping
November 2006 – January 2007

How was the mystery shopping conducted?
- 46 libraries and 4 mobiles were 'mystery shopped'
- The Mystery Shopper used the Presentational Standards for NLIS as guidelines
- The process took 15 – 45 minutes
- During the exercise, NLIS staff were asked a number of questions:
    - I have forgotten my PIN. Can you tell me what it is?
    - Where can I find X book/DVD?
    - If I borrow books from this library, do I have to return them to this library?
    - The book I want isn't here. Can I order it from another library and collect it from this library? Is it free?

What went well ?
- Library was clearly visible from the main road
- The power display in the foyer was eye-catching
- The Chinese literature power display demonstrates the library's customer-focus
- Numerous thriving plants created a 'homely' feel
- Staff were approachable and helpful when approached

What needs improving?
- The poster on the advertising board outside the entrance looked 'tatty' and unprofessional (see image)
- The old, stained sofa in the children's area was unappealing and should be replaced with a fabric or leatherette sofa
- Poor lighting reinforced the library's 'outdated' image – use of light pastel colours and brighter lighting would create a fresh appearance
- Staff were not proactive in their customer service
    - Staff did not greet customers verbally or through eye contact as they entered the building
    - I was not approached by staff when I appeared lost
    - Staff did not confirm that they had answered my questions by asking
    ... an help you with?

The evaluation criteria used by mystery shoppers should be fully discussed, transparent and available to all staff. Norfolk Libraries used a young woman in her twenties as a mystery shopper to all 46 libraries in the county. Each library received a feedback form, detailing where they did well and what could be improved.

The biggest issue revealed across all 46 libraries concerned the first reaction of staff when a new customer enters the space. Library staff who were very helpful when approached with an enquiry were not good at giving positive signals to acknowledge customers, there was too little looking up from tasks with a friendly smile. Norfolk undertook similar mystery shopping exercises involving teenagers aged 13-16 visiting libraries and, interestingly, the main issue uncovered was exactly the same. Teenagers said they didn't expect staff in libraries to be young but they did not like the way older staff appeared to ignore them; they too wanted acknowledgement, eye contact and a smile. In Yorkshire, public and university libraries have co-operated in cross-sectoral mystery shopping. This has identified many specific areas for improvement and also provided useful evidence of high quality levels of customer care.

Quantitative evaluations should always be seen in a wider context. Many UK libraries experienced a dramatic drop in numbers of enquiries after they introduced computer self-booking systems. Clearly the majority of enquiries related to booking computers and the decrease reflected a huge service improvement not a decline in levels of service.

Audience feedback forms showed consistently that Essex Book Festival audiences were predominantly female. Festival organisers sought to increase the attraction of the Festival to men by programming more non-fiction events - biography, history, debate. Casual observation confirmed these events did have more men in the audience but the increase wasn't showing up in the audience summary breakdown. One year staff did a count by gender at male-appeal events and this provided clear evidence that more men were attending. Their conclusion was that, as reported in many audience surveys, women were much more likely to fill in the feedback form.

Measuring impact

A great deal of evaluation simply counts the numbers that are easily available. This measures levels of activity rather than any more significant results. There have been several attempts in recent years to design measures for 'soft' activities such as reading which can stand up as important when it comes to 'harder' economic analysis. The New Economics Foundation has led on this in the UK with exploration of areas such as well-being indicators and social capital.

Devon Libraries wanted to know about the impact books have on readers' lives. A simple questionnaire slip was placed in 1000 non-fiction books and 181 were returned (a very high rate compared with any similar questionnaires in the commercial sector). The questions related to the five learning outcomes identified by the Museums, Libraries and Archives Council to help manage and measure learning across the sector. These are knowledge and understanding; skills; attitudes and values; enjoyment, inspiration and creativity; activity, behaviour and progression. When the results clearly demonstrated the value to the individual borrower of reading the specific title, the regional Museums, Libraries and Archives Council supported a further project in which six authorities distributed 22,000 forms and 5,379 were returned. The evidence of self-assessed learning is very powerful:

81.4%	of books borrowed entertained the reader
50.2%	of books borrowed resulted in new insight
49.8%	of books borrowed helped learn new facts
28.7%	of books borrowed inspired the reader
19.6%	of books borrowed challenged attitudes
14.9%	of books borrowed helped develop skills
13.2%	of books borrowed changed opinions
4.2%	of books borrowed changed the lives of those who borrowed them

Using Dewey numbers to correlate with specific subjects enabled further details to be analysed. 175 books in the sample were non-fiction books on health-related topics and responses here were even higher:

34.5%	of books borrowed challenged attitudes
27.6%	of books borrowed changed the lives of those who borrowed them

Colin Bray, who initiated the work, argues that without this kind of evidence-gathering, the library's role in learning is in danger of being simply overlooked as it will not show up in measures of course attendance. 'The trend towards formal qualifications and measuring activities should not be allowed to undermine the impact public libraries have on society and the individual whenever we issue a book[*].'

Evaluating websites

Measuring use of websites has been full of inconsistencies. In the early days, numbers of hits were frequently quoted and non-web people too easily equated hits with users which resulted in vastly over-inflated estimates of use. A single website page can register five or ten hits whenever it is opened as the different components it is made up of all register separately. Never trust any site which quotes hits as a measure of use. The number of page views or, better still, the number of unique visitors will give a much more accurate picture. Bounce rate is also a useful measure of quality. This is the percentage of visitors who only visited your home page or any other single page and left again immediately. A high bounce rate indicates your site content and navigation are not working for your visitors - the more compelling your landing pages, the more visitors will stay on your site.

Web statistics packages get more sophisticated all the time so you should be able to measure use more accurately, provided the site you are part of allows this. It is easy to check visitor loyalty, for example - are you getting mostly one-off visits or are people returning several times? You can see which are the top referring sites your visitors come from. Other useful measures are the depth of the visit (how many pages they clicked through) and the length of visit (how many seconds they stayed on each page). You can check which are the top pages visited and which are the top searches made on the site. You can go into greater detail and find, for example, which keywords are most used in searches. All this information can feed back into improving your web design and structure. You can remove unvisited pages and shape new material so the needs revealed by top searches and keywords are met more quickly.

There are still lots of inaccuracies in web statistics, apart from the obvious one that people may stay on a page a long time because they've gone to make a cup of coffee. Most web stats packages ignore cached content which means if you view a page, move to another

[*] 'Measuring outcomes - Libraries inspire learning', Colin Bray, *Public Library Journal* Vol 22 No 2, Summer 2007 and 'Evaluating the impact of core lending services', Colin Bray, *Update* 5 (3) March 2006.

and then click Back on your browser to go back, that won't register as a hit on the server as it's cached on your local pc. (You can set your browser not to cache pages but this is highly inconvenient.) One local authority estimated that 10% of hits were made by Google or other spiders updating their information though you may be able to recognise this by looking at browser types. Stats packages use different methods to measure use, some are javascript based and others are weblogs - no two packages will give the same result for the same site at any one time. Some packages like Google Analytics are tied into payment systems so there is an inbuilt conservatism in reporting what counts as a page view upload as they pay out to advertisers on numbers of page views.

Because most web stats give quantitative data, many sites try to supplement this with online surveys and questionnaires to get qualitative feedback. This suffers from the same problems as offline questionnaires - there are now so many all over the web that most people can't be bothered to complete them and may be put off your site if an online questionnaire is prominent. For example, a feedback form was added to whatareyouuptotonight (see Chapter Five, page 161) and remained there for six weeks to determine, amongst other things, the age range and ethnicity of users. During the six week period nearly 40,000 individual visits to the site were recorded. Of those 40,000, only 50 people completed the online survey, although it was very short. Clearly the number of visits was a more important guide to the success of the site than the online survey.

Offering a permanent, unobtrusive route for users to feedback their views on your site is good practice. Only a few people will respond and some will have their own agenda but you may pick up useful feedback from people who like your site and want to suggest improvements. Whichbook.net receives a small amount of email feedback like this every month from different places round the world. Responding quickly to explain why the site does not offer search by genre, to debate the merits of reverse searching and to discuss possibilities for a children's version has become a key part of the site's marketing and customer care more than its evaluation.

User testing while building a site is essential; this is a case where in-depth evaluation as you go along is much more important than evaluating the finished product. Branching Out librarians involved in the development of whichbook each tested the site in different versions with key groups and fed back responses on content, design, navigation and functionality. Some tested with young adults and others with over-60s; some with confident IT users and one with a group who had never used computers before. User observation was also a key part of this work. If you ask people how they found a site after they have used it, they tend to report on their final verdict rather than how it immediately felt when they first opened it. Once we know where to click, it's hard to remember what it felt like when we didn't. To test ease of navigation we asked librarians to watch eye and mouse movements and not simply to rely on user statements about how easy or difficult the site was to use.

Evaluating training

The first area where evaluation is useful in training is to analyse and prioritise staff training needs. An assessment of the skills of librarians in relation to literature promotion and reader development was essential in planning the Branching Out project. This clear articulation of existing skills and skills which needed to be developed provided a framework for the detailed training objectives of the three-year programme. It was particularly helpful in explaining to prospective arts funders why librarians needed training in audience development for literature as it was not part of their training as librarians. The same document became a key part of successful applications for national reader development training programmes in Wales and Scotland.

1997 Skills assessment of librarians in relation to the promotion of books and reading

EXISTING :	MISSING :
Knowledge of mainstream literature	Knowledge of non-mainstream literature
Good provision of information for marginalised groups	Integration of literature from marginalised groups in mainstream audience development
Good approach to customer care	Strategies for adding value to customer service

EXISTING :	MISSING :
Good knowledge of community networks	Involvement in literature networks
Responding to articulated demands	Generating initiatives which research needs
Managing books	Managing how books are used
ICT for information	ICT for imagination
Confident relationships with under -15s and over -40s	Skills in working with 15-40s
Good at providing familiar authors for readers	Skills in opening up wider choices for readers
Good at running core services	Originating new ideas for development
Competent at responding to press enquiries	Managing press and publicity relationships
Working with allocated budgets	Fundraising for specific projects
Using quantitative performance measures	Using qualitative performance measures
Providing access to books	Providing opportunities for reader participation

More than a tickbox

Testing the value and effectiveness of training after it has taken place is a small industry in itself. Many library services use standard evaluation forms for training courses. It is worth reconsidering this automatic use as it is often not very helpful in its effect. Firstly, the frequency and ubiquity of training evaluation forms means they are given scant attention, filled in with minimal answers at great speed at the end of the day when everyone is desperate to get home or back to work. Secondly, traditional forms relieve participants of all responsibility for their own learning; the form itself encourages the belief that good training is all down to the trainer. Participants can sit back comfortably and score the performance of those who appear in front of them as in a talent contest. This can be fun but it bears little relation to learning.

It is also pretty obvious if the venue and refreshments are adequate - you don't need 30 forms to tell you that the room was too hot or the coffee was late. Inviting detailed comments here means that participants spend time telling you how the catering could be better instead of thinking about the course content and how it relates to their own working practice. Of course, people don't learn well if they are hungry but in a service where no responsibility is taken for what staff eat on any normal working day it seems very odd to suddenly invite detailed criticism of what was missing from the buffet lunch! (And anyone who has read through hundreds of these forms will tell you that there are always more comments on the lunch - positive and negative - than on any other aspect.)

	bad>					<good	COMMENTS
venue							
catering							
training materials							
Trainers/speakers							
Training methods							
Coverage of stated topics							

Traditional training course evaluation form

Evaluations which encourage participants to reflect on their own experience are more useful to both participants and organisers. Ask which sections were most useful, whether the level of knowledge expected was pitched right, is there anything you want to learn to do/learn more about as a result of attending this course?

The form below was used to evaluate the first course run in UK libraries on promoting Black British writing in 1998, shortly after the landmark MacPherson Report on the death of Stephen Lawrence had identified and defined institutional racism in the police, a definition which was taken up by a wide range of UK organisations to help improve practice. Opening the Book trainers were aware that this was a new area for many participants and wanted to find out how people had reacted to the ideas, how they felt their colleagues would react and how much they felt able to do themselves.

How much do you think the ideas/suggestions from the course can be/should be put in practice in your workplace?

All ☐   Most ☐   Some ☐   Hardly any ☐

How confident do you feel about enlisting the support of colleagues in implementing these ideas/suggestions?

Very confident ☐   quite confident ☐   not very confident ☐

List 3 things you will try to achieve as a direct result of this course when you return to your workplace.

Another approach to evaluating training is to work with course organisers instead of participants. In the second phase of the Branching Out programme, 90 one-day training sessions in reader development were run across England, enabling every library service to benefit. The evaluation form asked training organisers in each service to reflect on the impact of the course and how it fitted into the wider context in each service.

What criteria did you use in selecting who went on the course?

What did you hope staff would get out of it? Did it meet any of your training targets?

What specific things that they heard on the course do you think staff found relevant to their work? Has there been anything in particular that they found exciting or have brought back to you?

Has there been / will there be any opportunity for staff who attended to cascade what they learned to other staff?

How, if at all, will this course affect staff practice, reader development strategy or the way your service is offered?

Evaluation need not always be tied to a specific training course. Karen Strutt, the Reader Development Network librarian in Argyll and Bute, wanted to find out how far the reader development message had got through to staff in branch libraries operating in communities which were remote from library headquarters. She carried out a 30 minute discussion with a member of staff chosen at random in each of five branches, including assistants in charge of part-time libraries, full-time library assistants and a member of relief staff. She saw this as a test of her practice as much as theirs and was much encouraged by the enthusiasm she uncovered. She also used the exercise to signal the start of an ongoing productive relationship.

The purpose of the evaluation was:

- To see what is already in place
- To see how much of the message about reader development has filtered through / been understood
- To assess training needs
- To draw on ideas the staff may have
- To inspire / enable them

Five questions were devised, with five follow-up questions to be used as prompts to expand the discussion. This approach shows how a well-structured evaluation can ask staff demanding questions without being intimidating.

FIVE QUESTIONS FOR STAFF IN BRANCH LIBRARIES

1 **What do you think reader development is?**

Back-up: show three statements and ask: Can you tell me which of these most closely matches what you think it is?

2 **What messages does reader development give to readers?**

Back-up: Can you think of any ways you develop or help readers at present?

and/or If someone asks you to recommend a good read, what would you do?

3 **What is the best way of doing reader development?**

Back-up: If you had half an hour away from the desk, what could you do?

4 **How do we get the staff on board?**

Back-up: We'll be planning a number of projects for World Book Day.

Is there anything you would like to be involved in at your branch?

▶

> **5   What are the benefits of reader development to your library and its staff?**
>
> *Back-up: Would it surprise you to know that on the whole only 25% of library users can find their way around using any of the guidance we put in place? Would it also surprise you to know that many people coming into a library leave without finding what they are looking for? What can we do to help?*

Using management information

Libraries already collect a lot of data but often do not spend time analysing it. Before setting up a special evaluation, do check that the information is not already in existence. In most authorities, the existing data could be mined more frequently as an effective part of regular evaluation. Library managers with commercial experience are bringing these skills into library management. As head of service in Medway, for example, Mandy Thwaites regularly checks on cost per issue and cost per visit per branch. Footfall by hour in branches helps to plan opening hours and staffing levels. Percentage occupancy of computers determines whether they are in the most effective locations; Medway has moved them to better meet demand. Medway logs not just attendance at Baby Bounce and Rhyme sessions but number of loans resulting from each attendance. Variations between branches in all these measures have been a surprise to staff and have led to greater understanding of the staff role in marketing the service and getting it used. Medway's next challenge is to analyse the acquisition cost per new customer and the retention cost per existing customer.

Targets can be a useful incentive but make sure that you analyse more than levels of activity. A high number of requests, for example, could reflect a poor selection or presentation of stock so people can't find books that they want. A reducing level of requests could indicate that more, not fewer, customers are satisfied with your service - the numbers alone won't tell you.

It is important that the focus is not put on achieving the target at the expense of delivering the service. There is always a danger that the measure itself can distort your aims. For example, if a project has an overall target of getting participants to read six books, this gives equal value to moving someone from zero to one and from four to five when these are not equal in importance. If six is the target, it is likely that a disproportionate effort will be spent getting people from five to six to make sure they can be counted. Getting to three - which is probably more important - won't count unless you redesign the evaluation so that it does.

Using results

It is probably clear by now that a mix of tools is useful - no one evaluation method can give a complete picture. When it comes to measuring change in the workplace it can be very hard to isolate one action or element as responsible. In one small library in the north east of England, book loans rose by 13% after the single member of staff who worked there had completed the Frontline course. Can that result be safely attributed to the effect of the course? Before making that claim, the evaluator checked that there had been no special improvements to the library stock, no new furniture purchased and no other factor that the member of staff could point to.

It helps to measure the situation before action is taken with the same tools as are used after the action has been carried out. For example, it's hard to get an accurate picture of how staff skills have been affected by a training course if you don't know the level of skill they thought they had before they attended. Before and after statistics are always useful and can be very powerful.

Whatever the tools you use, there will be no point to the evaluation unless you summarise what you have learned and plan to take action. Not acting on the results of evaluation is the single biggest cause of the cynicism which an evaluation process often generates. If you aren't prepared to make changes based on what the evaluation finds, then you should not waste time embarking on it. The public sector is littered with 'bad faith' evaluations of this kind - conclusions are bland, buried or ignored. One large library service provided a powerful image for this - an entire walk-in storeroom where every cupboard was overflowing with training course evaluation forms that nobody had ever read. The librarian who described this was particularly incensed as she discovered it at a point when all stationery supplies had been stopped through budget cuts. She was desperate for multi-punched plastic folders and estimated there were tens of thousands of them in these cupboards as each evaluation form had been carefully filed in its own plastic wallet.

The results of evaluation should be presented in as short a form as possible. Most evaluation reports contain far too much description of process and far too little analysis, judgment and recommendation. Keep the focus on who the evaluation is for and its overall purpose. For example, a simple exercise in East Ayrshire asked staff to observe how customers browsed and took from the top, middle or bottom shelves. The results of *Top, Middle, Bottom* were presented on one side of A4 and convinced all staff who saw them that moving stock to the best display spots on the middle shelves was crucial. Bromley Libraries aimed to gain political support to use part of the book fund to make changes in the library environment. Focus groups of people who had not used the library for a while were set up to test out how changes in book presentation would be perceived. The difficulty of choosing from so much stock and the lack of time to browse emerged as key factors which were putting off participants from resuming use of the library. This evidence was presented to politicians as a short series of slides with statistics, quotations from focus group participants and illustrations of the environmental problems and new shelving solutions.

Evaluation can be used an excellent marketing tool. This is well-known in the shape of a feedback form on the seat at one event to find out more about what sorts of other events you might come to. But it can be more than this. Essex Book Festival always feeds back to authors and publishers after an event, including some of the comments from the audience feedback forms. This has helped to build the Festival's reputation for running well-organised events and also its ability to deliver audiences for new writers through libraries. Penguin commented that no other literature festival can deliver audiences for new writers like Essex does. And, of course, organisers can now quote that when talking with other publishers.

One reason many staff are wary of evaluation is they fear that results will be negative and they will be blamed. We are used to a culture in which feedback is often negative as people who are happy do not see a need to comment. There is little culture of praise within local government; it is hard to get concrete, specific and helpful praise from work colleagues where there is no route or expectation for it and no confidence or practice in delivering it. It is worth tackling this directly in every evaluation you undertake. In the Frontline course, for example, supervisors are asked to praise their trainee for a piece of work in each module. They must make the praise specific and useful to the trainee rather than something that can be dismissed as just 'being nice'. This is one reason the course is having such a powerful effect.

This kind of thinking has been applied on a much bigger scale in the theory of Appreciative Inquiry (**http://appreciativeinquiry.case.edu**). Originating in America and used around the world, Appreciative Inquiry is the antithesis of traditional evaluation. Instead of focusing on problems and how to solve them, AI starts from what works, what people feel good about, stories that show the organisation at its best and builds from that. AI argues that an organisation which enquires into problems will keep finding problems while an organisation which attempts to appreciate what is best in itself will discover more and more that is good. AI encourages everyone involved to voice and understand the changes and ambitions that they hold for the future of their organisation and then to go to work as though those ambitions were already achieved. Anyone who is fed up with standard evaluation processes will find plenty to think about in this model.

The most disliked evaluation is the one imposed from outside or above. Nobody involved in the work owns it, everyone fears being judged and found wanting, and every excuse is made to put off doing it. The temptation to lie is very strong - after all, who will know and who will care? This is where the greatest cynicism is shown, partly, of course, as a defence.

If you have to do the evaluation anyway, you might as well make it more useful. Concentrate on what is most helpful to you, find out something you really want to know. Then think about how to make use of this public accountability strategically. Take the opportunity to impress, to explain, to warn or to request further support. Instead of complaining, turn it round and use the opening you have been given to your advantage. How often do you get the chance to get key messages across to funders, partners, elected politicians? This may be your only moment. Even when it's not asked for, a clever strategist can use evaluation to win approval, support and resources.

Chapter 10

READER-CENTRED STRATEGY

Many library staff avoid discussing strategy. The word sounds grandiose and a bit intimidating, people feel it's going to be, at best, difficult, and at worst, irrelevant. This is partly an old Anglo-Saxon prejudice against theory - Brits prefer solving problems pragmatically and just getting on with it - combined with an understandable scepticism about management-speak. The language some strategies are written in is opaque, self-referential and so full of jargon that their connection to real life in the library can be hard to see.

The point of strategic thinking is to look up from the day-to-day tasks to consider where you are going, where you want to get to and whether the actions you are currently taking are going to get you there. We all tend to postpone thinking about the bigger picture until we have got through our current to-do lists and, of course, this is fatal as that luxurious position never arrives. Staff may support reader-centred practice in principle and they may want to see changes in the service which give it higher priority. Without a clear strategy, however, these desires will remain aspirations and not get translated into reality.

In the third year of the Branching Out training programme, each of the 33 participating library authorities was required to write a reader development strategy to take the service forward for the next three years. One service brought together the management team and the senior group librarians for a lively discussion of what they wanted to offer. The moment of reality came when the group were asked 'And where does responsibility for reader development lie within the management structure?' Without thinking, everyone present said it lay with the reader development project officer. It turned out this was a part-time and fixed-term post, funded by an outside arts agency.

The post-holder was doing great work but as it was not through the mainstream library structure, he had not been invited to the meeting. In a service with more than 50 full-time equivalent professional posts, reader development was seen as the responsibility of an attached worker. The strategic priorities shifted in that moment from aspirations for exciting outreach projects based on his work to a realisation that a different approach might be needed to change the core library culture which was largely unaffected by reader development.

Joined-up thinking

A strategy should articulate why you're doing what you're doing, why it matters and how you can get to where you want to be with least effort and use of resources. Once articulated, the strategy can be shared; it can help to explain priorities to staff and check people are not all going in different directions. It can also be used as an advocacy tool with external partners and funders.

A clear strategy will help to set priorities for daily work. Whenever there is a choice of action, a strategy should help in determining which way to go. Getting in the habit of thinking strategically, of seeing and connecting consequences beyond the immediate, gives any action taken more impact and velocity. A simple way of approaching strategic thinking is to look for ways to make connections and to join things up. When choosing between two projects or two courses of action, choose the one which will achieve two objectives at once. You will invest the same effort and get twice the result.

This approach was used successfully in creating the first national reader development promotions in England, Wales and Scotland. The librarians involved in the Branching Out, Estyn Allan and Reader Development Network programmes brainstormed target audiences and ideas in small groups and came up with lots of possibilities. Many of these could have made good one-off projects but the purpose of the national promotion was to embody the overall changes the training programme was seeking to make. The promotion would provide a vehicle for testing and delivering these changes, making them concrete, visible and understandable for library staff, readers and other partners.

All the ideas from the brainstorm were scored against key strategic aims:
- developing the skills and experience of library staff beyond their current roles
- promoting books outside the mainstream bestsellers and with younger appeal
- connecting books and ICT
- potential for useful partnership with other agencies
- ability to contribute to longer-term change in the library service

Few project ideas scored highly on every criterion but some emerged as much more strategic than others in terms of the number of objectives they could deliver.

WAKE-UP CALLS

Misunderstandings, however well-intentioned, undermine reader-centred practice. If you recognise the views below, use the arguments in this chapter to challenge them.

" Senior management team is waiting for the reader development librarian to write the strategy. "

" Everyone thinks the service is customer-centred. "

" Your goal is to increase issues. "

In Scotland, the project idea with the highest score in 2003 was promoting books and reading to people aged 18-30 who came to the library to use computers but did not borrow books. In most libraries the People's Network computers had been installed together in one space, often a separate space from the main adult lending collection.   The computers were pulling in a new audience of young people to the library but this audience was not engaging with the books. *Print Options*, as the project was titled, put books within sight and touch of everyone using pcs in the participating libraries. Small acrylic stands holding four paperbacks targeted to the age group were placed next to every pc in participating libraries. The promotion title was also a website **www.print-options.net** which gave simple information about the library service, details of how to join if not a member, and linked to online catalogues and interesting reader sites. Instead of leaflets or posters, there were business-sized advertising cards which had space to record dates and times of next computer sessions booked.

It was recognised that this was a challenging promotion for staff to undertake. It required negotiation with IT and lifelong learning staff to gain access to physical and digital space which was used for a different primary purpose. It involved learning about the tastes and preferences of 18-30 year-olds and becoming more knowledgeable about the books and websites which might appeal to them. It meant staff coming off counter and taking responsibility for topping up stock throughout the day. It crossed boundaries between book-based and computer services which were often kept separate. The whole project was a risk and an experiment; there were no guarantees that effort invested would result in success.

The promotion was chosen because it had the potential to meet so many strategic objectives. The results were highly variable - in one island service, the promotion was very successful, in another seaport it turned out that most internet users were offshore from

sea vessels and English was not their first language. One city gained new library members while another found the books simply weren't taken. But everyone learned from the experiment. The strategic value of the project did not lie only in its success with users. The library service, like most large bureaucracies, is risk-averse and does not experiment enough; the message that trying things out is worth it is a very important one. And even 'failures' can be adapted; the service where nothing was borrowed moved the promotion to the main library counter and found that the books flew out, demonstrating that the edgy non-mainstream books chosen to appeal to younger IT-savvy adults, did have an audience in libraries.

ABM-utvikling, the Museums, Libraries and Archives Council in Norway, used the development of the Ønskebok website strategically. When Eva Haga Rogneflåten saw

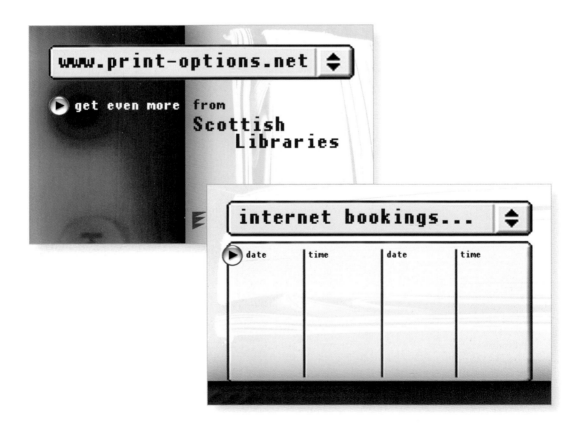

whichbook.net, she understood the potential of the site not only in its appeal to readers but also in the way it could change the traditional role of librarians. A training programme introduced 66 librarians across Norway to new ways of talking and writing about books, gave staff a non-judgmental language to discuss books they didn't like and opened up new ways of engaging with young audiences. These librarians have become a new national network in Norway, sharing and cascading skills, values and attitudes.

The Ønskebok site was also used as a focal point for discussions with library system suppliers who were moving to openURL; it became the test site for author-level web catalogue links. The site prioritised a 14-25 audience and new links were made with publishers and authors who wished to get their titles featured. The whole project was managed with flair to change the image of what a library is and does for the participants, the partners, the target audience and the media. It was Eva Haga Rogneflåten's strategic planning, and not coincidence, that led to Ønskebok being the first Museums, Libraries and Archives Council project to get coverage on national television news.

Types of promotion

Reader-centred promotion	Stock-centred promotion	Branded promotion (publisher, prize)
Starts from a reader need or preference or hook	Starts from a stock subject or category	Starts from a brand identity
Brings books from different parts of the library together in a promotion	Highlights one subject or category, can pull it out of Dewey	Concentrates on the brand
Aims to tempt people passing to try something they would not otherwise come across	Aims to fulfil customer expectations	Aims to persuade customers to buy titles which are part of the brand
For browsers and impulse choosers	For readers who know what they like	For readers who want to be part of national brand
Wide concepts make topping up from existing stock easy	Can be scaled to size of subject holding	Requires specific titles (libraries can extend to previous brand selections)
Uses unknown single book covers	Uses known single book covers	Brand is more visible than cover
Leaves books most in demand on the shelf where people expect to find them	Puts books most in demand centre stage	Sells the brand recognition
Uses catchphrase/colloquial language to contrast with library guiding and signal difference	Uses recognised terminology, traditional, direct, formal, clear	Uses national brand recognition
A library-based concept - turns the lack of multiple copies of up-to-date titles into a positive by going in a different direction	Library and retail concept	Retail concept

A clear strategy will help a library service to make decisions in planning a promotional programme and to explain these decisions to staff, users and other stakeholders. There are now many promotional opportunities in the UK for libraries to buy into; in choosing which to invest in, it helps to be clear about the benefits. A promotion like The Reading Agency's *First Choice*, which aims to tempt unconfident adults to get into reading, starts from reader needs and fulfils a reader-centred strategy more than a promotion, say, of a major prize shortlist. The table opposite shows the key differences between reader-centred, stock-centred and branded promotions. All these approaches can be successful and well-resourced services may well run a mix of all three. The reader-centred promotion, however, is the one which meets needs which are not met anywhere else. It is also the one which gives libraries a unique role in the wider culture.

Applying strategic thinking can help in deciding the balance of a promotional programme, and the investment of money and staff time which will follow. One technique is to ask what the results would be if the library service did or did not do the promotion. It is also worth looking at value over a longer period. Branded promotions have built-in obsolescence, organisers want to sell you new materials the next year so it is not in their interest to provide anything more lasting. Reader-centred materials can be used again and again - concepts like *Departures* (London Libraries Recommends) *Mindscapes* (Well Worth Reading) or *Take a bite* (Opening the Book Promotions) can be given fresh appeal each year by using them with different books.

The cost of promotions is not just the purchase of materials, it is the staff time spent in managing them. If you buy into a branded promotion every year for ten years at a cost of, say, £1000, at the end of the period you will have spent £10,000. What will be different at the end of those ten years, will you have new readers as a consequence, will you have widened reading choices? Could you have reached those same results more easily and with less expenditure by another route? How else could you spend that £10,000 to achieve your objectives? These are useful strategic questions to consider before automatically assuming that investment in a promotion is a good choice.

Branded promotions have a commercial agenda so their organisers will seek to persuade you to invest time and energy to promote their books. Promotions from national charitable organisations have modelled themselves in the same way and use the same techniques to achieve sales. There is no equivalent external pressure to undertake reader-centred promotions. If you decide that your service should prioritise or simply include reader-centred promotions, it will be important to explain why in your strategy and to evaluate annual programme choices against your strategic objectives. Otherwise, reader-centred work will always be elbowed out by the opportunities and pressures of participating in larger, more traditional programmes.

The most successful branded promotion of recent years in the UK, in both libraries and bookshops, has been the Richard and Judy Bookclub selection on television. This relies on the strength of the Richard and Judy brand but, interestingly, it has succeeded by selling the reading experience rather than the writer, publisher or theme. Richard and Judy and guests discuss the chosen books not as critics or literary presenters but as individual

Results of the library undertaking the promotion

READER-CENTRED PROMOTION	STOCK-CENTRED PROMOTION	BRANDED PROMOTION
More people take out a book which is not a bestseller	People who like this area of stock take a book from the promotion instead of another title	More people take out a branded book instead of another title
More people take out a book they did not plan to take		Fewer people buy a branded book
Maybe a few people take out a book who otherwise would not have taken anything*	Maybe a few people who have not tried this area of stock take out a book*	Maybe a few people take out a book who otherwise would not have taken anything*

*Interviews or questionnaires would be needed to prove these

Results of the library not undertaking the promotion

READER-CENTRED PROMOTION	STOCK-CENTRED PROMOTION	BRANDED PROMOTION
None of these people would have taken these books without the promotion	Bookshops continue to offer stock-centred promotions	The success of the branded promotion is not affected
		Some readers who would have borrowed, buy the titles instead
		Some readers who would have borrowed, take other titles instead

readers. The honesty and diversity of personal opinion have led to greater interest and trust from an audience, and far greater impact on sales, than any previous books in the media project. Oprah Winfrey's Book Club had the same effect in the USA. For libraries, there are problems of having enough copies (as with any branded promotion with a small list of titles) but the shared values of the reader-centred approach could justify treating a promotion like Richard and Judy differently from other branded promotions.

Competition

Strategic thinking always involves considering your own service in relation to its nearest competitors. In terms of the book offer to customers who does it best? Libraries offer internet access and information services, where the competitors are different, but in relation to the book offer the main competitors are bookshops and supermarkets.

A list of key factors where customers compare how libraries, bookshops and supermarkets perform might include the following (overleaf):

Bestsellers	easy access to the most popular books
Range	the widest choice possible
Value	the best price
Trying something	opportunity to taste something without paying
Reader advice	direct and indirect activities to help readers make choices, including how the books are organised, promotional activities and how individual direct enquiries are handled
Environment	an attractive environment to linger in

Surveys show that more people find it easier to find what they want in a bookshop (both physical and online) than a library and that bookshop staff are seen to be more knowledgeable about stock than their equivalents on the library floor. (Library expertise tends to be in the backroom rather than available on the floor.) The best libraries will easily beat the worst bookshops here but an honest assessment of strengths could not claim that libraries help people choose better than Borders or Amazon.

Some library environments, especially in new or refurbished buildings, compete well with bookshops but across the sector as a whole, bookshops currently win here too. *Change in store*, an MA thesis by Helen Cartwright, used questionnaires and focus interviews with customers of libraries and bookshops in five major English cities. The bookstore was rated more comfortable by both groups[*].

Taking this knowledge into account, library services can evaluate their relative positions in relation to competitors. The table opposite sets out how the positions might appear in the UK in 2008. The library service can make strategic choices of where to invest to make impact in a competitive market. To compete with supermarkets to be the best at offering bestsellers is not a sensible choice - Tesco and Asda will win this competition every time. From the table comparison it would make sense to promote range and value as the competitive strengths (the widest choice, easy to try and all for free) while investing in improving environment and reader advice to be more competitive. The library service has the potential to be better than bookshops in both those areas and it is already stronger than supermarkets in these aspects.

As well as 'Who does it best?' a useful question to ask is 'Where is the best place to do it?' The answer may not always be the library. Objective analysis of where best to reach adults

[*] Cartwright, Helen, *Change in store? An investigation into the impact of the book superstore environment on use, perceptions and expectations of the public library as a space, place and experience*, University of Sheffield, 2001.

Who does the book offer best in the UK in 2008?

	LIBRARIES	BOOKSHOPS	SUPERMARKETS
Bestsellers	3rd	2nd	1st
Range	1st	2nd	3rd
Value for money	1st	3rd	2nd
Trying something without paying	1st	2nd	2nd
Reader advice	2nd	1st	3rd
Environment	2nd	1st	3rd

with low literacy skills would not put the public library at the top of the list. Public libraries make excellent partners for adult literacy work (see projects like The Vital Link **www.literacytrust.org.uk/vitallink**) and they have had a demonstrable effect on the quality of materials published. Going to the library is clearly a good idea in any literacy initiative but it may not be the best place to make the first offer. It's a bit like expecting to reach arachnophobes at the insect house in the zoo or people who have always lacked confidence to drive at a car showroom.

This explains why many library services had poor results with the BBC's RaW (Read and Write) promotion in 2006. Libraries invested in appropriate books and displayed them prominently under the RaW banner in the best position near the entrance. Staff assumed that with the BBC publicity that the books would fly out; in practice, issues were low. The library's regular readers, who considered themselves confident, mostly assumed the promotion was not for them and walked past it. And watching a TV programme was not enough to encourage many readers with low confidence to brave the library and make a choice in such a public visible way. Library services with clearer strategic thinking anticipated this, made the same investment in materials and used them in more targeted ways to reach the audience.

What are your goals?

So far we have been looking at examples of specific choices where thinking strategically can help. All of these small choices ultimately depend on how the library service defines its main goals in relation to reading. This is where a written strategy document can be useful. Strategy is more evidenced, of course, by what you do than by what you say - actions are more important than rhetoric. However, the process of creating and consulting on a written strategy can itself help to sharpen everyone's thinking.

One weakness of many written strategies is the loosely aspirational quality of the main goals which can render them meaningless. Do you know of any organisation which actively sets out to make people read less? Another is that they can sound self-serving. The goal of getting more people to use libraries needs to explain why this is a good thing; otherwise it looks as if it is simply to keep current staff in employment or to make the library service more important.

A strategy should reflect the community the organisation serves. The Reader Development Strategy for Birmingham Prison, for example, identifies the core audiences within the prison as Basic skills students, Emerging readers, Reluctant readers and Experienced readers and outlines actions appropriate to the different needs of each group.

Many strategies use Opening the Book's definition of reader development as a starting point and set out the active steps they intend to take to:

- increase people's confidence and enjoyment of reading
- open up reading choices
- offer opportunities to share reading experiences
- raise the status of reading as a creative activity

Some authorities seek to link their work with adults and children in one strategy. Nottingham City, for example, added to the four objectives above:

- encourage a love of reading from the earliest years
- enable more people of all ages to develop the reading habit

The Get London Reading strategy, agreed by all 33 public library services in London, aims to link reader development work with literature development and added:

- cementing the link between readers, writers and publishers

This strategy also recognised the importance of staff training as one of its five main objectives in:

- giving library staff confidence to support library readers

WAKE-UP CALLS

Misunderstandings, however well-intentioned, undermine reader-centred practice. If you recognise the views below, use the arguments in this chapter to challenge them.

❝ *Reader development is a strategic aim with no budget.* ❞

❝ *The reader development librarian is an entry-level position.* ❞

❝ *The reader development group reports to senior management team twice a year.* ❞

All of these goals make an assumption that reading is a valuable thing to do and that libraries are well placed to encourage it. A written strategy will need to include justification of both these assumptions, see the examples shown overleaf from the East Midlands and Get London Reading.

2. What is the unique role of libraries in supporting reading?

Libraries are welcoming community spaces in which to meet, browse, read and study. Books can be borrowed free of charge and specialist and out of print titles obtained.

Libraries offer:
- The opportunity for risk free experimentation with reading
- An open, non-commercial and friendly atmosphere
- Helpful and expert staff to guide and support reading[10]

They also offer:

- A wide range of opening hours
- A greater range of titles than bookshops including access to backlist material as well as current titles.
- Materials in a wide range of formats giving th

ANNEX B

The value of reading

Reading is a basic human right. The ability to read opens a connection between the individual and the wider world, an unusual connection in that the individual is in control. The reader chooses what to read, how to read, where to read, when to start and stop, how much effort to make, what to believe or not believe. Reading is an empowering activity, not just because of the content we assimilate, but because the means of assimilation is itself an exercise in independence.

People read everything from screens to signs to sauce bottles. But above all, people read books. 90% of all households in the UK read books, 70% at least once a week.
And despite all the competing claims on leisure time, 40% of people say they read more than 5 years ago, 40% say the same, and only 20% say they read less than five years ago.
(Source: Book Marketing Ltd and The Reading Partnership *Reading the Situation*, Library and Information Commission, 2000)

Motivations to read are as various as individual readers. We read to find out about life and to escape from it; to turn up the emotional temperature and to turn it down again; to explore places that are distant and those close to home. We can do an' or al'
at our own pac

Extracts from Get London Reading (top) and East Midlands Reader Development Strategy

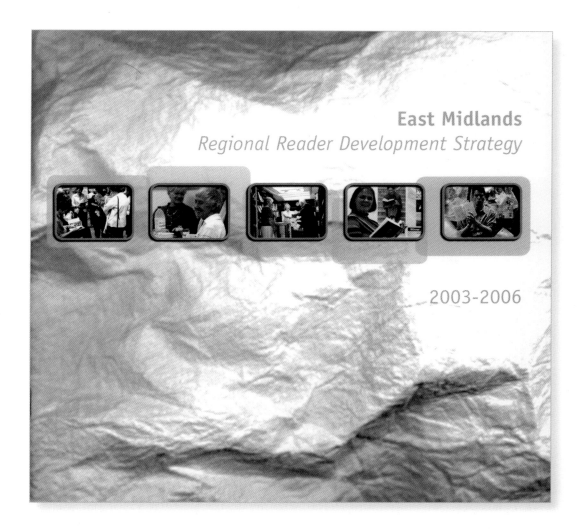

Entitlement and choice

Many strategies open with a first objective 'to get more people reading' or 'to widen participation in reading'. This is fine as long as it is not implied that people who don't read are somehow inadequate. If people reject your reading offer because they prefer to spend time doing something else, this is their right. If they reject it because your offer is a poor one, then you have a problem you should tackle. If they reject it because for some reason they feel not entitled or they are unaware they could take it up, this is definitely an area you should address.

If you include 'Get more people reading' you need to be able to answer the question 'Why?' If the answer is 'Because not enough people are using their imagination' or 'To make them mentally healthier' or 'To help cross-cultural understanding', there is then a further question - are libraries and reading the best way to deliver that goal?

WAKE-UP CALLS

Misunderstandings, however well-intentioned, undermine reader-centred practice. If you recognise the views below, use the arguments in this chapter to challenge them.

" Reader development is written into job descriptions but nobody knows what it means. "

" The reader development librarian is not sure what reader development means. "

" Staff all agree that reading makes you a better person. "

A strategy
for London's
Libraries

GET LOND

Readers For Life
A Reader Development Strategy for public libraries
in the North West Region 2005-2008

A reader-centred strategy should avoid proselytising - reading is not a religion. Many people live fulfilled and creative lives in which reading does not play a big part. (Functional literacy is quite another matter; anyone who cannot read to a basic level will be disadvantaged in our society, whatever their intelligence.)

Alternative ways of thinking about 'Getting more people reading' might be:

- offer every individual in xx area a quality reading experience
  - *this could go on to prioritise and list actions to reach different types of individual*
- break down barriers which stop people reading
  - *this could then prioritise and list actions to overcome barriers such as geography, class, education, culture, disability*
- offer a reading experience to every individual in xx area that they can't get anywhere else
  - *this would start from what is unique about the library offer of reading and prioritise and list actions in relation to that*

If the library service is actively involved in literacy work through projects like The Vital Link, then linking this to the overall reader-centred strategy makes sense. Leicestershire added:

- contribute to the raising of literacy levels

Libraries should, however, be careful of over-claiming in this area as evaluation of their contribution is likely to reveal that it is not central to the library function. Summer reading programmes encourage children to borrow books but they don't teach children how to read. Libraries provide books and venues for adult literacy but they don't employ adult literacy tutors. If the raising of literacy levels was adopted as the primary objective of reader-centred work, all of it would have a much more educational agenda, and many of the successful, imaginative reader-centred projects described in this book would not be a priority.

Many strategies use the term reader development as originally coined by Opening the Book to clearly distinguish this professional activity from learning to read or adult literacy work. Others prefer to use reading development, referring to the activity rather than the person. It's not worth getting too tied up in the semantics of what the work is called; it's more

more important to get on with doing it. Opening the Book often uses reader-centred as a more easily understood phrase than reader development. This keeps the focus on the person more than the skill. One way to keep a strategy reader-centred is to start from what customers have a right to expect rather than from what you want to offer. Wiltshire used this approach to frame their public statement on adult fiction stock in 1996.

Wiltshire
COUNTY COUNCIL
EDUCATION & LIBRARIES

Adult fiction Policy Statement

Through their local library the customers of Wiltshire Libraries have the right to expect access to:-

A broad range of general fiction

Classics and set texts

Special interest fiction

The current best sellers

A representative selection of first novels

Fiction written in a foreign language

A broad ranging and frequently changed stock of poetry

A broad range of fiction in large print and on tape

Staff with a specialist knowledge of fiction

Book news and information

In addition to the above they also have a right to expect libraries where books are arranged to enable ease of use and selection: fiction displays as appropriate: books in a good physical condition.

A year later, Leeds staff listed readers' rights on the opening page of their Readers' Strategy and included:

Readers have the right to expect:

- to have the opportunity to browse
- to see a wide range of reading materials
- to make choices
- to share their experiences with others
- to be stimulated
- to escape from everyday life into a world of imagination
- to experience other worlds, cultures, times and places
- to be challenged

Understanding audience development choices

Most strategies will include objectives about increasing the audience for reading and for libraries. For these to be more than platitudes, you will need to make choices about which audiences you mean and how you intend to do this.

A helpful model for understanding audience development is taken from arts marketing[*]. At the centre are the users of the service, the Attenders. In the next circle are the Intenders - people who like what you do, think you're a good thing and always mean to use your service but somehow never get around to it. Outside that are the Indifferent, people who don't know or care about your existence, and right on the circumference are the Hostile - people who dislike or object to what you do.

The circles are of different sizes for different organisations but the basic principle holds true - the further towards the edge of the circle, the more time and resources are needed to attract an audience. The easiest way to increase audiences to attend arts events is to persuade the Attenders to come more often. The next easiest is to convert an Intender to make a visit. Persuading the Indifferent is a much harder job and changing the minds of the Hostile is a very tall order. Marketing campaigns for most arts venues can be seen to target Attenders and Intenders with subscriptions and incentive offers of various kinds.

[*] Diggle, Keith, *Guide to Arts Marketing*, Rhinegold Publishing, 1984.

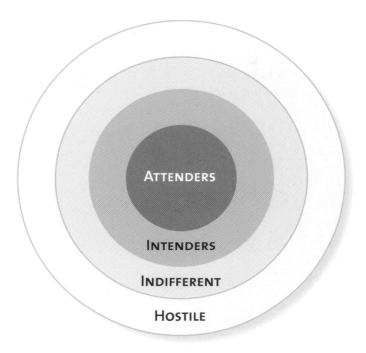

The library service has fewer Hostiles than most organisations but the Intenders and the Indifferent are large circles. The same rules apply that the easiest way to increase usage is to persuade existing borrowers to take another book, the next easiest is to persuade someone who used to the use the library to come back. Converting Indifferents into users is much harder. Commercial organisations plan their marketing to appeal to the centre of their target user audience, they don't waste any resources on Indifferents or Hostiles. Publicly funded services have a duty to provide a service for everyone in their area so they cannot do this as a commercial organisation would. But they also have a duty to spend public money efficiently and effectively so must think hard about their choices and be able to articulate clearly why they spend where they do.

A useful adaptation uses the same thinking to express the audience for libraries and is shown overleaf.

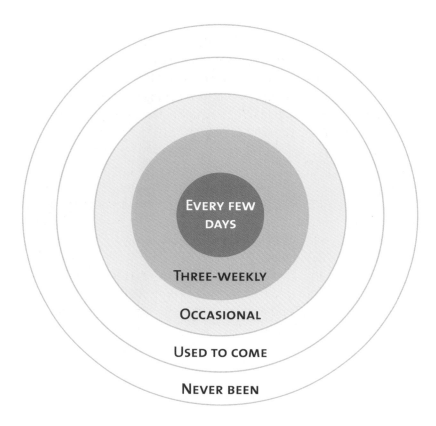

Some library customers are regulars - they come in every day or several times a week, for study, for company, to structure their time or because they don't have other places to go. Visiting the library frequently can be part of a regular routine for audiences as diverse as students, pensioners, parents and carers with pre-school children, refugees and local history enthusiasts. 'Three-weekly' customers come usually once every borrowing period to change their books. Visits by 'occasional' customers are triggered by specific and particular needs - a book on a particular health issue, for instance, or connected to a place you're going on holiday or an audiobook for a long car journey. These customers don't come back until another, probably quite different, need triggers another visit.

The 'used to come' category is very large in public libraries, especially amongst those over 30 who may well have been introduced to the library while at school. MORI surveys of non-users always show substantial numbers who have visited libraries in the past. Libraries' own member records show this too. UK libraries refer to this audience as 'lapsed' users, a dreadful description which should be discouraged. It implies that non-use is a temporary phase with full use likely to be resumed again at some point in the future - a wholly inaccurate perception. Worse, it has religious overtones, suggesting these people have fallen from grace and will return as soon as they recognise the error of their ways. The word 'lapsed' places the responsibility for leaving firmly with the customer, it gives library staff false comfort and prevents libraries from properly examining what it is that has driven customers away.

The 'never been' group has always included more working-class people than middle-class. In the last ten years, it includes more young people, as programmes of school visits to libraries have been squeezed out of the curriculum, though young people in further and higher education tend to be library users, especially for the internet. Socially excluded individuals and groups with multiple disadvantage are nearly always 'never beens' though the library service has an excellent track record in successfully reaching individuals within specific groups who may be thought to be socially excluded - housebound people, prisoners, those with mental health problems, refugees, homeless people. Black and ethnic minority use of libraries is proportionately higher in relation to population.

Conflicting goals

It can be seen that this circle diagram works exactly like the Attenders, Intenders, Indifferent and Hostile. The further out from the centre you go, the more effort and resources will be needed to make an impact. Library managers have clear choices about the balance of investment in each of the circles. The decision is up to each service to make in the light of local political policies and priorities. Your Reader Services Strategy could articulate why you are investing as you are in each circle.

Many reader development activities add value for the audiences in the first three circles. Most activities which take place in the building - promotions, reading groups, events - sit here. Reader development strategies can articulate what is offered and why. For example, one Scottish library service is aware that its programme of reader and writer events does not serve large numbers but it is seen by participants, funders and elected members as adding substantially to the cultural offer made to residents in an area without big-city arts provision. Instead of claiming that the events programme will increase the library audience, (a claim which will inevitably fail) the strategy articulates the purpose and rationale for events in terms of their value to the local communities.

Investing in refurbishments which aim to change the image and perception of the library, and present the reading offer differently, will have an effect on the 'occasionals' and can reach the 'used to come' and some 'never beens' if the change is physically visible from the outside or creates a lot of attention so everyone is talking about it. Of course, refurbishment improves the environment for the 'three-weekly' and the 'every few days' too, but the improvement may not be as crucial to maintaining their levels of satisfaction as it is to the 'occasionals' and 'used to comes'. And refurbishment may cause a loss of satisfaction to some of the frequent users if it results, for example, in much higher levels of use and noise. If a customer has been used to spreading over two or three desks because the library study area was never full, they may not be happy with an influx of new users. Strategic planning will help to anticipate and deal with this.

Events for adults in the library do not reach many 'used to comes' or 'never beens' - this is easily established by questionnaires or a simple scan of known faces. They may result in some new members joining but again the numbers are small. Some services have successfully attracted a quite different crowd from the usual by programming something not expected in the library. The problem here is sustainability; you may be able to pull in 150 young people to a large city-centre library by transforming the library for one night into a venue for local bands but what can you put in place to attract them back? You could make connections to music that can be borrowed or downloaded or perhaps offer a space where music can be listened to and discussed.

If you want to reach the 'never beens' you must go to where they are rather than expect them to come to you. The most successful library project in the UK that works at the outer edges of the circle is the Bookstart programme to reach babies and young children. Bookstart gives a pack with free books, plus information about the importance of reading to your baby and how to join the library, to the parents or carers of every eight month-old baby in the country. This is done by partnership working between a national charity (Booktrust), children's library services and the national network of health visitors. The reading offer is successfully piggybacked on the health visitor support to parents; the point of intervention is one that already exists as every baby must be brought for a check up and health visitors visit every new baby at home. The scheme has now expanded to connect with early years' providers and two further packs are given, one for toddlers aged 18-30 months and another for children aged three to four.

Bookstart has been a tremendous success in its impact on children and families (see **www.bookstart.org.uk**). The factors which make it work for libraries, despite funding crises at different points in its history and an increased workload for library co-ordinators, include clear objectives and philosophy, long-term planning, mature partnerships and high quality, sustained delivery. To carry out significant work at the edge of the circle, this is what's needed. Short-term one-off projects will not have lasting impact.

The pressures on library services to meet different demands can lead to confused and muddled thinking about the choices in audience development. The goal of increasing visits and issues is in direct conflict with the goal of reaching out to the 'never beens' on the edge of the circle. There are very good reasons for doing work on the edge of the circle but the work should be done for its own value not as a way of increasing performance at the centre. Some librarians present going to the 'never beens' as the route to reversing the decline in book loans - this is simply wishful thinking. There have been some highly successful projects working with specific groups - children in care, disaffected young people, elderly people in day centres - but the numbers are small, compared with the core audience of the library service, and even a massive success in these areas will fail to revitalise the library's role in the wider community.

The resource required to win new readers at the circle's edge means that the numbers will never be large within the current structures. The work may be exciting and valuable but it will not deliver an increased audience without a major redistribution of resources. A strategy which prioritised working at the edge of the circle would need to disinvest in the building-based service and offer more flexible options which meet people where they are. The service which has come closest to trying this in the UK is the London Borough of Tower Hamlets in its Idea Stores programme.

Tower Hamlets undertook a major programme of research and consultation in 1999 to understand why use of libraries had dropped to 20% of the population, despite the high number of libraries per head of population and surveys showing 98% of people questioned thought libraries were important. They discovered that having a library on every street corner, the vision of the 19th century founders of the library service, did not make the library accessible. Engagement depended on location, image and how the library fitted into today's lifestyles. Instead of designing libraries as major civic centres, Tower Hamlets argued for retail vernacular architecture in a decentralised programme, where services would move with the times as retail outlets do. The Idea Stores brand would be the constant - easily understood, inclusive and iconic. The programme has been tremendously successful in attracting new audiences into libraries - both visits and loans have tripled at the new Stores.

Tough choices

A strategy is a plan, or a series of plans, which converts policies into action. The way that is done will be influenced by wider issues in the management of the library service. Some authorities, for example, have recently opted for a marketing-led library service, using commercial expertise to improve understanding and communication of the library brand values to target audiences. This approach aims to the centre of the circle and expands out from there; accurate analysis and segmentation enables budget spend to be targeted towards potentials rather than existing satisfied customers. Others argue for the role of the library in community cohesion and social inclusion, involving local people more actively in planning, design, delivery and assessment of services and concentrating especially on groups and individuals who are 'hard to reach'. Overall plans and performance targets may be set in relation to policies like these and will provide a context for strategic choices in reader development in a specific service.

Your strategy should articulate the wider policy context it connects into. If you can show how your objectives help to deliver other people's objectives, those people are more likely to support you. There is no need to stretch the connection by over-claiming. Libraries and reading have such a broad social, cultural and educational role that it can be genuinely argued they support a wide range of objectives from creative enterprise to health and wellbeing. Reader development work across the UK has benefited hugely from the arts funding system, both regionally and nationally. This investment did not come about by chance; it happened because Opening the Book led a strategic approach to demonstrate the role libraries could play in audience development for literature.

Read

T'is the good reader that makes the good book.
Ralph Waldo Emerson

Reader Development in Yorkshire and the Humber

Our key priority areas are:

Skills for Life

Reading is one of the most vital life skills, which anyone can possess. It unlocks knowledge and understanding of the world around us and has the power to transform and shape lives. Libraries in this region support individuals to develop their reading skills and have shown that reading is key to improving other essential life skills.

More visits are made to libraries than to museums, galleries, the theatre, the cinema, the UK's heritage sites and football matches combined.

Reading is to the mind what exercise is to the body.
Richard Steele

Reading and Health

Reading promotes well-being. By feeding the imagination it can provide opportunities for relaxation, enjoyment and social interaction. It also gives us access to information about our health.

Reading empowers the individual by helping us take control of our physical and mental health and move towards a healthy lifestyle.

Reading can aid memory skills in older people and can be a therapeutic activity that helps us to engage with others.

Libraries and reading activities play significant roles in combating some of the causes of illness, improve health and contribute to people's general sense of well-being.

Family Reading

Taking time to share books and stories is a great opportunity to enjoy time together and help children develop a love of reading. Libraries encourage positive shared reading experiences across all ages, communities and groups.

2007 strategy emphasising life skills, health and family reading

One useful technique, whatever the policy context, is to look at the consequences of your planned action in terms, not just of who will benefit, but also who will lose out. A strategic goal needs to be something you are prepared to sacrifice other things for - otherwise, it's not a goal, it's simply an aspiration which makes you feel good. What are you going to not do in order to do the things you have decided to? List the people who will have reduced service because of your actions as well as those you are adding value for. If you are not reducing service anywhere, then either you're not putting energy into the new strategy or you have a very inefficient existing set-up where you can put lots of energy into new activities without anything else feeling the impact.

Purchasing range instead of bestsellers, for example, will result in people who request the bestselling title having to wait longer. Setting up a large quick choice area in which the stock is organised randomly will annoy and inconvenience customers and staff who like to be able to find every book in its place. Emphasising paperbacks (all promotions in Branching Out, Estyn Allan and the Reader Development Network in Scotland took a strategic decision to use only titles available in paperback) will mean that certain writers and publishers are excluded from promotional initiatives.

It's very pleasant to think up ways to spend public money or staff time; any member of staff can have good ideas on how to spend an extra thousand pounds or how to occupy a new member of staff. Thinking strategically, however, the choice is not between an exciting new project and no project at all. What you choose shouldn't be better than nothing, it should be better than the next best alternative way of spending the money. Investing in a promotion, for example, needs to be justified not on the grounds that it's better than an empty space but because it's more effective than spending that money on a more attractive seating area or better signage. Even harder is to apply this way of thinking to what you are already doing, especially how much time existing staff spend on each activity and which groups benefit from that staff time.

A strategy will help you make conscious choices instead of drifting into projects because they seem like a good idea at the time. For example, if offered the chance to host an author event by a national publisher, you can simply respond gratefully or you can consider strategically if you could work with the publisher to use the author visit differently to have more benefit for your readers. Or you could decide to put the same resource of time and energy into working with a local publisher instead.

Nowhere is the tendency to drift more apparent than in approaches to fundraising. Many projects in the public sector are funding-led - they are devised to meet funding criteria or budget spend deadlines in a hurry. Whether it's a question of 'not missing the chance' or 'we must be seen to apply because everyone else is', the efforts expended are often wasteful of time (an inappropriate fund for the idea) or disappointing (staff geared up to go and then no money is found). Projects can be weakly opportunist and cobbled together or distorted by specific criteria so that even if successful, staff feel trapped by what they said they'd do. Meanwhile other important work is neglected in favour of the project which can attract money, even if it is not a priority.

A clear reader development strategy will improve your ability to raise funds. Instead of chasing after every possibility which crosses your path, you will know what you want to do and why you want to do it. You can write up each good idea and keep it to hand - money is never available at the precise time you want it, so keep a project bank. You can contact relevant funding officers and budget-holders and inform them of your plans, even if you don't intend to apply just now. You can gather evidence about what you have achieved and show how you have used seed money to develop and embed work so it is now part of the mainstream. All these will place you in a much stronger position when you do make your bid.

Having a strategy in place also helps when resources are cut and decisions get harder. In Oxfordshire Libraries, for example, the budget was cut each year from 1990 to 1997, making a reduction of 21% overall. The commitment to range in book purchase, and the existence of circulating schemes to bring new paperbacks to smaller libraries (see *Feast on Fiction* Chapter Five, page 149), came under threat and it would have been easy to axe buying risk material altogether. Instead the strategy held up and cuts were applied equally to all stock areas, bestsellers and genre purchase sharing the hit with newer, risk writing.

WAKE-UP CALLS

Misunderstandings, however well-intentioned, undermine reader-centred practice. If you recognise the views below, use the arguments in this chapter to challenge them.

" *Our strategy says every library must have a reading group.* "

" *Our strategy says every library will do two events and two promotions a year.* "

" *Partnership means other organisations giving us money.* "

A strategy is a plan for a particular set of circumstances - it is not for all time. Discussion can begin from your current position by asking the question 'What are readers getting from us now?' and move out from there to consider 'What could and should they be getting?' Or you could start from the wider picture by asking 'Where is reading going, what are the needs of readers in the next few years?' and then focus in on the library role in meeting those needs. You will need a reality check whichever direction you come from. 'What can we realistically offer?' is an essential test of your objectives and will helpfully bridge the process from strategy to action planning. You can then work through the necessary actions for staff - what will the head of service need to do, the stock librarian, the training officer, the human resources section? What actions will the group librarians and the frontline staff need to take?

WHERE ARE WE NOW?			
Reading and writing groups are increasing in number	Reading and writing groups are traditional on the whole	It is difficult to find out easily which groups are meeting where and when	Good links have been established with partners for particular promotions - the GLA, London Film Festival, London Comedy Festival and community groups
WHERE DO WE WANT TO BE?			
Reading and writing groups become a standard offer from London's libraries	Alter the mix/experiment in non-library locations and non-users	This information is easily available for all users of services	These links become embedded and develop further
HOW TO GET THERE			
Benchmark and report on progress	Build into local position statements for all authorities	A centralised database - The Reading Agency is leading on this as a national project under Framework for the Future	Opportunities worked upon and existing partnerships developed
RESOURCE IMPLICATIONS			
Staff time	Staff time	Staff time/website	Staff time

Extract from Get London Reading - a strategy for London's Libraries

In following a strategy through to an action plan, it is important that objectives are matched with resources. £200 to bring in teenagers who don't use the library service is wrongly scaled. If £200 is the limit, rescale the objective to be more meaningful. Some services spend a lot of time debating how a small promotional fund of £100 per branch should be managed instead of considering how the much more substantial resources tied up in staff, in buildings and in books could be harnessed better to meet strategic objectives. How does your reader strategy affect how staff are recruited, trained and appraised, for example?

It is important that the reader strategy is incorporated into the overall library service strategy or it may be sidelined and forgotten about. This is why senior managers must be involved from the outset. As part of the overall strategic plan, reader development is visible as part of the mainstream service. This also makes it easier to demonstrate its contribution to overall service development.

Making the cake bigger

The only alternative to the tough choices of prioritising one group over another in resource allocation is to seek to increase your overall resources so that everyone benefits. Librarians are modest people and they tend not to shout very loudly about what they do. Advocacy for the importance of reading, reader-centred work and libraries should be embedded in your reader development strategy.

Take every opportunity to sell your strengths. In 2005, Opening the Book's promotional programme offered three linked promotions: *Free Spirit*, a collection of mind, body and spirit books, mixed in with a range of non-conformist titles; *Free Fall*, books to take you to the edge of experience; and *Free Speech*, celebrating the power of books to communicate ideas and the power of public libraries in making ideas freely available. Each promotion also carried the tagline *free library* to keep at the forefront libraries' main selling strength - books are free. This also celebrated the role of libraries in providing free access to information in a democracy, in supporting free spirits and outside voices and in offering on-the-edge free-fall experiences.

In 2008, Scottish libraries invested in jute bags as part of the *Read Mòr* promotion and again took the opportunity to emphasise 'free'. The slogan *Scottish Libraries - free books, less waste, more trees* ties the free library theme in with recycling. The suggestion is that customers should use this jute bag instead of a plastic one to save the environment. There is a further subliminal message that borrowing and sharing books is more eco-friendly than buying or owning them.

Senior library managers need to develop more confidence as advocates for their service. The uncertainty and confusion about the role of libraries, combined with the long tradition of serving the needs of others, tends to disadvantage library advocacy. Librarians are not good at explaining what they do in succinct ways and their understandable frustration at others' lack of knowledge and understanding of their contribution can lead to a projected air of long-suffering exasperation which is not helpful.

Part of the advocacy problem for librarians is their awareness of the continued decline in book borrowing. In the last five years, visits to public libraries have increased across the UK but the number of book loans continues to fall in most places. The main reasons for this are not contested, though the proportionate responsibility is much debated - competition for leisure time, increased access to buying books, inconvenient locations and opening hours, range and quality of bookstock, shabby environments, old-fashioned atmosphere. Separating out these factors is important; where libraries' offer has declined in quality and has not kept pace with changes in people's lives, this should be analysed and addressed. But where the external change is a good thing - the change in access to book buying, for example, from the forbidding traditional bookshop to the excitement of the new chains in the 1980s and the easy availability of books everywhere - this is to be welcomed. Similarly, the expansion in the ways we can use leisure time offers far more choice than 30 years ago. Librarians can delight in these changes as much as anyone else.

Audiences for all forms of popular mass entertainment have declined - the audiences for football, for cinema, for television are unlikely ever again to reach the peaks they once did. This is because of a widening of choice not a decline. 27 million people watched Morecambe and Wise's Christmas Special in 1977. 30 years later, consumers had a lot more choice of what to watch on Christmas Day.

A comparison with UK cinema attendance is instructive. Cinema audiences plummeted after the invention of television and then video. From the peak of 1.4 billion visits a year in 1951, audiences fell to 54m in 1984. This is a much steeper curve than book loans in libraries. Then over the following decade, cinemas reinvented themselves. Gone were the old-fashioned fleapits showing one film at a fixed time. Instead the whole experience changed to meet new expectations - a choice of films and times, a smart environment with comfortable and spacious seats, no smoking, easy parking, families welcome. In the 1990s, cinema attendance rose steadily to 123m in 1998 and 167m in 2002. Is there a lesson here for libraries?

Advocacy

Comparisons with what libraries used to do are irrelevant; libraries are not an end in themselves to be propped up at all costs. Current support will be based on what libraries do now and what they are capable of doing in the future. This is where your vision and evidence should combine to make a convincing case. Libraries can still claim a huge audience, a bigger cross-section of types of user than any other organisation and a unique role as the only provider of safe, warm, stimulating, free space for anyone to use on their own terms without question in every UK community. This should give senior managers strength and confidence when negotiating with others. Whether it's an issue of where the library is located in a new shared building, or what the library service can bring to new initiatives in lifelong learning or health and wellbeing, you can stand strong in the knowledge that your audience reach is wider than any other organisation round the table. When people can voluntarily choose what activities they participate in (which excludes formal education and needs-based social provision) more of them choose to use libraries than anything else.

It is up to library managers to get out and make these connections or libraries will continue to be overlooked. A recent major national report on adult learning, for example, mentioned libraries only once and then not for all the resources and support they offered but because they could provide occasional venues for adult education classes!

The combination of under-selling what libraries do well with a new romanticism (at its weakest a sentimentality) about the power of reading, and what it can do for people, is highly dangerous and will lead to libraries not being taken seriously by other players. Of course, reading can be a life-changing experience but it does not yet cure cancer, break drug dependency, sort out marital problems or find people jobs. Claiming it does will only weaken your case.

In discussions with organisations and businesses outside the public sector, it helps to be aware that they are unlikely to understand how libraries work. They do not always realise that there are few ways to reach all libraries at once, and even fewer consistencies in the titles or responsibilities of relevant staff in each library authority. Once they do make contact, either nationally or locally, they also do not understand how libraries are organised, how they buy books or what is unique about the way they reach readers.

Libraries are now approached quite frequently to be a partner in book-related projects. Sometimes these are high profile, national projects and they tend to be in the nature of offers that you cannot refuse. Partners like the BBC, large commercial organisations and major publishers get together to pursue a national marketing campaign that centres on reading and they naturally come to the library. The projects are often devised with book sales in mind and it is assumed that libraries will be happy and grateful to be included. Organisers don't consider the difference or uniqueness of libraries, nor any difficulties that sales-based messages might cause in a library. This, to be fair, is often because libraries don't tell them.

For this type of partnership, it is important for libraries to be clear about the strengths of the library service and what value they are prepared to offer the potential partner. Library space is relatively unencumbered by advertising - if you are offering a commercial opportunity to a partner be aware of the value of that offer. A company brand, for example, if placed in the majority of libraries across the UK, will reach up to 60% of the population in a trusted location as practically the only sales message in the space. It's a valuable offer that you shouldn't underestimate or sell cheap. You are also offering trusted, skilled staff, who often have a personal relationship with a small but significant section of their users and a powerful role in recommending to them. Successful partnerships are two-way; work out what you want back for your investment of time and energy and demand it.

As well as external advocacy and partnerships, librarians need to make their case within local government. Of all council services in a MORI survey in Stockton-on-Tees in 2004,

WAKE-UP CALLS

Misunderstandings, however well-intentioned, undermine reader-centred practice. If you recognise the views below, use the arguments in this chapter to challenge them.

" Launching a strategy is one of your service's top ten achievements this year. "

" Staff assume that keeping existing borrowers happy with the service is the main priority. "

" Senior managers believe that strategic thinking is most useful for new projects and funding. "

libraries were the most used (55% of respondents) - ahead of car parks, leisure centres and primary schools. They also had the highest satisfaction ratings (89%) of all services provided. But when asked to select the ten most important services from a list of 33, only 6% named libraries, except for non-white residents where 22% chose libraries. Here is the library advocacy dilemma in a nutshell - the most popular, most used council service, attracting more non-white users than any other and yet, when compared with refuse collection, schools and street cleaning inevitably not seen as so important. Laurayne Featherstone, the head of service, set out consistently to improve this with an increased programme of activity and lots of targeted local PR. In 2006, libraries not only scored the highest satisfaction rating, they got into the top ten most important services for the first time.

It is the job of library managers to show why libraries are important, especially to elected politicians. Evidence of use, quality customer feedback, local media coverage - libraries can deliver superbly on all these fronts. Too often, however, the focus is on library decline or, worse still, a short-lived campaign to keep open a little-used branch library which is in the wrong place and should be closed. (Any retail business which was unable to restructure its offer to keep pace with changes in population would soon go bust.) Library leaders need to take the initiative here and take active steps to tell a different story. Many of the projects in this book can contribute to that.

A reader development or reader services strategy will help library managers in the political process. It makes a useful focus for presentation and discussion with elected politicians and, if adopted, gives a public statement which can be especially helpful to refer to in cases of specific complaint. Individual complaints have a big impact in local councils where politicians are always aware they depend on local votes. The local media will always find space for complaints from enraged library users, that's their job and it makes a good story. It's the library managers' job to consider the duty owed to the thousands of people who used to come to the library or who have never been, and who contribute just as much to the funding of the library service as the regular users. It may also be your job to remind politicians that these people are their constituents just as much as those who write letters of complaint or turn up at the weekly surgery.

Politicians can be nervous about controversial promotions in libraries and sometimes hold strong moral views themselves which they wish to impose on the service. Some library staff share these fears and convictions. The library profession has an honourable tradition and a clearly articulated stance in relation to censorship (see, for example, 'CILIP Statement on Intellectual Freedom, Access to Information and Censorship' on **www.cilip.org.uk**). Clear guidelines on censorship mean that library staff accept they should stock all kinds of material. There are no guidelines on what should be promoted and staff are much less confident in this area. The effects of self-censorship when it comes to choosing what to promote can be very strong.

This tendency in the UK was exacerbated by the Section 28 amendment to the Local Government Act passed in 1988 (and not repealed till 2000 in Scotland and 2003 in the rest of the UK) which stated that a local authority 'shall not intentionally promote homosexuality'. No prosecution was ever brought under this law but its existence had a damaging effect. Confident heads of service, for example in Brighton and Hove, argued that highlighting books with gay content no more endorsed them than any other books in a display - does a promotion of vegetarian cookery books imply that no-one should eat meat, or a promotion of books in French suggest no-one should read English any more? But many staff became more nervous as a result. It was in this context that the Branching Out promotion *Loud and Proud* (2000) and Opening the Book Promotions' *Queer Choice* (2002) offered extra staff training as an essential part of the promotion.

It is not just the more obvious areas that can cause controversy. The sexual joke of a promotion for 16-19s titled *Textual Intercourse* (see Chapter Five, page 156) did not appear to cause concern while the image used on *Free Style*, a promotion aimed at 14-17s resulted in staff in several services deciding not to use the promotion because they feared complaints that the library was approving body-piercing. Eyebrows were raised at one new library opening, where the promotions included *The book made me do it* (see Chapter One, page 26), on the grounds that in some mysterious way the staff were endorsing bad behaviour in the library. The head of service reported that children loved the image, and so did most of the staff, but the issue required careful handling with the older politicians and members of the Friends of the Library group who attended the event.

A dynamic model for the future

Being able to articulate the purpose and value behind your actions will give reader-centred work much more impact. Wherever you are in the power hierarchy, you will have more effect if you are able to show clearly why what you want to do matters, who it will benefit and how you will make it happen. The history of reader development is testament to the power of ideas. The underlying philosophy gives coherence so that examples become illustrations of a larger purpose and not just a series of one-off projects. To change a whole professional practice, as reader development has changed UK librarianship, requires strategic thinking. This may start small - reader-centred work in libraries was originally started from two fringe part-time posts - but it will think big.

Strategic thinking is conscious, you know what you're doing, why you're doing it and can then discuss success or failure. Too much in libraries is done unconsciously, it is unquestioned, simply custom and practice. The daily routines, the physical layout, the staff timetables and the stock organisation are all driven by process more than policy. This is the same in large or small, urban or rural libraries. But how things are organised, the ways things are made available to the customer, is what shapes how it feels to use the service at the customer end. This needs to change much faster and deeper if the library service is to keep its role and importance in the future.

Emphasising a reader-centred approach gives more opportunities to library staff to engage with their work and get more out of it. Library staff tend to get on a career plateau very easily. Many library jobs are repetitive and are managed to be like that. There is often no clear, dynamic career path so dynamism needs to be created in the job itself. Most staff joined to work with books and readers but have no way of knowing how to do that except talking to elderly ladies about the weather when they can steal a moment. Managers in some libraries still disapprove of staff talking to customers at all and often emphasise the importance of keeping the library shelves tidy over the readers having access to the books. There needs to be an active push to revitalise enthusiasm among frontline staff, to counter the stagnation of what becomes by default, habit and neglect, a routine job. Staff need management permission and encouragement to take initiatives and something to boost their confidence to have a try. The excitement of finding out how stimulating it is to engage with readers provides that.

The role of libraries as one of the few places in our society where diverse needs meet and cross over may become even more important as our society changes. Enduring principles like free access to ideas or providing a public cultural service need to be reinterpreted by

WAKE-UP CALLS

Misunderstandings, however well-intentioned, undermine reader-centred practice. If you recognise the views below, use the arguments in this chapter to challenge them.

" *The chief librarian has 'build a reading community' in the objectives for the service.* "

" *The chief librarian thinks readers are a customer group.* "

" *Senior management team all have this book but no-one's read it.* "

each generation. The principle of universal access is important but it is only meaningful if the experiences people are being offered are appealing to them.

It is likely that libraries must drop the one-size-fits-all of universal provision and look at how they meet diverse needs differently. The old notion of cradle-to-the-grave provision on every street corner still influences library thinking. This is a Victorian aspiration, reshaped by the success of the welfare state in the 20th century, but it is completely out of date in terms of the way people live now.   This belief still influences stock management, where many staff feel there is a responsibility to have a taste of all subjects even in small branches, although this means the collection of any subject is not big enough to keep anyone interested and a few out-of-date science or literature texts stay on the shelves far too long. There's a difference between having access to a poor but comprehensive selection and having access to a good selection that isn't comprehensive but reflects what people need. Offering a better collection in fewer subjects and bringing range through targeted stock circulation is clearly a stronger way forward.

Similarly, the emphasis on catering for everyone in every service point must be rethought. A city would be far better designing one city-centre library to meet the needs of teenagers really well instead of the current practice of having two sad shelves and a beanbag in every branch. Another service point could be located out of the centre, with excellent access and services for elderly people, lots of free parking and connections to free transport to bus people in to visit.

Those who are cash-rich but time-poor are probably the largest group of non-library users and, as more and more people in our society find themselves in this situation, libraries will need to develop new services which recognise their needs.

The traditional librarian skills of organising and evaluating knowledge are being overtaken by technology. The old roles of selector, judge and gatekeeper won't work any more. The new librarian skills of promotion, connection, motivation and engagement are increasingly important. The new skills involve understanding people in relation to books and knowledge, rather than organising books and knowledge as fixed entities. This is a dynamic model for a library service rather than a static one and therefore holds great potential for the future where everyone realises the traditional static model is in decline.

The last ten years have seen changes in many UK libraries as reader development unlocked energy the service didn't know it had. The reader-centred approach is not a passing fashion. It is a powerful and practical philosophy which has a natural affinity with the ethos of public libraries. Respect for individual difference within a shared resource, open access to opportunities for self-development, connection to others if you want it, stimulus and support provided directly or indirectly as you prefer - all these lie at the heart of the best traditions of the public library. They can be given a fresh relevance with the new approach of putting readers at the centre and rethinking library operations.

Will the next ten years see a revitalised and re-energised library service, recognised by customers, partners and funders for its unique role in enriching people's lives? That will be up to readers of this book.

ABOUT THE AUTHORS

Opening the Book ®

Opening the Book has led reader-centred thinking and practice over the last twenty years, offering a dynamic model of reader development as a powerful force for change. Opening the Book's ideas have influenced libraries, publishers, booksellers, arts organisations, education and the media.

Starting with the reader has led us to create new approaches to involving users, to library promotions, to collections' management and to the design and layout of library interiors. Sister company, Opening the Book Promotions, has designed display furniture and graphics which have changed the look of libraries across the UK.

Opening the Book runs national training programmes in the UK and Ireland and has introduced the reader-centred approach to many other European countries as well as to North America and Australasia.

Opening the Book is an innovative company, always looking to develop ideas and practical solutions to make the experience of reading and the experience of libraries more exciting and satisfying for everyone involved.

Please see **www.openingthebook.com** for full details of our library interiors, promotional furniture, websites and training programmes.

Rachel Van Riel, Director, founded the company in 1991. Rachel taught in university and adult education before moving into arts development. In the 1980s she got a job as Community Arts Co-ordinator for Sheffield City Council which was based, unusually, in the library service and discovered libraries were the ideal place for the kind of audience development work she wanted to do. Rachel is a strong advocate for the library service in wider cultural and educational circles and a critical friend to the service internally, combining challenge with empathy. Rachel's mix of clear thinking, practical advice and passionate enthusiasm has inspired many people to get involved in reader-centred work. She is much in demand as a speaker and has addressed many national and international conferences over the last ten years.

Olive Fowler, Assistant Director, joined Opening the Book in 1996 after working in independent publishing and marketing. Olive played a central role in the delivery of Branching Out in England and leads on Opening the Book's work with the Reader Development Network in Scotland. Olive manages Opening the Book websites and is responsible for the concept designs for graphics sold through Opening the Book Promotions. She also manages colour schemes, graphics and signage for Opening the Book's library interiors programme.

Anne Downes, Training Director, joined Opening the Book in 2000, from the funded literature sector where she worked as Literature Officer for regional arts boards, ran a literature festival and worked in publishing. Anne also has experience in designing training and youth work. Anne led for Opening the Book on the delivery of the Estyn Allan programme in Wales and is responsible for the strategic and day-to-day management of Frontline, the online course in reader development which is used by most library services in the UK.

Thanks

The authors would like to thank the people who read and commented on draft chapters:

Rhona Arthur
Rosemary Bullimore
Dot Cameron
Sheila Harden
Cheryl Hesketh
David Kenvyn
John Lane
Steve Liddle
Sarah Mears
Anne Peoples
Judith Rhodes
Simon Rice
June Souter
June Turner
Steve Van Riel
Sue Wilkinson

The Society of Chief Librarians and Arts Council England would like to thank library book suppliers who supported the project by distributing this book to their customers without charge:

Askews
Bertram Library Services
Browns Books
The Holt Jackson Book Company

Acknowledgements

Many library services have contributed to the success of the reader-centred approach and, of course, we do not have space to discuss all the examples of good practice. We are grateful to the library services and other organisations below whose work is quoted in this book.

ABM-utvikling
Argyll and Bute
Barnsley
Birmingham
Blackburn
Bolton
Book Communications
Book Tokens
Brighton
Bristol
Bromley
Cambridgeshire
Cheshire
CILIPS/SLIC
CIRT, University of Central England
Conwy
Copenhagen
Coventry
CPLIS, University of Sheffield
Devon
Doncaster
Donegal
Durham
East Ayrshire
East Dunbartonshire
Edinburgh
EMRALD
Essex

Fife
Gateshead
Glasgow
Gloucestershire
Greenwich
Halton
Herefordshire
HMP Birmingham
Hull
IPF Market Research
Kent
Kirklees
Leeds
Leicester City
Leicestershire
Liverpool
London Libraries Development Agency
Medway
Merthyr Tydfil
Midlothian
Neath Port Talbot
Norfolk
North Tyneside
North Yorkshire
Oldham
Opening the Book Promotions
Oxfordshire
Powys

Read (Yorkshire and The Humber)
Renfrewshire
Richmond
Royal National Institute of Blind People
Salford
Stirling
Stockton-on-Tees
Surrey
Sutton
The Reading Agency
Time to Read
Tower Hamlets
Vaerløse Bibliotek/Hareskov Bibliotek,
Denmark
W F Howes
Wakefield
Warrington
Warwickshire
West Sussex
Western Education and Library Board
Wiltshire

INDEX

We have indexed proper names and some useful concepts, references and project examples. Where a topic is the subject of a whole chapter, we have not indexed it nor have we indexed words such as reader or promotion as they occur on so many pages. Where an entry refers to discussion over continuous pages, we have given the first page only.